MW01079327

Praise for *Own the A.I. Revolution*

This book is a godsend for those of us that struggle with the disruptive nature of A.I. It is a roadmap to embracing its impact to the betterment of our professions, including law.

—SENATOR JOE DUNN (retired)

A practical and thought-provoking understanding of artificial intelligence (A.I.). A.I. will enable us to rethink how we analyze data and use the resulting insights to improve customer engagement and experience.

—LYNN HEMANS
Vice President of Customer Data &
Business Intelligence, Taco Bell

Still confused what A.I. really means and more importantly what impact it's likely to have on your business? In accessible language, Neil Sahota demystifies A.I. bridging the gap between theory and application, from evolving forms of artificial intelligence to practical solutions. Neil has produced the necessary primer for understanding the enormous change coming with A.I.

—MIKE KILANDER
Global Managing Director, Experian

Wondering what the future holds? This enlightening book shows what people are doing today to shape the future driven by A.I. More importantly, it explains how those people are implementing today. A must read for those who want to innovate and disrupt.

—PAUL KIM
Virtual Reality Content General Manager,
Samsung

Dining disrupted by A.I.? This book will help you understand why every industry will be disrupted by A.I., and help *you* be the disrupter. Incredible examples and a simple guide on how to apply A.I. make this book a must have!

—STEVE JOYCE
CEO Dine Brands (Applebee's and IHOP)

Sahota and Ashley offer us a compelling guide to the challenges and choices that the unprecedented power unleashed by artificial intelligence means to the next generation and every business. This is one of the most practical and insightful books on A.I. that provides guidance for the road forward and helps the reader form their own opinion without intimidation.

—AMIR BANIFATEMI
Senior Advisor and General Manager,
XPRIZE

In *Own the A.I. Revolution*, the authors provide an enlightening and entertaining view of how A.I. has evolved to become a force that is set to reshape our personal and professional lives. It is an exceptional read for business leaders who are looking to formulate strategies for success in an A.I.-driven world.

—ANDY NORONHA
Director, Strategy and Thought Leadership,
Cisco & Author of *Digital Vortex* and
Orchestrating Transformation

A thought-provoking and well-written book on how machine learning and A.I. affects our lives today and tomorrow as technology develops faster than our social norms can keep up. Neil's book gives the reader a historical prospective of where A.I. fits into the evolution of technology and the possibilities of what's to come.

—JAY WITZLING
Vice President (retired),
The Boeing Company & Special Advisor
to Discovery Science Center

Neil and Michael provide an epic opportunity juncture for those wanting to understand, capture, and benefit from this technological revolutionary giant called artificial intelligence. I walked away from this book mesmerized and excited about the A.I. market forces impacting business industries across the globe. *Own the A.I. Revolution* simplifies an often-complex subject as it provides a window into the changes that are dramatically redefining the "transhumanism" boundaries of our world. A terrific read!

—JOSEPH HOPKINS
COO, Strathspey Crown

This book defines variations of emotional, intellectual, and artificial intelligence which provides a profound analysis of natural and formulated decision making. It's an eye-opening revelation of the moral obligation we have to humanity (and ourselves) when implementing systems theory, Big Data, and machine learning.

—MARCI TREVINO
Vice President, Tilly's Life Center

There is at present considerable confusion within the professions (including the legal profession) about the nature and impact of A.I. Some are blissfully ignorant, some over- or underestimate the timing and scope of the changes to professional practice that A.I. will bring about, and many simply don't appreciate the full potential of A.I. This book makes a most welcome contribution to the conversation about A.I. by providing a thorough, well-informed and, importantly, engaging examination of the A.I. phenomenon. Written in an accessible style that avoids the use of technical jargon, this book will be of interest to anyone who wishes to quickly and authoritatively get up to speed with contemporary A.I. discourse.

—NICK JAMES
Executive Dean of Law, Bond University

This book is the intersection of Art + Sustainability + Technology! Want to change the world? Then learn the path from this book!

—ANTONY RANDALL
Executive Producer and Director

I believe A.I. will affect the legal system more than anything since the Seventh Amendment. It is truly extraordinary to be able to procure such important knowledge and to be able to guide clients in the right direction. Wish we had this book 40 years ago!

—TOM GIRARDI
Founding Partner, Girardi & Keese

As an educational leader, I look at how the job market and higher ed are trending. We then create programs and curriculum to serve as a strong foundation for our students to matriculate into current industries as well as industries of tomorrow. We rely on experts like Neil to guide us through this process. This book allows the layperson to understand what A.I. is and how it can impact our world.

—BOBBY MENDOZA
Sr. Vice President & Headmaster,
Fairmont Preparatory Academy

In today's world where the term Artificial Intelligence is used in such a careless way, Neil manages to break down its framework and provide a hands-on guidebook for those seeking to finally grasp A.I.'s disruptive force.

—CHRISTOPH AUER-WELSBACH
Founder, City.AI

Balance and insight! The authors have masterfully presented "A.I. for Good" and "A.I. for Bad" through a crystal-clear lens of societal perspective and supported by their impressive experience and powerful interviews. The result is a set of amazing solutions for business and social enterprise. More than knowledge, it's a guide on how we can build a brighter future with one of the greatest tools that humankind has ever yielded.

—HANS KEIRSTEAD
CEO & President, Aivita Biomedical

This book is a must read for anybody interested in A.I. It doesn't try to "sell" you Artificial Intelligence but shares facts about the future. Inspiring examples and deep insight in our own intelligence will greatly impact organizations and change society as a whole.

—FRITS BUSSMAKER
Chairman, Institute for Accountability
in the Digital Age

This book is an absolute *must read* for those that want to disrupt their industry, drive profitability, and impact the world as we know it.

—CHERI TREE
Founder & CEO, Codebreaker
Technologies, Inc.

Own the A.I. Revolution is brilliant. Sahota and Ashley provide an optimistic look into the ways A.I. can be leveraged to effect positive change in the very near future. They make a compelling case for the fact that if trained to be inclusive, A.I. has the potential to be a real equalizer by uplifting the most underrepresented communities in the world. Access to resources and opportunities for all.

—DAVID RIXTER
Founder & CEO, One United Globe

Open the pod bay doors . . . Neil Sahota and Michael Ashley have written a must-read intro for anyone considering Artificial Intelligence.

—TONY CRISP
CEO, CRISPx

"Taking a new step, uttering a new word, is what people fear most." Dostoevsky's 19th century quote perfectly applies to the 21st century A.I. revolution. We're afraid of the power of this new technology. We're unsure how to implement something so mysterious. But it is coming, and Sahota's book is the best guidebook out there for joining this revolution. And he somehow succeeds at getting us off the fence and into the camp of enthusiasts. Excited about the cultural Renaissance coming out of the time A.I. will free up. Relieved that A.I.'s dynamic insights will help fend off problems my companies don't see coming. Inspired by the thought of turning managers into super-managers, engineers into super-engineers. I find myself agreeing with Sahota that, "We live in exciting times, exponential times. Never was a moment riper for disruptors and innovators to dream big human dreams, assisted and enhanced by our A.I. collaborators."

—GRANT VAN CLEVE
President, Tech Coast Angels OC

Own the A.I. Revolution offers the definitive blueprint for seizing the power of artificial intelligence to succeed in today's competitive landscape. Filled with illustrative case studies and thought-provoking interviews with today's most innovative experts—yet written in an easy-to-follow, compelling fashion—it is a MUST read business/tech book.

—JOE GARNER
Six-Time *New York Times*
Best-selling Author

Sahota and Ashley have written a must-read primer for anyone considering A.I. They tackle the tough questions and empower people to create the next generation of products and services. Read this book and learn from one of the best.

—BRENDAN KANE
Author of *One Million Followers*

A provocative, interdisciplinary, integrative analysis of science, technology, business, economics, politics, history, psychology and philosophy that helps us better understand A.I., how we think as human beings, our businesses and ourselves.

—JEFF AU
Managing Director & General Counsel,
PacifiCap Investment Management

This is not a book about IT. In plain language, Neil Sahota clearly describes the power A.I. brings to society and the promise of a hopeful future we can unlock through its use and application.

—NOAH KROLOFF
Principal, GSIS & former Chief of Staff, U.S.
Department of Homeland Security

As an educator, I believe we constantly have to stay on the cutting edge of what students will need to be successful in an ever complex and evolving global society. This book delivers a comprehensive and easy to follow guide to understanding artificial intelligence and gives a realistic picture of how we can prepare today's students for their roles in this new world.

—CAROLYN LUCIA
Director of Education,
Fairmont Preparatory Academy

Are you caught somewhere between amazement at the potential of A.I. and worry that it might just be the end of humankind? This is just the book you need to make sense of it all. Neil Sahota and Michael Ashley cut through the hype, covering the history, the ethics, the science in a down-to-earth way that will leave you with practical advice for harnessing the power of the A.I. revolution for yourself.

—JEANNA MATTHEWS
Associate Professor, Clarkson University
& Co-chair, Subcommittee on AI and
Algorithmic Accountability, US Technology
Policy Council, Association for Computing
Machinery (ACM)

For those of us who need guidance on where A.I. will lead us and how we can harness the immense possibilities within, Neil Sahota takes us on a journey into our fascinating future where we will coexist with A.I. applications that will be embedded into our very beings and will be carrying out most tasks that we do today, thus leaving us to be more creative, productive, and effective. Perilous if you don't read it!

—SURINDER AND JAVIER OBEROI
Founders, Zinx

Finally, we have a book that helps nontechnical people understand how they can use A.I.! This is a must read for anyone wondering how A.I. will reshape businesses, international politics, our future jobs, national security, and the very fabric of our societies. The book presents amazing stories of regular people building novel A.I. solutions!

—IRAKLI BERIDZE
Head of the Centre for Artificial
Intelligence and Robotics

Neil makes "artificial intelligence" very real. As with any new horizon, there are shamans and prophets; ideologues and exploiters. But with every revolution or societal transformation, we look back and find the clear-eyed few who made that better future real and achievable. Neil Sahota is that pathmaker for this future.

—JAY CONNOR
CEO, Learning Ovations

In their book, *Own the A.I. Revolution*, authors Neil Sahota and Michael Ashely have provided an excellent resource for those who are curious about Artificial Intelligence and its application to business and society. They begin the book with a description and history of Artificial Intelligence and end it with practical recommendations for your organization. Neil Sahota is uniquely qualified to write about Artificial Intelligence and its applications, based on his experience as an IBM Master Inventor, United Nations (U.N.) Artificial Intelligence (A.I.) subject matter expert, and Professor at UC Irvine teaching Entrepreneurship. Don't let the A.I. Revolution leave you behind: read this book.

—JIM KLINGLER
CFO, Multiple Companies

Neil Sahota deeply understands how the emergence of artificial intelligence will transform our civilization. He clearly explains the integration of these transformative new technologies into our lives and offers us a fresh perspective on how they will better us. He also offers us a view into the challenges these technological breakthroughs pose. This book is a valuable and needed addition to our understanding of artificial intelligence in our world.

—SCOTT STEWART
CEO, Innovative Lending Platform
Association

The absolute best resource for all business and tech leaders without question and for years to come. Interesting, engaging, transformative, exciting, amazing—the superlatives boundless.

—STEPHEN IBARAKI
Futurist & General Partner REDDS

OWN THE

A.I.

REVOLUTION

**UNLOCK YOUR ARTIFICIAL INTELLIGENCE
STRATEGY TO DISRUPT YOUR COMPETITION**

NEIL SAHOTA
MICHAEL ASHLEY

New York   Chicago   San Francisco   Athens
London   Madrid   Mexico City   Milan
New Delhi   Singapore   Sydney   Toronto

1 2 3 4 5 6 7 8 9   QVS   24 23 22 21 20 19

ISBN   978-1-260-45837-4
MHID   1-260-45837-7

e-ISBN   978-1-260-45838-1
e-MHID   1-260-45838-5

McGraw-Hill Education books are available at special quantity discounts to use as premiums and sales promotions or for use in corporate training programs. To contact a representative, please visit the Contact Us pages at www.mhprofessional.com.

For "Kini," who always reminded me to
"Uber myself before I got Kodaked."
Thanks for always believing in me!
—NEIL

For Valerie, my partner and best friend.
Thank you for always believing in me.
—MICHAEL

Contents

SECTION II

Conversations with Today's Thought Leaders on A.I.

Foreword

re you prepared for the digital earthquake, tornado, hurricane, and tsunami (all wrapped into one) about to engulf our world? If you've read the headlines, you know that artificial intelligence (A.I.) threatens to disrupt every domain of human existence. So how can you forecast the stratospheric possibilities and endless opportunities? How can you mitigate the risks? More importantly, how can you avoid the unintended avalanche of consequences accelerated by A.I.?

It's just impossible to plan for something this big, you might be thinking.

Not so. The following pages break through the challenges and implications surrounding A.I. Before you read the definitive primer on this fascinating subject, it's my honor and privilege to provide a glimpse of the magnitude of change that's coming. (Also, please note I use the term "A.I." as an umbrella framework encompassing robotics, machine learning, and many types of Big Data analytics.)

It's been my honor to keynote, moderate, and guide more than 100 global engagements surrounding this topic recently, impacting more than $10T (trillion) of U.S. investment in alignment with the United Nations Sustainable Development Goals (SDGs). Whenever speaking, I always try to present myself as the only chairman/founder/board member with roles in business, finance, venture capital, serial entrepreneurship, global computer science, history-making U.N. innovative programs, top industry organizations, think

tanks, and summits. Such an interdisciplinary perspective informs my assertion that *Own the A.I. Revolution* must be read now by today's business leaders or others who want to participate in the revolution. Believe me, your fortunes—and those of your descendants—depend on your understanding and
putting to good use the information contained in this book.

Still unconvinced that your business is tied up in A.I.? Let's do the math.
Into 2019, A.I. infiltrated every industry and is being adopted into small and
midsized organizations. Countries such as Finland are challenging 1 percent
or more of their populations to be A.I.-educated. A.I. will increase to $20T in
wealth creation and impact, integrating more than a trillion sensors through
the Internet of Things, all within 15 years. Moreover, A.I. is the centerpiece of
what's been termed the "Fourth Industrial Revolution" and "Second Machine
Age." This movement is now Society 5.0 or what I call the Fifth Machine Age
Unlimited X-Revolution (5MUX, for short). We stand at a unique moment in
world history—an inflection point out of which we shall witness an unprecedented growth of economic, cultural, and societal change, the following
aspects of which I term the ACCC:

- *Automation*
- Time *Compression* in new innovations
- *Convergence* in all domains and existences
- Ubiquitous *Connectivity*.

The underlying catalyst for ACCC is the digital artificial intelligence (A.I.)
mesh created by the growing deployment of machine learning, or the *A.I. of
Everything*. But A.I.'s rapid advancement and even its ubiquitous presence in
our daily lives portends far more than mere technological innovation for its
own sake. A.I. is already exhibiting a potential to yield exponential overlapping
amplification of value to a myriad of interrelated sectors, including government, industry, media, and education. Even so, a growing wariness surrounding the negative unintended consequences for society, economic development,
and prosperity will increase as long as people view it as a threat.

To counter such concerns and better gauge the global impact of A.I.
throughout all aspects of industry, it's helpful to review a matrix of the types of
innovation A.I. is rampant in such as the development phases of:

- **Concept.** The source of ideation and exploration of new ideas
- **Research and Development (R&D).** The stage in which ideas convert
  into proof of concept

- **Transfer.** Proof of concept commercializes into working products and services
- **Production and Deployment.** The production of commercial products and services scaling for distribution
- **Usage.** Consumers and end users find more value in products and services

A.I., coupled with machine learning, promises positive structural reorganization when it comes to business and organizational models. To better witness A.I. in action, it's helpful to understand how it will bring new and improved innovation in the following areas:

- Products
- Services
- Organizational models
- Operational processes
- Social media outreach

However, as I said, to simply view A.I. through the business lens is to mistake its full potential. A.I. is different from any other tool mankind has developed in its short tenure of this planet. Humans won't just employ artificial intelligence, they will be shaped by it. *They will be transformed by the technology.* Various thought leaders interviewed for this book, including Peter Diamandis, Ben Goertzel, and David Hanson, have suggested we are witnessing the dawn of transhumanism in which we evolve our physical and mental faculties far beyond our current levels through biological integration with A.I. Likewise, leading proponents witnessing this change envision humanity splintering into four categories under the banner of what I call "CASAL": Classic, Augmented, Synthetic, Artificial Life.

1. **Classic.** Represented currently by 7.3 billion of us, this is the modern form of our species which has existed for tens of thousands of years.
2. **Augmented.** Those individuals augmented by technological wearables and implants. (Full disclosure, I am augmented and am a founding member of a think tank created by a top five corporation in which augmented humans participate.)
3. **Synthetic.** New forms of life where the genome for the species is artificially produced suggest a new version of humans will be possible within 15 years. At the same time, human cloning is possible, as well as embryonic inheritable genetic editing.

4. **Artificial Life.** Early A.I. children (evidenced by humanoid robots or avatars hinting at what is to come). These individuals will be able to share/accelerate their development and knowledge through a mind-cloud.

If the above section didn't boggle your brain just a bit as to what's possible through A.I., perhaps it's worth taking a stroll down the future lane, contemplating life in the year 2030.

TIME STAMP: 2030.07.14

"It's time to wake up, Sue," says FIA (acronym for Financial Intelligent Agent). "You weren't sleeping well. Your happiness quotient is lower today. Would you like to sleep an extra hour and we'll talk again at 9 a.m.?"

Sue says yes and sleeps until her scheduled meeting. By the time 9 a.m. arrives, she is dressed, drinking a cappuccino, which her smart kitchen began brewing for her the moment she exited the shower. Now ready to face the day, Sue listens to FIA through a mind interface.

"While you were sleeping, I performed a self-upgrade, enhancing my participation in a 360-degree holistic view of your life. This helps me improve your well-being and your financial status—a top priority for you."

Sue nods her head as she sips her drink and stares out the window.

"I am making continual micro-adjustments to your investment portfolio based on dynamic trends being monitored on a continuous 24/7 basis," FIA continues. "I am redistributing your savings through micro-auctioning to the Top Ten-ranked services for best spot interest rates."

Sue suddenly realizes she forgot to schedule a flight to her nephew's birthday party next month and thinks her concern.

"Also, no need to fret over missing little Tommy's get-together. I examined your calendar and through UIA (United Intelligent Agent), I booked flights for August 20 at the lowest rates."

"Whew. Thank you, FIA!"

"Also, I am sensing a 90 percent probability for a high flu outbreak in Amsterdam when you arrive. Using IIA (Insurance Intelligent Agent), I was able to negotiate spot health insurance for the 23.3 hours of risk."

"That's smart. No use in paying for the whole weekend if I don't need it."

"Next, I booked you an autonomous rental car with the best safety record, thus the lowest insurance. You can call him SAM. Your hotel is handled the same way through their intelligent agents (IAs)."

"Perfect."

"And just so you know, I will handle via IAs all of the fund transfers and payments with the best-negotiated lowest fees. From my analysis of your thought patterns, I know you worry about this. We can get all this information in one place, updating continuously, with the best deals and rates, lowest fees, no minimums, and no overhead infrastructure since it is all virtual."

FIA knows Sue only too well. A worrier, she is concerned about the costs.

"But best of all, Sue, you and I can go through everything together using embedded, augmented, and virtual reality, so there will be no surprises."

"Good. You know how I feel about surprises."

"By the way, your health index is down to 94.2," says FIA.

FIA senses Sue's biometrics go on high alert.

"But no need to worry. I will ensure the needed supplements get added to your meal plans today when ordering via RIA (Restaurant Intelligent Agent). Your life index is also down to 102.4, so I will make a gene adjustment via the nanobots. Concurrently, I will ensure micro-adjustments to your retirement savings plan and life insurance via IAs."

"Sounds good," says Sue, grabbing her things to head out the door.

"And just so you know, your work schedule today entails devising multiple project bids on creative design with robot guides."

Sue thanks FIA at the same time that updates are implanted in her memory from FIA via direct neural communication. She is now ready to face her day.

SO . . . MADNESS OR REALITY?

Though the above scenario may seem far-fetched, the necessary elements are already here projecting out just to 2020, all based on an A.I. foundation. Just try to imagine what the year 2030 will look like. It may seem impossible, but already brain signatures exist for predicting emotions, thoughts, words, and images, as well as new theories for explaining consciousness. Likewise, labs are experimenting with direct brain interfaces and implantable neuro devices, injectable nanochips, brain modulation and recordings, and advanced computer chips modeled on human brains.

Smart sensors using Big Data analysis can also predict climate, disease, crime, political, and economic trends with more than 80 percent reliability and provide prescriptive tactics. It's only a (short) matter of time before our forecasting abilities improve to godlike levels inconceivable just a generation ago.

Still, despite so many beneficial opportunities for the progress of humanity, danger lurks. The propensity for discriminatory bias looms large, whether it involves hiring decisions, police profiling, or insurance underwriting. Autonomous weapons systems threaten countries the world over, endangering the relative state of peace the globe has enjoyed in the more than 70 years since the end of World War II. Besides these concerns, one of the most vexing issues to consider is how so much innovation will impact the future of the workforce. The latest data suggest a net employment increase, though jobs will change. Similar to how the Internet created industries people couldn't imagine in 1990, A.I. will generate professions we can't imagine today. Overall, the effect will be a net positive. In the years to come, productivity is likely to skyrocket, and we'll end up with a much richer society than we can possibly imagine.

Have I piqued your curiosity so far? I hope so. These are just a fraction of the many themes and questions *Own the A.I. Revolution* addresses. It is my firm belief this book is needed now more than ever to prepare not just the savvy businessperson for what's coming—but also the savvy citizen of Earth, who dares to wonder what will come next.

—STEPHEN IBARAKI

Introduction

Artificial intelligence is the stuff of nightmares. Or so many people believe. In 2017, shortly before his death, the celebrated British physicist Stephen Hawking, the man who postulated the existence of black holes and wrote the international best seller *A Brief History of Time*, warned that the development of artificial intelligence could be "the worst event in human history," noting that, without proper safeguards, "we could conceivably be destroyed by it." This same year, billionaire entrepreneur Elon Musk, the man behind the Tesla electric auto company, SpaceX, and PayPal, warned, "With artificial intelligence, we are summoning the demon."

Mankind's fear of intelligent machines traces its history at least as far back as 1818 and the publication of *Frankenstein* by Mary Shelley. This seminal tale of a scientist who imbues dead tissue with life, only to be killed by his creation, became the template for every "technology run amok" story told in print or on celluloid for the next two centuries. The 1920 play *R.U.R.* by Czech writer Karel Čapek was not only one of the first works of twentieth-century literature to depict a revolt of mechanical slaves against their human masters. It also introduced the word "robot" to the English language.

In 1968, science fiction author Arthur C. Clarke and director Stanley Kubrick introduced us to HAL 9000, the soft-spoken, ultimately homicidal A.I. in *2001: A Space Odyssey*. A couple of decades later, writer-director James Cameron gave his fictional SkyNet computer network control of America's atomic weapons in 1984's *The Terminator*, only to have the system become self-aware and turn the Earth into a blasted, radioactive wasteland. The 2015 film *Ex Machina* featured an intelligent android in female form learning to use empathy, guile, and sensuality to secure freedom from her brilliant but egotistical creator. Currently, HBO's original series *Westworld* vividly depicts the lethal chaos that ensues when robots created for human amusement decide they will no longer live as slaves.

As essential as "evil A.I." is to science fiction, the popular depiction of artificial intelligence as something dangerous and malevolent does the field a serious disservice. After all, the scientists, engineers, and entrepreneurs working to develop artificial intelligence certainly aren't doing so to fulfill some twisted doomsday fantasy, but because they see this technology as a means to better the human condition. For example, imagine if a computer could:

- Review a patient's medical tests and instantly produce an accurate diagnosis?
- Serve as "eyes" for the blind and vision-impaired?
- Act as a personal therapist, demonstrating all the emotional intelligence of a trained psychologist?
- Accurately translate nuance and meaning between multiple languages in real time?
- Provide expert legal advice in seconds?
- Serve as a digital personal assistant, doing everything from booking theater tickets to cooking meals based on voice commands?
- Accurately predict stock market activity based on the sociopolitical zeitgeist?
- Find your perfect mate?

Sounds like science fiction again, doesn't it? But guess what: all of these amazing services are available *right now*, due to advances in artificial intelligence. A.I. is already with us. And there's not a runaway killer robot in sight.

In the coming chapters, we're going to explore where A.I. stands today, apart from its science fiction roots, exploring the potential this revolutionary technology has to make monumental changes in the way every one of us works, plays, and even, yes, thinks. Through better understanding of what A.I. is, and what it is not, hopefully we can shed our pop culture-fueled fears and learn to embrace a technology promising to be as revolutionary as the invention of agriculture, the harnessing of steam, the mastery of electricity, and the splitting of the atom.

Acknowledgments

Writing my first book has been an incredible journey. I need to thank my incredible co-author, Michael Ashley, for guiding me through his wisdom on what it takes to write a great book. Likewise, my deepest thanks to Donya Dickerson and the rest of the McGraw-Hill team for believing in us and powering through a very aggressive publishing schedule to get this book ready in time for the United Nations AI Summit for Good. I owe a very special thanks to each of our interviewees, who took the time to share their knowledge and insights with Michael and me so we could share them with the world. (I would name you all—however, I've been told I've got a character count . . . yeah, I got Twitter-fied.) Most of all, I wish to extend my sincerest thanks to you, the reader, for taking the time read this book. (I hope it was useful and inspiring!)

Through this entire journey, there are three special people I wish to share my most heartful thanks with. First is my very good friend Stephen Ibaraki. He was amazing when it came to brainstorming ideas, engaging his network on our behalf, and being our number one cheerleader. Second is another great friend, Steven Kotler. Since the day we first met, he was always telling me, "Neil, you need to write a book!" Steven is a great inspiration and amazing mentor on being an author. Third is yet another great friend, Senator Joe Dunn. Joe's support has been a pillar of strength, and he opened some incredible doors for us. His help was a huge accelerator for us. I truly feel blessed by all the great people who made this book possible. To all of you: THANK YOU!

—NEIL SAHOTA

A big thanks is due to Neil Sahota for bringing me into the fascinating world of artificial intelligence. In the course of collaborating you have taught me so much, opening my eyes to the possibilities of this incredible technology. Moreover, you have shown me how A.I. can be used as one of humanity's greatest tools for good, offering a better quality of life to our brothers and sisters as well as all creatures on this planet.

I am deeply grateful to Donya Dickerson and the entire McGraw-Hill team for bringing forth our vision. Thank you for being our cheerleaders and partners, allowing us to achieve our very ambitious publishing schedule while developing a high-quality book we can all be proud of. I am also very grateful to the United Nations for participating in our book and promoting it.

I wish to thank the many participants in this book who so graciously gave their time to create amazing, inspiring, and thoughtful interviews. I so appreciate your insight and knowledge, especially the ways in which you affected my thinking, ultimately helping our readers to better understand this special time we are experiencing.

In particular, I want to mention several individuals who went above and beyond in helping Neil and me create and share this content. Thank you to Stephen Ibaraki for a wonderful Foreword, for making influential introductions, and for continually supporting us. A big debt of gratitude is due to Lisa Wood of Cognitive World for opening the door to *Forbes* and for championing our work.

Thank you to my good friend Joe Garner for your continuingly sagacious advice throughout the writing and publishing process. I am also appreciative of the talented Chase Geiser for assisting with the marketing presentation. Thank you to Allen Ury for your invaluable research, and thank you to Senator Joe Dunn for making such a helpful introduction to Donya, kicking off our partnership with McGraw-Hill.

On a personal note I would like to acknowledge the following individuals who continually support me. Your love and guidance make all the difference in my life: my parents, Garry Seltzer and Leslye Louis; my children, Teddy and Sammy; my second mother,: Janet Brakensiek, Cynthia Seltzer; my brothers, Kevin Seltzer and Blake Hamilton; my mentors, Behzad Mohit, David Crespy, Paul Wolansky, David Kost, Ron Friedman, Lorna Collins; and my second family, Carla Shepherd, Don Shepherd, Ashley and Tyler Dockins.

—MICHAEL ASHLEY

SECTION I

The A.I. Frontier

Chapter 1

"Who Could Have Imagined . . . ?"

O n the morning of Tuesday, September 11, 2001, the Western world's complacency was shattered when two hijacked commercial airliners slammed into Towers 1 and 2 of New York's World Trade Center, soon reducing the iconic monoliths to piles of smoking rubble. Minutes later, a third hijacked airliner, American Airlines Flight 77, nosedived into the western side of the Pentagon in Alexandria, Virginia, demolishing a good section of the building's outer ring and the Naval Command Center within.

Forty-five minutes later, a fourth jetliner, United Flight 93, also believed to have been headed for Washington, crashed in a field in Somerset County in southwest Pennsylvania after its passengers, wise to their captors' intentions, rebelled and overwhelmed the four hijackers who had taken command of the cockpit. In all, more than 3,300 people lost their lives in these four related terrorist incidents. In the months following, government spokespeople often cited a "lack of imagination" among defense and intelligence department agencies for failing to anticipate an attack of this nature, often saying, "Who could have imagined such a thing happening?"

Ironically, imagination was not the issue. For at least a decade, Hollywood screenwriters had concocted numerous scenarios in which terrorists had commandeered civilian vehicles, including commercial airliners, converting them into weapons of mass destruction. Perhaps the most infamous of these prescient scenarios was writer/producer Chris Carter's pilot episode for his *X-Files* spinoff *The Lone Gunmen,* which climaxed with a commercial airliner being remotely hijacked and flown straight into the World Trade Center as part of a bogus "false flag" terrorist attack, only to be diverted at the last possible second by the gunmen's heroic actions. The episode aired on March 4, 2001, a mere six months before the same scenario played out in real life—with a tragic ending. That same summer, analysts within the U.S. intelligence community, having intercepted troubling communications between al Qaeda cells throughout Europe and America, submitted a report to President George W. Bush, titled, "Bin Laden Determined to Strike Inside the United States."

The report was summarily ignored.

"Who could have imagined such a thing happening . . . ?" Indeed. Failing to ignore warnings of disaster is, of course, no new phenomenon. Greek mythology tells us of Cassandra, daughter of the king and queen of Troy, who, after offending the god Apollo, is saddled with an unusual curse: She will possess the power of unfailing prophesy . . . but her decrees will fall on deaf ears. Ignored at best, disparaged at worst, poor Cassandra's life is doomed to be a never-ending series of avoidable defeats and maddening frustrations.

It's tough to be right when no one believes you.

The Cassandra Syndrome lives on with us today, not only in Washington, where warnings of emerging military threats, looming deficits, crumbling transportation infrastructure, leaking entitlement programs, and accelerating climate change are met with "What—Me Worry?" shrugs worthy of *MAD Magazine*'s Alfred E. Neuman, but also in the boardrooms of America's most powerful corporations. Either leaders lack the tools to predict coming challenges or, even when they are warned of impending danger, they choose to ignore such admonitions, clinging stubbornly to their previous modes of behavior.

It is difficult for people to change their minds, to open themselves up to new possibilities, even when faced with conclusive facts and compelling arguments. Even at the highest levels of business, government, and, yes, even science, there is a powerful, almost hardwired compulsion to resist change and meet anything smacking of radical disruption with skepticism, if not outright hostility.

The landscape of American business is littered with the bones of companies that achieved great success meeting the needs of a market at a particular time, only to ignore warnings of disruptive technologies, emerging competitors, and changing consumer demands. How many people born in the twenty-first century have ever heard of the Pullman Company, Woolworths, Marshall Field, Kodak, or even Blockbuster Video?

While operating in disparate sectors, ranging from transportation to retailing to consumer electronics to entertainment, all these once-great American brands had one thing in common: they failed to see the signs of coming disruptions. Even when they did react, they tended to cling to increasingly outmoded ways of doing business until they were either shuttered or absorbed by nimbler and more foresighted competitors. Each of these companies stand as a cautionary tale for what happens to businesses lacking the ability or willingness to sense what's coming and meet the future on its own terms.

Although its name is barely known today, the Pullman Company once enjoyed monopolistic control. Founded in the early 1860s by George Pullman of Chicago, the organization made its fortune crafting luxurious sleeper cars during the height of the country's railroad boom. Anyone who traveled cross-country during the late nineteenth and early twentieth centuries—trips often requiring several days of travel by rail—was intimately familiar with Pullman's iconic coaches.

In fact, Pullman grew so large and powerful, it actually built its own company town on Chicago's South Side, a community where employees lived, worked, shopped, and educated their children all within its municipal confines. However, after World War II, Pullman fell on hard times when the advent of the Interstate Highway System and affordable airline travel made city-to-city passenger train service passé.

It took nearly two decades for passenger train travel to completely fall out of favor with the American public, but even with the future staring it in the face, Pullman made only token efforts to adapt. With demand for its product virtually nonexistent, the company finally folded in 1968—just over 100 years after its founding—its name quickly disappearing into the mists of history.

F.W. Woolworth is another once-great brand virtually unknown to today's younger generation due to its inability to recognize and respond to changing market conditions. Founded in 1878 in Utica, New York, F.W. Woolworth & Co., often referred to as simply Woolworths, was the first of the low-price general retailers known as five-and-dime stores. (Initially, many of Woolworths' products actually did retail for just five or ten cents.) The precursor to Walmart, you could walk into any neighborhood Woolworths with the expectation of buying everything from a pair of pants to a set of glassware to children's toys to gardening tools, all at low discount prices. If you were hungry, you could take a seat at Woolworths' famous lunch counter, where a soda jerk could make you an ice cream soda or fry you up a juicy hamburger.

At its peak in the mid-twentieth century, Woolworths operated more than 800 stores in the U.S. and U.K. and served more meals than any other restaurant in the world including McDonald's. It also built what was, at its time (1912), the world's tallest office building, for which the company paid in cash. However, in the 1970s, the face of general retailing changed rapidly with the surge of so-called "big box" stores, such as K-Mart and Target. At first dismissive of this trend, Woolworths later tried to compete by opening its own "big box" chain, Woolco, but it was too little, too late. The last Woolworths in the United States closed its doors in July 1997. While the name can still be found on some storefronts overseas, the company, once an American icon, is now just a footnote in the history of American retailing.

Marshall Field & Company was another Chicago-based retailing icon that dominated its field for decades, only to fall victim to changes in retailing trends it failed to anticipate. Founded in the mid-nineteenth century, Marshall Field grew to become as synonymous with the Windy City as Macy's was to New York or Neiman-Marcus was to Dallas. Field's flagship State Street store, occupying an entire city block and distinguished by a dramatic multilevel atrium topped by original Louis C. Tiffany glass skylights, was built between 1891 and 1892 and became a world-renowned model for the modern department store. Its iconic Great Clock at the southeast corner of State and Washington streets became a Chicago landmark and was immortalized in a famous *Saturday Evening Post* cover illustrated by Norman Rockwell.

However, Field's decline came in two distinct waves, both of which were predictable to anyone paying close attention. The first hit in the 1950s and '60s as, in the boom years following the end of World War II, retail activity moved out of the central city to the expanding suburbs. In reaction, the company opened satellite stores in most major Chicago-area shopping centers, but these scaled-down facilities failed to capture the majesty and allure of the original downtown location.

Much later, in the 1990s and early 2000s, Field fell victim to the same plague to shutter so many other retail operations during this period: the rise of the Internet. Failing to take e-commerce seriously, Field made only a token attempt to go online. As a result, its income dropped quickly into the red, and the company was ultimately acquired by Federated Department Stores in 2004, which dropped the Marshall Field moniker entirely, renaming it Macy's. Despite passionate protests from longtime Field aficionados, it failed to revive the iconic brand, which now lives on only in the form of the store's famous Frango Mint candies.

While Woolworths and Marshall Field imploded because they failed to anticipate changes in retail trends, the demise of Rochester, New York-based Kodak can be traced to its myopic executives' refusal to see the future even when handed to them on a silver platter. Since Kodak was for decades the world leader in photographic film manufacturing and print processing, many people assume the company was killed by the invention of the digital camera.

But in fact, Kodak *invented* the digital camera—*twice*—but then twice decided not to actively pursue this burgeoning technology. Company engineer Steve Sasson created the world's first digital camera in 1975 in Kodak's own R&D facility, but his superiors viewed it as nothing more than an amusing toy. A few years later, company engineers perfected the first mega-pixel camera, considered a breakthrough in producing sharp, clear photographic prints, but again company leadership gave it a pass.

In 1981, in response to Sony Corporation releasing the first all-digital camera, Kodak commissioned an in-house study concluding that in 10 years, digital would come to dominate the consumer photography market. However, still wedded to their chemical and paper-based business model, Kodak's executives remained in denial. As late as 2007, the company boasted, "Kodak is back," predicting a resurgence in the traditional film-based photography market. Sadly, it was not to be. In January 2012, Kodak finally filed for Chapter 11 bankruptcy and over the following year shed most of its assets, including its multi-million-dollar patents. Today, Kodak remains a going business concern in name only, a shell of its former self.

Finally, let's examine the tragic rise and fall of the company everyone loved to hate, Blockbuster Video. Founded by David Cook in Dallas, Texas, in 1985, the VHS, DVD, and computer game cartridge rental conglomerate hit its peak in 2004, when it had more than 9,000 stores operating around the world. Although the company ostensibly made its money by renting movies and videogames in 24-hour increments, the real money—about 16 percent of revenues—came in the form of (the rightly despised) late fees.

The first major challenge to Blockbuster's dominance in home entertainment occurred in 1999, when Netflix arrived, offering two things Blockbuster didn't: mail-order delivery and, perhaps even more importantly, a subscription service with no late fees. Whereas Blockbuster made money betting you would fail to return your rental on time, Netflix encouraged you to hold onto your rental disc indefinitely. Why? You couldn't get a second one until you returned the first.

As customers began drifting away from Blockbuster's brick-and-mortar model toward Netflix's Web-based mail-order experience, Blockbuster was hit by a second tsunami in 2008: streaming video. Although Amazon and Hulu had offered Internet-based video-on-demand a year earlier, it was Netflix—with its already sizeable subscription base—that proved to be most customers' provider-of-choice. True, Blockbuster eventually attempted to copy Netflix's online model, but the public wasn't buying an also-ran, and they succumbed to bankruptcy in 2010. As of July 2018, there is only ONE Blockbuster left (down from about 9,000 during its peak in 2004). The last store is in Bend, Oregon, and it's more of a tourist attraction now . . . people like to take Instagram photos in front of it.

The tragedy in all these stories is that it didn't have to be this way. People still travel. They still buy consumer goods, take photographs, and enjoy home entertainment. The failure leading to these companies' demises was not a lack of growth opportunities. In some cases, the problem was a simple lack of information. When information *was* available, the problem was decision makers simply didn't understand the messages the information contained. And even when the information was understood, the problem was that well-placed people chose not to act on key information.

Well, nobody's perfect, you might say. And, sadly, this is true. While we fancy ourselves to be rational beings, the fact is, most people are driven by emotions. This is true even at the highest levels of business. Instead of basing business decisions on cold calculations rooted in solid data, many, if not most, are the result of pride, ambition, ego, spite, anger, stubbornness, and misplaced hope.

Enter artificial intelligence (A.I.).

When it comes to A.I., a business, any business, *your* business, can better identify the market forces already at work and, perhaps more importantly, predict coming trends with amazing precision. A.I. can help you understand what these trends mean to you and your customers and provide guidance on how to adapt your business operations accordingly. As A.I. becomes more sophisticated, it will not just offer advice, but will proactively change your business model *without prompting* to anticipate challenges well before they become problems. And it will do all this without the emotions, prejudices, myopia, and egoism clouding so much human judgment.

Today, companies like Amazon, Uber, Tesla, and Netflix rake in billions thanks to A.I. algorithms that, historically speaking, are just in their infancy. Their leaders—visionaries like Jeff Bezos, Travis Kalanick, Garrett Camp, Elon Musk, Reed Hastings, and Marc Randolph—took to heart Apple Computer's slogan, "Think Different," first introduced in a 1997 commercial. They learned to think differently and therefore transformed their businesses. You should too. To fear or reject A.I. is to go down the same dark road as did Pullman, Woolworths, Marshall Field, Kodak, and Blockbuster, names once associated with success, now forever tinged with the patina of failure. To embrace A.I. is to welcome a future that, well, to coin a phrase, you can never even imagine.

Chapter 2

How Did We Get Here?

Before we can discuss the potential of A.I., we need to define our terms. Just what *is* artificial intelligence? Merriam-Webster's Dictionary defines it as "the theory and development of computer systems able to perform tasks that normally require human intelligence, such as visual perception, speech recognition, decision-making, and translation between languages." *Science Daily* offers a somewhat more nuanced description: "The study and design of 'intelligent agents,' where an intelligent agent is a system that perceives its environment and takes actions that maximize its chances of success."

The fact is, while artificial intelligence has been studied for decades, there is as yet no widely held consensus on what the term actually *means*. Defining the first part of the term is fairly simple. *Artificial* means, "that which is not found in nature; man-made." The second part of the term, *intelligence*, is significantly more problematic.

Since the time of Aristotle, philosophers, psychologists, and research scientists have struggled to identify just what it is that makes someone or some*thing* intelligent. As children, we tend to think of "intelligence" as simply "knowing stuff." We consider someone who can memorize and spit back facts like the names of all the American presidents or the batting average of every player on the 1938 New York Yankees baseball team intelligent. And if that's all intelligence requires, then we would have had A.I. 40 years ago. After all, if there is one thing computers have always been good at, it's storing and retrieving information.

But most psychologists now recognize intelligence is far more than just the ability to acquire and regurgitate facts and figures. Intelligence can exist on many levels. When a high school senior whips through the math portion of the SAT and scores a perfect 800, this is an indicator of *mathematical intelligence*. When a politician delivers a speech stirring emotions with lofty ideas and poetic turns of phrase, it's an example of *verbal intelligence*. A military commander who can eerily predict enemy movements and prepare effective countermoves clearly enjoys the gift of *strategic intelligence*. Likewise, artists from Michelangelo and Annie Leibovitz to architects like Frank Gehry and I.M. Pei show clear signs of possessing *creative intelligence*. Finally, when Sidney Crosby nails a puck into the goal, or when LeBron James sinks a three-pointer or Serena Williams demolishes her opponent with an unstoppable overhead smash, it's a demonstration of *physical intelligence*.

THINKING SYSTEMS

Even recognizing intelligence is not such a simple thing. Today's A.I. engineers often speak in narrower terms, focusing on creating machines capable of mimicking only certain aspects of human intelligence, such as the ability to run an obstacle course or write a sonnet, without necessarily duplicating all other human capabilities. While most people tend to think of artificial intelligence as a relatively new phenomenon, it actually has been around almost as long as electronic computers themselves. In fact, it might be said the development of A.I. has progressed *in parallel with* the evolution of electronic computers, as the two are similar, but not strictly equivalent, fields.

The big difference between the two is that while most computers were developed to simply do, to perform one or more assigned tasks according to their strict instructions, A.I. systems in contrast are designed to *think*, to find solutions on their own by freely associating with whatever information their inputs permit them to acquire. Traditional computers have been historically limited by the skill and creativity of their systems designers and programmers. (You have no doubt heard the old phrase, Garbage In = Garbage Out.)

On the other hand, true A.I. has no set limits precisely because it can modify the *way* it thinks—it can draw meaning from information and experiences to complete an assigned task. True A.I. might even be able to reject or change assignments based on its own judgment. In other words, while traditional computers will forever be little more than "order takers," true A.I. may develop the electronic equivalent of *free will*. And this is when things will *really* get interesting. But before we go there, let's take a step back to understand how this all began.

ORIGINS

Since the invention of the first ENIAC vacuum tube-powered computer in the early 1940s, computer technology has focused mainly on creating machines smaller, faster, and cheaper with each iteration. Moore's Law, coined in 1965 by Gordon Moore, cofounder of Fairchild Semiconductor and Intel, observes that the density of integrated circuits tends to double every 18 to 24 months, making each generation of computer roughly twice as powerful as the one before.

But while computing speed and capacity has increased exponentially since the mid-twentieth century, most computers are still basically "stupid," capable only of executing their prewritten instructions. Even the so-called "smartphone" in your pocket is pretty dumb. Yes, it can play games, provide turn-by-turn navigation, respond to voice queries, and even make phone calls, but it's still fundamentally the same kind of number cruncher the military used to crack enemy codes and figure out ballistic trajectories during World War II.

On the other hand, the mark of artificial intelligence is a machine's ability to *learn* and *adapt*. If a conventional computer's programming is buggy or otherwise flawed, it will continue to make the same error over and over again, regardless of how many computations its central processor can perform per second. A computer incorporating A.I., by contrast, will recognize its error and attempt to fix it. Another distinction of true A.I. is that it can *anticipate* its users' needs, something even the most powerful super-computer cannot accomplish. This is what makes A.I. such a game-changer.

THE TURING TEST

Back in 1950, British computer pioneer Alan Turing, a key member of the top-secret British team responsible for cracking the Germans' Enigma code, posited the following experiment to test machine intelligence: An "evaluator" would sit in a closed room. Using only a keyboard and monitor, the evaluator would communicate with two other parties by text, asking questions, posing challenges, soliciting opinions, making small talk, and so on.

One party providing responses would be human, the other a computer. If the evaluator could not tell the difference between the two, then the computer could be said to have passed the "Turing Test." (A test similar to Turing's was dramatized in Ridley Scott's 1982 sci-fi-noir classic, *Blade Runner*. In that film, subjects suspected of being "replicants"—artificial humans—were read a series of scenarios involving people or animals in various states of distress. If the subject responded with signs of empathy, this was a sign of authentic humanity. A replicant could not, by design, "feel" for anything but him- or herself.)

As even *Blade Runner* can attest, the criteria for success in a Turing Test involves not so much the accuracy of a participant's responses but that they mirror natural human behavior. Any well-programmed computer can deliver correct information; however, only true A.I. can demonstrate empathy, deliver a joke, appreciate a *double entendre*, tell you why the latest *Star Wars* movie sucked, or display frustration.

DARTMOUTH COLLEGE: SUMMER 1956

Most historians of science date the field of A.I. back to the summer of 1956. This is the year John McCarthy, then Assistant Professor of Mathematics at Dartmouth College, the private Ivy League research university in Hanover, New Hampshire, hosted an eight-week-long symposium on a subject he artfully coined as "artificial intelligence." (This appears to have been the first use of the term.)

Designed to merge the separate studies of cybernetics, automata theory, psychology, and complex information processing, McCarthy's symposium was designed, according to his original 1955 funding proposal to the Rockefeller Foundation, to consider how far computers could go in matching the performance, capabilities, and flexibility of the human mind. Topics covered included computers, natural language processing, neural networks, the theory of computation, abstraction, and creativity. McCarthy had been inspired to host this event by Claude E. Shannon, a mathematician at Bell Laboratories who, five years earlier, had published two seminal papers on how computers might someday be programmed to play chess. McCarthy wanted to know if, indeed, a computer could learn to play chess, could it learn to do more? *How much more? How quickly? And at what cost?*

Originally, only 10 of the world's top thought leaders in these fields were invited to attend. About half of those on McCarthy's original list demurred, but other leading researchers, upon hearing of the event, volunteered to attend in their stead. In all, 20 of the nation's leading computer and behavioral scientists participated in the symposium at some point during its eight-week run. Its impact reverberated throughout the scientific community for decades, influencing, perhaps most notably, psychologist and computer scientist J.C.R. Licklider, whose symposium-derived theories on universal networks led to the creation of the Internet.

DARPA GETS INVOLVED

In 1958, responding to the Soviets' launch of Sputnik, the world's first artificial satellite, the previous year, the U.S. Department of Defense (DOD) created the Advanced Research Projects Agency (ARPA) to direct and fund cutting-edge scientific research projects at such universities as MIT, Stanford, and CalTech. Later renamed the Defense Advanced Research Projects Agency (DARPA), the group became a major supporter of A.I. research during the 1960s.

In 1962, DARPA created the Information Processing Techniques Office (IPTO), which helped fund research-and-development projects in A.I. as well as such breakthrough fields as computer time-sharing, computer graphics, networking, advanced microprocessor design, and parallel processing. Perhaps most famously, in 1969, DARPA launched the ARPANET, a precursor to the Internet, a network allowing research computers at universities across the country to "talk" to each other via a common communications system.

However, while A.I. theory was advancing rapidly, practical advances were being hampered by the technology's failure to advance quickly enough to put the theories into practice. With data storage and processing speeds still in their relative infancies, funding for A.I. research waned throughout the 1970s —a so-called A.I. Winter, so designated because of reduced public interest and funding.

RISE OF EXPERT SYSTEMS

However, by the 1980s a thaw set in as more technology caught up with theory, kicking A.I. development into high gear. Perhaps the most notable advance in the field was the development of "expert system" software. These are decision-making tools users employ to direct actions based on large volumes of data. They require a large knowledge base—that is, a collection of facts and assertions accurately describing the real world—and an inference engine, a logic system using existing knowledge to deduce new information.

Usually written in an *If/Then* format, inference engines possess the advantage of being intuitive, easily understood, and, if necessary, modified by laymen, not just IT specialists. Paired with the powerful mainframes and then personal computers (PCs) entering the market, expert systems became extremely popular with banks, health-care facilities, manufacturers, real estate developers, financiers, and other companies needing to make decisions and accurate forecasts based on large volumes of information. In the 1980s, typical uses for this type of rudimentary artificial intelligence included everything from approving mortgage loan applications to diagnosing diseases to designing toxic spill response plans. With computing power rising and costs plummeting, the only factor limiting the power of expert systems was the acquisition and reliability of the knowledge base itself. Again, it was an issue of "Garbage In = Garbage Out."

MAN VS. MACHINE, ROUND 1

By the late 1990s, due largely to the availability of increased computational power, A.I. was being used widely for logistics, data mining, marketing, and medical diagnosis. Perhaps the era's most dramatic demonstration of how far A.I. had progressed may be found in the epic showdown between the reigning world chess champion, Russian Garry Kasparov, and Deep Blue, then the most advanced super-computer yet developed by IBM.

The first match occurred in Philadelphia, Pennsylvania, on February 10, 1996. In the first of six games, Deep Blue, playing white, beat the Russian grandmaster. However, Kasparov came back in game two, tying the match. The next two games were draws by mutual agreement. In game five, Kasparov, playing black, offered to draw after the twenty-third move, but the IBM team managing Deep Blue rejected the offer. In the end, Kasparov defeated the machine, and did so again in game six, clinching the match. For the moment, man still held the title as unchallenged master.

Believing his status secure, Kasparov subsequently agreed to a rematch in New York City on May 11, 1997. Kasparov, playing white, won the first of six games, but then lost the second when he switched to black. The next three games ended in draws by mutual agreement. Which meant it all came down to game six. As he had in game four, Kasparov opened with what is known as the Caro-Kann Defense. But Deep Blue, in a seemingly erratic move, sacrificed its own knight, shattering Kasparov's confidence along with his game strategy.

Sweating bullets, Kasparov resigned in less than 20 moves. The Russian grandmaster was furious. This was the first time in history that a computer had defeated a reigning grandmaster under tournament conditions, and he could only believe the victory was illegitimate. At first, he accused IBM of hiding an actual human grandmaster behind the scenes to feed moves to the computer. When this charge was disproven, he still insisted IBM had cheated, but offered no evidence of how this might have been done.

In fact, Deep Blue had won by making a very human decision. Based on an overwhelming number of possible chess moves, it simply chose one at random, the computer equivalent of throwing its hands in the air and saying, "What the hell, let's roll the dice." Resorting to such a capricious, irrational, and utterly *human* move broke Kasparov's concentration and conviction, leading to his downfall.

MAN VS. MACHINE, ROUND 2

The next *Eureka!* moment in the evolution of A.I. occurred 14 years later, when IBM put "Watson," its next-generation successor to Deep Blue, on national television to play the most famous answer-and-question game of all time, *Jeopardy!* With the classic Turing Test in mind, the director of IBM Research approached the show's producers, Merv Griffin Productions, who immediately recognized such a contest as a ratings bonanza and agreed.

While chess ultimately requires decision-making based on rapid mathematic computations and foresight, to win on *Jeopardy!*, Watson would need to manipulate vast amounts of data—basically the contents of the entire *Encyclopedia Britannica,* as well as every back issue of *People, Billboard,* and *Entertainment Weekly* magazines—all while trying to understand complex, conversational language, including puns, metaphors, homonyms, and idiomatic phrases.

Watson's task was no walk in the park. Just consider it is often difficult enough for a husband and wife—even those who have been together for decades—to communicate effectively. Now imagine how hard it is for a computer to understand a sentence like, "Honey, I'm feeling blue because it's raining cats and dogs." The challenge can be likened to the one non-native speakers face when learning the conversational version of any foreign language, although at least people, having once learned their own language's idioms, are more predisposed to glean the concepts behind figures of speech.

After gathering 200 million pages of data, learning to understand linguistic nuances, question-answer exchanges, and practicing against 100 past *Jeopardy!* winners, Watson made its national TV debut. Its challengers consisted of *Jeopardy!*'s biggest winners, Ken Jennings and Brad Rutter, who had between them earned more than $5 million on the program. Although Rutter had won more money than Jennings, Jennings was a seasoned veteran who had dominated an unprecedented 74 games in a row.

With a $1 million prize at stake, the contestants squared off in a special set built at IBM's T.J. Watson Research Center in Yorktown Heights, New York, providing questions for answers in such categories as Alternate Meanings, Beatles People, Olympic Oddities, Name the Decade, and Final Frontiers. The three contestants—two carbon-based, the other silicon—engaged in a heart-stopping trivia battle royal. During the three-day-long tournament, Watson proved itself formidable, but not flawless. It answered many questions incorrectly and even repeated other players' incorrect responses. But what the machine lacked in omniscience, it more than made up for in speed.

Jeopardy! players can only buzz in when a signal light flashes the moment the question has been fully read. Even the most practiced of contestants take about 0.10 seconds to make this quick physical move. Watson, having no eyes or ears, was fed the "go" signal electronically . . . and responded in kind, usually in just a few nanoseconds, flummoxing the human contestants even when they knew the answers. In the end, Watson won the tournament handily with a three-day total of $77,147 against Ken Jennings's $24,000 and Brad Rutter's $21,600. IBM gave its $1 million prize to charity, but went away with something more valuable: public trust in the future of A.I.

In a later interview, Jennings confessed he saw his losing to Watson as the beginning of his own obsolescence. The engineers at IBM had quite a different interpretation. They saw Watson's impressive victory as just one more stepping-stone on the road to true artificial intelligence.

Chapter 3

The Machine Learns

homas Edison, America's most prolific—and celebrated—inventor, happened to be a great believer in the value of experimentation. While trying to perfect the electric lightbulb, he famously experimented with hundreds of different materials before finding one to provide illumination long enough to be commercially viable. Later, when asked by a reporter what it felt like to fail hundreds of times, he replied, "*Fail?* I never failed! I found hundreds of things that don't work." In another version of this story, Edison was asked why it took him 700 tries to invent the lightbulb, to which he replied, "Because inventing the lightbulb was a process with 700 steps."

The Edison story, along with countless other tales of innovation, illustrate how knowledge is gained through the accumulation of facts, experiences, and observable reactions in the physical world. Together, we call this process "learning." The ability to learn is essential to the survival of higher-functioning species, especially humans. If early *Homo sapiens* had not learned how to make fire, fashion tools, distinguish edible plants from poisonous ones, hunt prey, dress wounds, and avoid predators, we would have vanished from the planet many years ago.

But while learning has been essential to humanity's success, our arguably greatest creation, the computer, has so far lacked this essential ability. Even as computers became more powerful and capable of storing vast amounts of data, they still couldn't acquire information on their own. For years, computers also failed to make the great leap forward by approximating anything close to what we would call an educated guess about the meaning of events. A computer's brain power was limited to the operating instructions contained in its programming and the data people chose to feed it. For computers to be truly intelligent, they needed to *learn how to learn*. Which is no easy thing.

THE THREE WAYS WE LEARN

In nature, animals acquire knowledge in one of three ways: instinct, instruction, and experience.

Instinct

Instinct is the most common and rudimentary of these processes. When a spider spins a web, a bird builds a nest, or a beaver constructs a dam, it's not because these creatures consciously believe such efforts will aid them in their daily lives. Neither is it because they were given detailed instructions by their parents.

According to the modern understanding of animal behavior, such organisms do so based on compulsions buried deep in their genetic code. Along the same lines, a puppy shaking itself to get dry, a newly born sea turtle crawling from its nest across a sandy beach to open water, or a baby kangaroo climbing into its mother's pouch, exemplify the instinctive behavior found throughout the animal kingdom. Even without parents or other members of their species to show them the way, animals spontaneously display instinctive behaviors evolved over millennia.

Even humans—the only species we know of to possess free will—exhibit instinctive behaviors, although these are not nearly as complex as bees dancing to direct others to sources of food or avian mating rituals. Usually, we call human instincts "reflexes." For example, put your index finger on a newborn's palm and it will instinctively grip it. Babies will also instinctively cry when hungry. As we've seen in innumerable cartoons, just tap a leg below the kneecap and a person will instinctively kick forward.

In this respect, most animals—even humans—are much like computers in the sense that they will behave in ways dictated by their programming—in this case, genetic programming. Computers, however, have no instincts. When a computer rolls off an assembly line, it is nothing but a finely engineered collection of transistors and circuits. It has no knowledge, no abilities. Turn it on, and all you get is a blank screen. It is, for lack of a better word, lifeless. To do anything at all, a computer must receive instructions.

Instruction

Instruction is the second way animals can learn. So far, only a small number of animal species—mostly mammals—have been observed learning in this fashion. Africa's meerkats, for example, possess a step-by-step process for teaching their young to hunt and handle scorpions, one of their main food sources. Golden lion tamarins, small monkeys with lionlike manes, will summon their young to trees where prey can be found. And, of course, humans have had great success training animals, like dogs, dolphins, chimpanzees, and sea lions to perform complex tricks. Undoubtedly, the ability to follow instructions would not have evolved if it did not offer some survival applications in the wild.

Humans, of course, have turned instruction into a billion-dollar industry. From preschools to universities to MasterClass online learning, instruction is the primary way humans learn about the world and themselves. Societies have developed complex rituals governing everything from courtship to eating to religious worship, all of which must be carefully taught. In most developed countries, one's income potential and social status is also tied to the amount of formal education one receives. Earning the illustrious title of "Doctor" may only be achieved through years of formal and rigorous instruction—one of the highest social ranks a person can achieve.

Since their invention, computers have learned almost exclusively through instruction. Programmers had to work out in painstaking detail every step of every operation a computer was intended to perform. Unlike a human, if a computer didn't work, you couldn't ask it what's wrong or how to fix it. In fact, even the smallest coding error in its operating system could result in a machine that, for all intents and purposes, was just an expensive paperweight. In this respect, even the most advanced computers were still "dumb."

Experience

The third way animals learn is through experience. One such sub-category of this is "social learning." Observed in insects, fish, birds, amphibians, and mammals, social learning occurs when young animals mimic behaviors they observe in those around them. Many learn most of their species' hunting and feeding techniques by watching and copying the behaviors of their more experienced elders. Biologists believe young marine mammals, such as whales and dolphins, acquire their species' complex languages by repeated exposure and imitation rather than through actual "teaching" by adults.

The other major subcategory of experiential learning is called "individual learning" or "asocial learning"—learning through trial and error. An expensive and painful way to grow, this has been rightly dubbed "The School of Hard Knocks." If a lion in the wild encounters fire for the first time, he may be initially attracted to it—until it burns his paw. Ever after, this lion will know to steer to clear of orange flames. Likewise, if a lab rat accidentally hits a button and receives a food pellet as a result, the rodent will quickly learn to press the same button each time it is hungry.

Of course, we humans employ both social and asocial learning to acquire knowledge and skills. Walking upright is not necessarily a natural behavior; most so-called feral children—boys and girls raised in the wild without other humans to learn from—more often than not walk on all fours. As toddlers, we learn to walk upright by imitating adults and older children around us. Likewise, much of our verbal language skills—and certainly all of our regional accents—are acquired through imitation.

On the other hand, humans are particularly adept at self-learning. Since the invention of literacy, and especially since the explosion of mass media in the nineteenth and twentieth centuries, anyone thirsting for knowledge has encountered fewer obstacles acquiring it. In fact, some of our most accomplished inventors, artists, scientists, and businesspeople of the last 200 years were self-taught, acquiring knowledge and skills outside the established systems of formal education. Known as autodidacts, here's just a few self-taught geniuses.

- **Authors:** Hermann Hesse, Truman Capote, Jane Austen, Harlan Ellison, and Doris Lessing.
- **Musicians:** Frank Zappa, Keith Moon, David Bowie, Anna Calvi, Jimi Hendrix, and Paul McCartney.
- **Filmmakers:** Stanley Kubrick, Woody Allen, Quentin Tarantino, Andy and Lana Wachowski, Steven Spielberg, and Orson Welles.
- **Inventors:** James Watt, Nikola Tesla, Margaret Knight, Henry Ford, Benjamin Banneker, and, of course, our friend Thomas Edison.
- **Scientists:** Charles Darwin, Mary Anning, Benjamin Franklin, George Washington Carver, and Buckminster Fuller.

Until recently, self-learning had been the "Holy Grail" of computer science. Most A.I. researchers believed that for a computer to be truly intelligent, it had to be able to learn from experience. Just like these brilliant autodidacts, a computer had to recognize what it *didn't* know, to search for sources of additional knowledge, and, when necessary, to ask for help.

As impressive as the expert systems discussed in the last chapter were, they did not involve self-learning. The applications could analyze copious amounts of data with near humanlike skill, but they had no ability to expand their knowledge base by themselves. Likewise, though IBM's Watson possessed the ability to process idiomatic English, it still required humans to feed it knowledge. (It also didn't have the sense to realize that while Toronto may host an American League baseball team, the city is actually in Canada.)

Breakthrough

It took the A.I. computer AlphaGo to show the world what *real* artificial intelligence looks like. First unveiled in 2016, AlphaGo ushered in far more than an incremental change in A.I. technology. This thinking machine, capable of playing the ancient Chinese game of Go, took computing a quantum leap forward into unchartered territory.

Before we discuss what happened, let's pause to remind ourselves what the IBM engineers accomplished with Watson. They taught it to use natural language processing (NLP) to interpret, manipulate, and comprehend human language. This was critical to winning *The Jeopardy! Challenge*—and to Watson's applications in the commercial sphere. As you have no doubt observed, people speak differently than they write, and in each language, individuals use different idioms, expressions, colloquialisms, and jargon to communicate. NLP, which we will discuss in greater detail in future chapters, by its nature, enables computers to break down language into its component parts to interpret meaning, understand written and verbal communication, and even determine emotions and priorities. We already experience NLP in our everyday lives when we talk to Alexa, Siri, or Cortana, or when we dictate text messages via our smartphones.

When it came to Watson competing on *Jeopardy!*, its engineering team took the computer's NLP ability to the next level, adding a layer of sophistication to make their machine's responses almost humanlike. However, something even more impressive occurred in March 2016, when AlphaGo, developed by Alphabet Inc.'s DeepMind Technologies division, beat legendary Go player and 18-time world champion Lee Sedol in a five-game match.

Not nearly as popular in the West, Go is a Chinese board game light-years more complex than chess. Mathematicians have posited that the possible moves in Go "exceed the number of atoms in the universe," and the game requires skills, such as creativity and abstract thinking, once deemed uniquely human. Chess grandmasters, who must think many moves ahead, can say with certainty why they made a particular move and how it fits into their overall strategy. However, expert Go players use a different approach to playing their game. When asked why they have made a particular move, they often respond, "It just *felt* right."

Undoubtedly, the sophisticated nuances and layers surrounding Go made for a high-stakes showdown between Sedol and AlphaGo in 2016. All around the world, the highly anticipated match piqued the attention of programmers, scientists, gamers, and everyday people alike. On one side, the invested engineering team hoped their creation might prove once and for all the power of A.I. to employ humanlike, intuitive thinking. On the other side, traditionalists clung to their faith in the indefatigable nature of human thinking to slay the computer upstart.

It was truly a battle between man vs. machine.

But there was no contest. In the first game, AlphaGo won in 186 moves. It trounced the second game in 211 moves and the third in 176 moves. Yes, Sedol came back to win game 4 in 180 moves, but the computer crushed its human opponent in the final game in an exhausting 280 moves. AlphaGo's triumph was so dramatic that the Korea Baduk Association awarded it the highest Go grandmaster rank, an "honorary 9 dan." Experts in artificial intelligence called AlphaGo's stellar performance "A.I.'s version of landing on the moon."

DEEP LEARNING, DEEP IMPLICATIONS

So what distinguished AlphaGo from Deep Blue, the computer that beat chess grandmaster Garry Kasparov in 1997? The fundamental difference is that while IBM engineers taught Deep Blue to play chess, AlphaGo *taught itself* to play Go. Practicing against human players and other, less advanced Go-playing computers, AlphaGo tested and evaluated strategies. *On its own.* It took chances. It *learned from its mistakes.* It accomplished this feat because IBM engineers built into it an artificial neural network facilitating "deep learning."

Sometimes called "deep structured learning" or "hierarchical learning," deep learning is a subset of machine learning based on understanding what data *represents* rather than task-specific algorithms. Inspired by the human nervous system, deep learning models allow computers to not only learn from data, but more importantly, make informed predictions—surpassing the intelligence limitations of every animal species on earth, except humans.

Ultimately, AlphaGo was a phenomenal demonstration of A.I.'s power to not only learn the rules of a fantastically complex game, but also, most remarkably, to *teach itself* in the same way Thomas Edison learned from his experiences, one mistake at a time. Not only that, this event proved something to the world: for the first time since their invention, computers demonstrated that they have the potential to equal, if not surpass, their human creators.

The new question became: where do we go from here?

Chapter 4

Special Sauce:
Decisions, Decisions

When making even minor decisions, people will usually consider a variety of factors before committing to a course of action. For example, when deciding what movie to see on a given Saturday night, a couple might consider such factors as:

- **Preferred genre.** Do they like superhero movies? Romantic comedies? Horror films? Indie dramas?
- **Stars.** Everybody has a favorite actor or actress whose mere presence can excuse a host of other cinematic failings.
- **Critic and/or audience ratings.** A quick trip to Rotten Tomatoes or Metacritic may provide guidance.
- **Buzz.** What are friends and coworkers saying? What's the word on Twitter and Facebook?
- **Awards.** Did the film win any Oscars or Golden Globes? Did it at least receive nominations?
- **Convenience.** Is the theater close by? Are the showtimes convenient?
- **Box office performance.** Who wants to watch a box office bomb?
- **Importance.** Is this a visually impressive film demanding to be seen on the big screen or can it wait six weeks to be rented from Red Box?

OPPORTUNITY COSTS

Fortunately, if our hypothetical couple ends up making a bad decision, the most they will lose is a few hours of their time and perhaps $25 to $30 (not counting overpriced popcorn and soft drinks).

When making *major* decisions, however, the list of variables can seem endless. Consider the U.S. Department of Defense (DOD). When evaluating a contractor to build a new weapons system such as a tank, fighter jet, or destroyer, the process can take years and cost tens of millions of dollars, requiring competing companies to submit complex cost proposals, complete mountains of paperwork, and even build pricey demonstration prototypes.

Even then, the system the DOD selects may not perform up to expectations, leading to further expenditures and, in worse-case scenarios, significant loss of life. (The Lockheed-Martin F-35 Lightning II supersonic jet fighter program is an example of just such a DOD boondoggle. Despite a lengthy procurement process, the program's development, as of mid-2018, is reported to be $163 billion over budget and seven years behind schedule.)

Now, wouldn't it be nice if there was a machine to make decisions for us? Especially complex decisions with Lightning II-type opportunity costs? A kind of "Magic 8 Ball" that was actually *right* more often than not? Imagine how much time, money, and aggravation might be saved if a thinking machine—a computer—could acquire and evaluate every factor impacting a choice, then recommend the best possible action course. Such a device would be the next best thing to an authentic fortune-telling machine.

SOOTHSAYING DEVICES

In fact, accurate forecasting and intelligent decision-making is one of the centerpieces of current A.I. research. And we would bet you've already experienced it in its currently limited form. Computer-based decision-making accounts for the explosion of personalized recommendations found on retail sites, like Amazon.com, or streaming services, like Netflix and Hulu. No, Netflix didn't read your mind to know just because you liked *Orange Is the New Black*, you might enjoy *Glow*.

Instead, these companies use complex algorithms to track our previous buying decisions, constructing a model of our preferences and long-term buying habits. Based on ongoing evaluations, cross-referenced with those of customers with similar selection patterns, it dynamically chooses shows—or products—it believes we will find attractive. This ability to "read our thoughts," or anticipate our unspoken desires, is a key reason for the success of so many A.I.-driven companies, including Facebook, which uses similarly complex algorithms to suggest friends and populate our news feeds.

But computers initiating consumer behavior-based buying suggestions is just the tip of the iceberg as to what's coming, a simple demonstration of artificial intelligence's astounding decision-making capabilities. Things will really get interesting when A.I.-based systems connect with the Internet of Things (IoT).

EVERYTHING'S GONNA GET A LOT SMARTER

So just what is IoT? Before explaining, let's return to the early '90s, when the Internet first became popular. It sounds antiquated and even a little lame now to remember the Web's running tagline back then was "The Information Superhighway." By connecting computers worldwide, allowing them to communicate in a common language, HTML, anyone anywhere suddenly gained access to what amounted to the accumulated knowledge of the entire human race.

In the last decade of the twentieth century, it suddenly became possible to access information on virtually any topic imaginable, just by typing in a keyword. Type "Beethoven's 5th" into a then-current search engine like Gopher, Infoseek, or Yahoo!, and you would find links to articles about the history of the early nineteenth-century symphony, biographies of the composer, and perhaps even an audio file of the music itself. Enter "pizza restaurant," and listings of several local pizzerias would instantly appear. Unfortunately, the programming behind such early search engines was still somewhat primitive. Because they were almost entirely keyword based, a query like "local restaurants not pizza," would likely still bring up pizza parlor recommendations.

Later, more sophisticated engines, such as Google, created primitive A.I. systems capable of anticipating common questions based on just a few keystrokes. Type "pizza," and you'd be offered a series of query options, such as "Pizza Hut," "Pizza Near Me," and "Pizza Delivery," all based on the frequency such questions are asked. In addition, Google pioneered the concept of ranking responses based on website popularity, figuring that the more popular a site was, the more useful its content was likely to be. The power of Google's A.I. helped it break away from the pack—which initially also included such sites as Ask Jeeves, Lycos, and AltaVista—and become a now nearly $1 trillion company with a virtual monopoly in the search engine realm.

Fast forward to today and another race for anticipatory supremacy is on. Digital assistants, such as Siri (Apple), Alexa (Amazon), and Cortana (Microsoft), use sophisticated voice recognition software to both understand our instructions and act on them. Eschewing the keyboard for a more direct person-to-machine experience, these interfaces allow users to acquire information not via tedious text keystrokes, but rather through natural verbal commands.

Though the term "Information Superhighway" is now far in our cultural rearview mirror, the acquisition and dissemination of information is still the Internet's main purpose. Enter the IoT. Whereas the "old" Internet merely delivered information, the IoT promises to reach deep into the physical world and control virtually anything with an On/Off switch.

If this sounds a little spooky or too much like far-out speculation, let's consider how the IoT *already* impacts people's lives in myriad ways. Many people possess television sets linked to the Internet via either add-ons, like Roku, Google Chrome, and AppleTV, or via smart apps built directly into TV sets. Likewise, wireless home security systems allow anxious homeowners to monitor their property from their cell phones and receive automatic alerts, including live video feeds, whenever anyone ventures into sensor range. In the not-too-distant future, everything from our refrigerators and dishwashers to our cars and bedroom table lamps will likely be connected to the web, providing endless actionable data and unparalleled control over the technology with which we interact on a daily basis.

IT'S HEEERE

Of course, much of this so-called "smart home" technology is already available. Go to any big box DIY store, like Home Depot or Lowe's, and you'll find gadgets enabling connection to all manner of appliances synced to a smart phone. Where A.I. will make its biggest impact is in providing behind-the-scenes control offering valuable efficiencies without personal intervention or even knowledge.

As an example of such a phenomenon, let's consider energy management. Already, smart thermostats, like Nest, not only adjust heating and air conditioning demands when we enter/leave the house, these systems can adjust accordingly as occupants move from room to room using proximity sensors. Soon, A.I. will communicate with an area's electric utility to ensure power consumption is perfectly balanced with grid capacity on a second-by-second basis. By interfacing with our water company as well as the weather service and sensors buried in the soil, these devices will even ensure the lawn receives the optimum needed water to remain green and healthy. Connected to emergency service centers, an A.I.-equipped house will eventually shut off water and gas lines in the event of imminent natural threats, like earthquakes or tornadoes.

Outside of the home, the IoT of the future will deliver astonishing efficiencies on a national or global level. For example:

- In agriculture, data on temperature, rainfall, humidity, pest infestation, and a thousand other variables could be used to automate farming techniques, minimize risk and waste, and more accurately predict future crop yields.
- Sensors monitoring air and water quality could communicate with manufacturing and transportation companies, creating feedback loops mitigating pollution and stemming the rise of global warming.
- Within just a few decades, private automobiles could give way to autonomous cars communicating with not just surrounding vehicles, but the traffic grid as a whole, allowing vehicles to move at much higher speeds while virtually eliminating traffic jams. (For more on this topic, see Chapter 16's A.I. Town in China.)

EVEN GREATER VISTAS TO COME

And while these A.I.-driven improvements may seem impressive, connectivity and data acquisition are just stepping stones on a path to something greater. Though radical to many of us, especially those who grew up in a world before television, these incredible applications barely scratch the surface of what artificial intelligence is capable of. Trained correctly, A.I. has the potential to solve age-old problems, like poverty, inequality, and injustice, as well as to offer the kinds of revolutionary guidance and wisdom the likes of which have eluded humans since our ancestors first climbed down from the trees.

Even more important, A.I. has the potential to *answer questions we didn't even previously know to ask.* In 2007, then Defense Secretary Donald Rumsfeld famously said, "There are known knowns. These are things we know that we know. There are known unknowns. That is to say, there are things that we know we don't know. But there are also unknown unknowns. There are things we don't know we don't know."

Though nearly universally panned as a clunky way to explain military foreign policy, Rumsfeld hit on something key. The limitations of our intelligence preclude us from asking questions about things we haven't yet even considered, precisely due to our limitations. Therefore, a thinking machine capable of processing vast amounts of data—recognizing complex patterns in ways our minds have yet to approach—could open avenues of inquiry we have yet to even conceive.

It is currently impossible to anticipate what will happen when IoT networks become more and more interconnected. When your home security system begins to interface with millions of home security systems across the world, and these connect with A.I.s in law enforcement, transportation, power distribution, energy exploration and extraction, climate monitoring, disease control, and every other human activity on this planet—and beyond—we are likely to discover patterns, impending hazards, and potential solutions of which we cannot yet even conceive. By connecting umpteen million dots together, A.I. has the potential to open up vast new markets, technologies, and fields of inquiry as unimaginable to early twenty-first-century humankind as the Internet itself would have been to Thomas Edison, Henry Ford, and the Wright Brothers. And, perhaps most amazing of all, it is likely to happen within most of our lifetimes.

Fascinating, right? And perhaps even a bit frightening. Advancements in A.I. are likely to put issues like privacy and individual liberty at the forefront of our political discussions. With A.I.-predictive powers, it's easy to imagine a scenario straight out of Steven Spielberg's *Minority Report* (2002) in which artificial precogs have people arrested for crimes they have yet to commit.

Certainly, like any new technology, A.I. must be carefully controlled and regulated—but as this book will continue to suggest, it needn't be feared. Especially not if we take the time to view the emerging new reality with both open eyes and an open mind. After all, this is the real world, not some dystopian sci-fi film. Like the development of the steam engine, electricity, the internal combustion engine, antibiotics, atomic energy, telecommunications, and Big Data, A.I. is likely to cause radical changes throughout society—and even pain in the transition—but the end result will hopefully be a safer, cleaner, healthier, and more prosperous world for us all. To better appreciate this new world and what A.I. can bring us, we need to first step back and consider how our own minds operate, the subject of our next chapter.

Chapter 5

Theories of the Mind

An artificial plant may not look exactly like its natural counterpart, but we recognize the thing it is designed to represent. It has a brown stalk. Stems. Green leaves. The flowers are red or yellow or violet. *It looks like a plant*. Now, if the stalk were candy-striped, the leaves checkerboard, and in place of flowers we found pinwheels, we would all agree that the manufacturer had done a poor job of creating an artificial plant. Likewise, an artificial flavor may not taste exactly like its natural analog, but we still recognize artificial strawberry as strawberry, artificial blueberry as blueberry, and artificial lemon as lemon. We know what real strawberries, blueberries, and lemons taste like. The relevant question is how well the white-coated scientists in their laboratories have come to duplicating their natural counterparts.

But when it comes to artificial intelligence, evaluating success becomes more muddied. This is because, unlike with plants or flavors, no two people can agree on exactly what "intelligence" is in the first place. For millennia, academics, philosophers, artists, and scientists have struggled to define this term—its nature, its source, and its manifestations—and, of course, they have yet to arrive at a definitive answer.

We can all agree that *Homo sapiens* are intelligent; after all, the very name means "wise man"—but from where does our intelligence spring? Our brains? Virtually all other animals have brains. Chimpanzees have brains. Cats and dogs possess brains. Even fish and worms do. Does this make them intelligent? Likewise, we would all probably agree a nuclear physicist or a surgeon is intelligent, but what about an illiterate dirt farmer? A recidivist drug abuser? A two-week-old baby? *Are they intelligent?* How do we know? How can we measure their intelligence? What standards are we to use?

As these examples suggest, it is a tricky business assigning a universal definition of intelligence differentiating one being's mental aptitude from that of another. Still, this book is all about understanding A.I. In order to fathom what this field entails, we must grasp what our brightest minds have said about well . . . our minds. We must first explore natural intelligence. And to do this, we need to examine the various schools of thought surrounding consciousness, perception, and intellect.

THEORY OF MIND

Theory of mind pertains to the ability to recognize beliefs, desires, and intentions, in one's self and in others, and to use this ability to predict actions. This ability is critical to all social interactions. For example, a married woman may wish to go to a popular diner for brunch on Sunday morning. However, from past experience, she knows so many other people love this place too that it's bound to take hours to get a table. She also knows one of her husband's pet peeves is waiting in line for anything. Even suggesting they go to this spot will probably lead to an argument. Therefore, she suggests they try a cute new bistro instead. There will be no chance of a long line there. Her careful reasoning staves off a fight—thus preserving the tranquility of her marriage. Here's another example to illustrate this concept: Imagine you go shopping for a new pair of pants. Approaching the checkout counter, you place your bootcut jeans before the cashier, then reach into your wallet for your debit card in the belief that the cashier will accept it as payment. In fact, you believe the cashier will likely be eager to do so.

Now, let's step back to examine *why* you might think this. Even though this scenario may seem so commonplace as to hardly warrant investigation, it's actually highly complex, founded upon a string of theory of mind assumptions we often take for granted. The fact is, you don't know this cashier. The two of you have never met. Yet you feel confident she knows what a debit card is, how to process it, and will be happy to do so. To believe otherwise would be to question the very foundation of the twenty-first-century economy—how humans relate to each other in our mutually agreed-upon capitalist system.

In either of the above scenarios, the subjects recognize their own desires, yet also perceive the other person in the situation possesses wants of their own. In order to best navigate their respective social spheres, they must weigh both intentions against each other and behave accordingly. Although we have no way to enter another person's mind, much less confirm that another person even has one, we can infer their states of consciousness based on our own observations and experiences. Such inferences supply the foundation to the social order we interact with every minute of every day. They form the crucial, yet invisible structure behind our daily existence, which we might well overlook if we didn't stop for a moment to ask why things are the way they are.

Beyond the capacity to consider others' wants, another key aspect of theory of mind is the ability to recognize someone may hold *differing* beliefs or assumptions. In a classic experiment, a five-year-old child is shown a Band-Aid box. Asked what is in the box, the child naturally says: "Band-Aids." But when she opens the box, she finds it contains not adhesive bandages, but a pack of gum. The experimenters then bring a second child into the room and also show him the same Band-Aid box.

"What do you think the boy will say is in the box?" they ask the girl.

"Band-Aids," she replies.

From experience, she knows this particular box contains gum, not Band-Aids. But she also knows that the boy doesn't yet know this. Going "inside his mind," she believes he will make the same mistake she did. And she will probably be right. Even at the age of five, the girl knows other people often hold beliefs at odds with objective reality.

Again, we practice this skill every day, often without recognizing it. Approaching a four-way stop, we carefully check the cross traffic in the event another driver does not see the signs and blows through the intersection like a missile. In a public place, we keep our voices low when discussing hot-button topics like politics or religion, in case someone with differing views might overhear. We warn an unsuspecting coworker not to put money into a vending machine we know is out of order.

In this sense, theory of mind is linked closely with *empathy*. We assume other people have thoughts and feelings just as we do, and while their opinions and values may be different, we are still all bonded by the same rudimentary emotions. Another person's joy becomes our joy. Another person's sadness becomes our sadness. Even psychopaths, infamous for lacking empathy, still recognize that other people harbor thoughts and feelings apart from theirs; in fact, such recognition is key to the psychological and emotional manipulation psychopaths often use to hide in plain sight and ensnare their victims.

BUILDING BLOCKS OF CONSCIOUSNESS

Now that we have a framework to better understand how our minds function in reality, particularly in social situations, we will learn some of the leading theories of consciousness put forth by experts in the field. These concepts will return throughout the following pages as building blocks for us to understand how artificial intelligence operates in the real world.

Primary/Secondary Components

The author of the book *Consciousness*, renowned physicist Dr. J. Allan Hobson, theorizes that all mammals, including human infants, experience *primary* components of consciousness: sensation, perception, attention, emotion, instinct, and movement. For example, a baby is aware it feels uncomfortable when hungry and responds to this unpleasant sensation by crying. Babies are attracted to bright, shiny objects like a set of car keys and will even reach out to grab them. However, this is pretty much the limit of their primary consciousness. A crying infant does not yet understand the concept of "food." It only knows that when it sucks from its mother's breast, it feels satisfied. Likewise, while babies may find a set of car keys attractive, they have no concept of what a "car" is, nor do they understand that these jagged metal objects are required to operate it.

On the other hand, *secondary* consciousness components, such as memory, thought, language, intention, orientation, and volition, only emerge in humans as they mature. As an infant grows into a toddler, he will begin not only to understand the concept of food, but will also develop names for its various forms as well as preferences. He may remember he does not like the one called broccoli, but greatly enjoys the one called chocolate. Likewise, a different child will not only come to learn that keys can start the engine of the four-wheeled conveyance called a "car," but by the time she is 16, will ask for one.

According to Hobson, most of the secondary components we experience after infancy are a type of "elaborative processing," involving mentally retrieving, reflecting, symbolizing, representing, and recording information. Two components not included in processing are volition and movement. Hobson classifies these as "output actions," including our decisions to act. Let's now look to one of the principal theorists responsible for understanding the motivations behind our behavior.

Freud

The late Dr. Sigmund Freud, the father of modern psychotherapy, expanded the binary concept of theory of mind by asserting that the mind is composed of not two, but three levels of consciousness: 10 percent conscious, 50-60 percent subconscious, and 30-40 percent unconscious. He posited that our conscious mind controls both our attention and our imagination. When we read a book, prepare a meal, or ponder the details of next week's Hawaiian vacation, we are using our conscious mind. Meanwhile, our subconscious, the ultimate storage space, holds information, habits, and feelings. The skills necessary to read a book, prepare the meal, and picture the resort hotel where we plan to stay are contained in this subconscious realm. If called upon to explain how to read, sauté a trout, or fly to the Big Island, we could probably do so, even though we regularly employ this knowledge with little conscious thought.

Lastly, the unconscious mind holds our memories and experiences, influencing our behaviors and emotions. This is where impulse behaviors, compulsions, and phobias arise. If asked to explain why we stared at an attractive man or woman passing on the sidewalk but ran screaming when a harmless garter snake appeared in our path, we may not have a rational explanation other than that we "felt" like doing this. In psychoanalysis, Freud focused on the unconscious, which he viewed as the seat for so many of these seemingly inexplicable things in our day-to-day life. This is also the same nexus he believed could most enact tangible behavioral change in the real world.

Freud's trinity explanation extends to his breakdown of consciousness into three distinct personality parts: the id, ego, and superego. In his formulation, the id relates to instincts, ego to organization and realism, and the superego to moralizing. Of course, Freud lived in an era before computers, one in which the best explanations for theory of mind came from the analog phenomena surrounding him, but what might an expert of our Information Age have to say about consciousness and its power to affect reality? For this, we must turn to a nuclear physicist who once worked for NASA, Tom Campbell.

MY BIG T.O.E.

In his book *My Big Toe,* Campbell explains his Theory of Everything (T.O.E.), covering such diverse topics as relativity, metaphysics, and the origin of consciousness. Employing more of an engineering mentality than psychiatric analysis, Campbell likens thinking to the functioning of a computer. He asserts that consciousness is a dynamic information system capable of being reprogrammed by the individual experiencing it. Because we can control our conscious state, our consciousness can evolve just as nature selects for the fittest organisms.

It is Campbell's belief that humans, as well as other animals, are all individuated units of consciousness with varying degrees of awareness. Consciousness itself is therefore information originating from other minds and shared among its participants. Trained in quantum physics, Campbell takes an "observer's view of reality," meaning that there isn't an objective world. Instead, the way the world behaves depends on how we look at it. Most famously demonstrated in the double slit experiment, in which a beam of electrons was affected by the act of being observed, he believes consciousness and reality aren't separate but instead affect each other, one acting on the other.

Since Campbell believes that subjective reality exists only in our consciousness, it can also be simulated to the point it becomes indistinguishable from objective reality. In fact, because of theorists like Campbell and the futurist Elon Musk, who has suggested reality may be a simulation, there continues to be a long-standing debate over whether or not the universe itself may be nothing but a massive computer simulation inside some alien super-computer. (As Musk said in an interview, "The strongest argument for us probably being in a simulation is the following: 40 years ago, we had Pong, like two rectangles and a dot. That was pretty much what games were. Now 40 years later, we have photorealistic 3D simulations with millions of people playing simultaneously, and it's getting better every year.")

Though Campbell's Theory of Mind ideas may seem far-out, they are grounded in concepts explaining the way computers work. It may also be instructive for developing functioning artificial intelligence based on the intersection of consciousness and reality. Now that we understand the idea our minds may be programmable much like a computer, let's consider how such programming may have occurred with a controversial theory.

The Bicameral Mind Theory

In 1976, psychologist Julian Jaynes published his highly contested book, *The Origin of Consciousness in the Breakdown of the Bicameral Mind*. Based on his study of ancient literature, Jaynes argued that up until 3,000 years ago, humans were guided not by self-awareness, but by commands they thought they heard from afar. Jaynes contends that the ancient gods, such as Zeus and Apollo, now viewed in modern times as fictional characters from myths, could actually have played such a significant role in early human history as "voices within our heads."

According to Jaynes, this part of the mind that "speaks"—expressing needs, desires, and judgments—was "heard" by a second "chamber" of the brain, and the individual obeyed. (In this sense, these commands are akin to the "voices" heard by modern-day schizophrenics.) However, around 1,000 B.C., toward the end of the Bronze Age, the two parts of the human mind merged, and the "gods" fell silent. Afterward, humans became the conscious masters of their own destinies.

Though this notion goes against everything science says about how the world works, it is interesting to note that the word ""genius" actually dates back to Greece, not as a *quality* of the mind, as when a person is said to be a genius, but rather, a person possesses a "genius," an invisible entity that transmits information directly to our brains. No less than Socrates, the founder of Western philosophy, claimed to be guided by his own genius, an entity that spoke to him alone, his personal "daemon" or divine nature spirit.

Bestselling author Anthony Peake, in his book *The Daemon: A Guide to Your Extraordinary Secret Self*, delves deeply into the bicameral mind theory, explaining how each person has two distinct consciousnesses: one we recognize as "daily consciousness" and the other what he calls the Daemon, a "higher being possessing knowledge of future events." Interestingly, in HBO's *Westworld*, a popular show about A.I., the robot creators utilize aspects of the bicameral mind theory to bootstrap consciousness in the fledgling thinking machines.

In our final theory of mind discussion, we will look at yet one more attempt to extrapolate a functioning model for how intelligence works.

Brain as Model Theory

In his book *The Future of Mind,* another celebrated physicist, Dr. Michio Kaku, explores telepathy, artificial intelligence, and transhumanism. In this seminal work, he proposes the consciousness theory that all sentient beings create their own model of reality to understand the world and predict the future. Kaku views consciousness as a series of feedback loops placing one's self in space, in relationship to others, and in time. Like Campbell, he suggests sentience levels. Each organism increases in sentience complexity from simple one-celled organisms to humans at the apex.

Kaku goes so far as to say that we can even rank intelligence by counting the number of feedback loops involved in each of our behaviors. Not only do all carbon-based organisms have a level of sentience, so do physical objects as they operate in the world. (This explains how the IoT discussed in the previous chapter works.) For instance, a smart thermostat may possess one unit of consciousness measuring temperature. A flower, on the other hand, might have 10 units of consciousness because it measures data like temperature, sunlight, gravity, and moisture. A more advanced creature, though, such as a guinea pig, will possess even more units, maybe several hundred, because it can create a model to locate its position as it travels, as opposed to a plant. Monkeys have even more units of consciousness because they can construct a mental model explaining their ranking in their hierarchal society.

Of course, humans possess the most intelligence units of all because they can create mental models incorporating all of the above and much more. Not only can we develop understandings of our positions in time, we have the ability to imagine and plan for the future. Throughout our discussion in this chapter, we have often returned to the subject of sentience. No matter which theory of mind is involved, each thinker has invested much care into formulating a concept viewing intelligence as an aspect of expanding awareness—the more intelligent the organism, the higher its awareness. Let's now turn.to sentience in greater detail, as it remains the lynchpin to all of our theories.

SENTIENCE: THE CAPACITY TO PERCEIVE

To be sentient is to be "self-aware." To some degree, all sentient beings have the ability to be subjective: to separate themselves from their surroundings, to understand there is a difference between "me" and "you," and to make choices. Today, scientists recognize that virtually all complex animals, including mammals, reptiles, and most fish, amphibians, and birds, feel emotions of one sort or another. They can all experience fear and anxiety. Many also show the ability to experience joy, sorrow, and even love. Any dog owner will tell you his pet is sad when he leaves the house, and positively joyful upon his return. Likewise, a trip to the vet is likely to trigger anxiety in a pet and even fear, long before the veterinary clinic comes into view.

While the Abrahamic religions—Judaism, Christianity, and Islam—separate humanity from the rest of the animal kingdom, many other faiths do not. Buddhism, for example, holds that any creature that can suffer and has a fear of death is, by definition, sentient, and therefore capable of rebirth through reincarnation.

Are plants sentient? For centuries, most scientists scoffed at the idea. Today, many are not so sure. Many plants exhibit signs of anxiety and joy just as animals do. Mycologist Paul Stamets contends that mushrooms possess sentience. In fact, he believes we are all fungal beings and that mushrooms are "network-based organisms" with incredible communicative power. Many of the bacterial infections affecting fungi also affect us, he notes. He thinks that by trying to define consciousness in other beings, we are being hypocritical as we were raised by the very nature we now dismiss as nonsentient.

No matter which organisms we designate as sentient, as Kaku suggests, not all sentient beings are created equal. Varying levels of awareness exist, ranging from the ability to store information, to formulating objectives, experiencing emotions, and, last, developing self-awareness. This final component may be thought of as the gold standard of sentience. As far as we know, humans are the only creatures with the ability to self-reflect. *For now.* There may come a day when A.I. possesses the same or greater sentience levels.

As these various theories of mind demonstrate, psychologists, physicists, and philosophers haven't yet agreed on a unitary system of consciousness, mind, and intelligence. For developers working to artificially duplicate or even improve upon human intelligence, this makes the challenge more daunting. However, not being able to agree on a definition won't preclude them from pushing the bounds of what's possible. Though we cannot say for sure how consciousness works, our brightest minds are hard at work fashioning thinking machines that may one day tell us. In the next chapter, we will learn how artificial intelligence is aided by our newfound theoretical foundation.

Chapter 6

Just What *Is* Artificial Intelligence?

O ver the last five chapters, we toured the history of artificial intelligence. We explored the origins of thinking machines and examined the progress scientists and engineers have made in duplicating aspects of human consciousness and reasoning. However, before discussing the future of A.I. and the impact it is likely to have on our daily lives, it's important we pause to define what is meant when we speak of artificial intelligence.

In the last chapter, we witnessed how tricky it is to define intelligence. As it turns out, nailing down a precise definition of *artificial* intelligence is just as hard. As philosophers, psychologists, biologists, and brain researchers continue to squabble over the nature of organic intelligence, so do computer scientists, engineers, and theoreticians continue to debate what artificial intelligence means and how it can be measured.

WHAT IT IS NOT

With so much disagreement, perhaps we will find it easier to first discuss what artificial intelligence is *not*. To begin with, artificial intelligence is *not* just the gifting of computers with greater memory or faster processing power. When computers went from 10 kilobytes to 600 terabytes of memory, or from operating at 33 MHz to 4000 MHz (4 GHz), it didn't make them any more "intelligent." It just allowed them to do more work in less time. Also, artificial intelligence is *not* the ability to mimic human speech or behavior. When Siri, Alexa,

or Cortana respond to your queries in a human voice, or a robotic chef prepares a delicious hamburger, the machine is merely executing a set of complex
algorithms designed by its human programmers. No independent learning or
decision-making is involved.

WHAT IT IS

All this leads us to ask: is a computer capable of independent learning and
decision-making "intelligent"? Perhaps. At present, there are two types of artificial intelligence currently in development. The first, what most people think
of when they hear the term A.I., is *artificial general intelligence* (AGI).

Artificial General Intelligence (AGI)

Popularized in science fiction, it is evidenced by computers or humanoid
robots speaking and behaving in ways similar to and, in some cases, indistinguishable from human beings. HAL 9000 in *2001: A Space Odyssey*, C-3PO
in the *Star Wars* franchise, or Lt. Commander Data in *Star Trek: The Next
Generation*, are all examples of AGI. So far, scientists and engineers have not
even come close to achieving this ideal. However, the other type of A.I., *artificial* narrow *intelligence* (ANI), has been with us for some time.

Artificial Narrow Intelligence (ANI)

ANI describes any system using algorithms to make decisions regarding a
single subject or, as the name implies, a very narrow range of subjects. For
instance, AlphaGo, the Go-playing computer discussed in Chapter 3, is an
example of ANI. The machine did a brilliant job of teaching itself a game and
honing its competitive skills to the point it could beat even the best human
player, but it would still be helpless if asked to compose a limerick, paint a
sunset, or prepare sushi. Likewise, companies, utilities, and government agencies now regularly employ ANI systems to pick stocks, determine insurance
rates, and allocate electrical power, but these systems would be useless against
problems they weren't specifically designed to address.

Another example of real-world ANI is the "expert systems" we discussed
back in Chapter 2. First developed in the 1980s, these programs were designed
to mimic the expertise of subject matter experts (SMEs) like medical diag-
nosticians, financial planners, and nuclear plant engineers, and thus aid in

decision-making. Again, these applications were very specific and useful only in a very narrow range of activities.

Robotics, one of high-tech's fastest-growing fields, is highly dependent on ANI. Using sensors and physical actuators, modern robots now perform a wide range of functions independent of human operators. On a small scale, you are probably familiar with robot vacuum cleaners like the iRobot Roomba, the Samsung POWERbot, or the Shark ION. On a larger scale, many warehouses, shopping centers, and stadiums now employ robot security guards to navigate corridors, detect and report intruders, and interact verbally with visitors. As of this writing, intelligent robots are being introduced into restaurant kitchens, surgical operating rooms, and onto the military battlefield. And, of course, autonomous automobiles, which may be ubiquitous within 10 years, are actually mobile robots equipped with, among other things, "computer vision," a branch of A.I. allowing computers to "see," analyze, and understand the nature and significance of physical objects such as pedestrians, lane dividers, and stop signs.

Again, it's important to note the robots discussed above are specialized machines employing equally specialized ANI. In fact, ANI is now so common it has made the definition of "artificial intelligence" a moving target. As computers become ever more capable and algorithms more complex, tasks once thought of as requiring "intelligence" have one-by-one been removed from the list of functions under the rubric of A.I. The best way to think of this is to consider computer scientist Lawrence Tesler's famous theorem, "A.I. is whatever hasn't been done yet."

To understand this idea better, let's consider optical character recognition (OCR). Originally, the ability to identify a written or printed character was considered a function of A.I. The fact that a computer program could distinguish a "B" from and "8," an "I" from a "1" and an "O" from a "0" was once considered revolutionary. Now, OCR is so commonplace it has been removed from the list of A.I. descriptors. The same is true with voice recognition and artificial speech. In the 1970 movie *Colossus: The Forbin Project*, giving the super-computer a voice was a major technological endeavor portrayed as the pinnacle of scientific achievement. Even so, the voice that emerges is dull, mechanical, and lifeless. Contrast this with today's cheery turn-by-turn GPS instructions possessing no shortage of available accents: Irish, Swedish, British, American, Australian—not to mention the wide array of celebrity voices, such as Burt Reynolds, Kim Cattrall, Morgan Freeman, and the effervescent John Cleese of *Monty Python* fame.

Before we put these descriptors of artificial intelligence into some historical context, let's discuss the third and highly controversial form of artificial intelligence that is not yet here (and may never be—depending on who you ask). This is called artificial *super* intelligence (ASI).

ASI

Leading A.I. thought leader Nick Bostrom defines superintelligence as "an intellect that is much smarter than the best human brains in practically every field, including scientific creativity, general wisdom, and social skills." Though not explicitly about artificial intelligence, the 2014 film *Lucy,* starring Scarlett Johansson, offers a jaw-dropping demonstration of what might happen should one individual (or computer) suddenly acquire such profound mental powers.

In the movie, Lucy (Johansson) undergoes a freak mishap that explodes her intelligence to inconceivable levels, allowing her to run circles around everyone in the movie with her mental prowess. Funnily enough, Johansson was also involved in another A.I. movie called *Her,* about similar themes. In *Her* she plays an evolving operating system that eventually transcends her original programming to become something unfathomable to her owner/love interest Joaquin Phoenix—a kind of disembodied pure-being entity on par with *2001: A Space Odyssey's* Dave Bowman—who leaps evolutionarily forward to become a starchild.

The fact that all three of the above movies deal with evolutionary transcendence to levels difficult for most people to envision, much less comprehend, speaks to the grandeur behind ASI. When futurists such as the late Stephen Hawking warn about the perils of A.I., they are often referring to a future in which, for the first time in history, someone—or rather, some*thing*—is at least far more intellectually superior to us. As Tim Urban writes in the Wait But Why blog, *The AI Revolution: The Road to Superintelligence,* "The superintelligence of that magnitude is not something we can remotely grasp; any more than a bumblebee can wrap its head around Keynesian economics. In our world, smart means a 130 IQ and stupid means an 85 IQ—we don't have a word for an IQ of 12,952."

Regardless, even though this idea is thought-provoking, to say the least, this book's scope pertains to *actionable information* regarding A.I., so for now we had better return to the broader history of computing to place the former two categories in a larger context.

A.I.'S EPOCHS

Many historians of technology view computing as occurring within three separate (but largely overlapping) waves:

- *The First Wave of Computing* was characterized by giant computers limited to tabulation and calculation. ENIAC (the Electronic Numerical Integrator and Computer), built in 1943, is considered the "grandfather" of digital computers. Filling a 20-foot-by-40-foot room and requiring a whopping 18,000 vacuum tubes to operate, it was by all means a gargantuan computing monstrosity. Its successor, UNIVAC (Universal Automatic Computer), built in 1951, the first commercially available computer for government and business use, wasn't much smaller. Weighing 16,000 pounds, it possessed 5,000 vacuum tubes and could perform roughly 1,000 calculations per second.

  Looking ahead optimistically, *Popular Mechanics* magazine predicted, "Computers in the future may weight no more than 1.5 tons." Luckily, by the mid-1950s, transistors invented by scientists at Bell Laboratories in 1947 began to enter the commercial market. Not only did they make devices weighing less than 3,000 pounds a reality, they expanded their uses beyond mere number-crunching.

- *The Second Wave of Computing*, which began in the 1960s and continues to this day, witnessed computers capable of programmable execution. Incapable of "thinking" in the sense of independent analysis and decision making, they simply executed the human user's instructions. Far more versatile than the hulking behemoths of the First Wave, they could produce photo-realistic images, detect intricate patterns, control complex mechanical systems, and analyze physical environments.

  Key breakthroughs of the Second Wave include:
  - **1964.** Douglas Engelbart's graphical user interface, which would eventually make computers accessible to the general public.
  - **1970.** Intel's introduction of the first dynamic random-access memory (DRAM) chip.
  - **1973.** The invention of the Ethernet, allowing multiple computers to be linked to each other.
  - **1974–1977.** The advent of the personal computer.
  - **1975.** Paul Allen and Bill Gates found Microsoft.
  - **1976.** The release of the Apple I.

- **1985.** The introduction of Microsoft's Windows, soon to become the operating system standard for business worldwide.

  During this Second Wave, computers grew exponentially faster and more powerful, following Moore's Law, which predicts the number of transistors in a dense integrated circuit will double about every two years. Computers also became ubiquitous in homes and offices of all First World countries.

- *The Third Wave of Computing* features artificial intelligence, characterized by machine learning. Rather than blindly executing instructions, the Third Wave concerns training (or the enabling) of computers to discern how to perform actions without human intervention or guidance. Though scientists have been working on artificial intelligence since the 1950s, it is only in the last several years that the two limiting factors, lack of availability of sufficient data and insufficient processing power, have been solved, enabling A.I. to reach its tipping point.

FULLY EMBRACING THE THIRD WAVE

Drawing upon such varied fields as mathematics, computer science, psychology, philosophy, and linguistics, experts in the growing field of A.I. have set out to achieve a number of challenging goals in recent years. Broadly, these include creating machines capable of reasoning, knowledge representation, planning, learning, natural language processing, perception, and the ability to move and manipulate objects. As of 2018, A.I. has proven itself capable (or nearly so) of understanding and communicating in human speech, competing in strategic games, like chess and Go, driving autonomous cars, utilizing intelligent routing in content delivery networks, and conducting military simulations.

Yet so far, no comprehensive system has yet been devised capable of accomplishing *all* of these functions at once. At present, such diversification remains the sole province of the human brain. In the future, this may not be the case. Such awe-inspiring capability centers upon something elusive that has been—until now—a pie-in-the-sky chimera. However, recent advancements are changing this. How? By generating computers capable of learning. In the next chapter, we will explore how we learn and how machines are being taught to replicate this amazing process.

Chapter 7

Learning: The Key to Artificial Intelligence

ewborns are blank slates. Fresh from the womb, they have no way to communicate beyond primal screams, signaling everything from hunger to irritation from a wet diaper. As discussed in Chapter 5, babies are limited to primary components of consciousness. They cannot discriminate between themselves and the surrounding world. They have no concept of "self," much less of "mother" or "father." Likewise, they know nothing about such things as "doctors," "nurses," "hospitals," and especially not convoluted economic instruments like "health insurance."

Yet, in just a few days, an infant can recognize its mother's voice. In a few months, it can smile. It can reach for objects and orally signal more complex feelings, like pleasure and scorn. In less than a year, a baby will be walking; as the seasons roll by, now a toddler, she will advance to running, climbing, playing games, and speaking with a vocabulary containing thousands of words. This child's developing mind will grow to grasp abstract concepts including "fairness," "right and wrong," "good and bad," "love and hate," as well as "cause and effect." In a few decades, she will know enough to attend college and perhaps even seek postgraduate training as an OB/GYN specialist, helping to deliver yet more infants into the world.

So just how did this breathtaking learning life cycle unfold? It occurred through the process we call learning. As we have discussed, learning involves more than just the acquisition of data. As defined by Peter Vaill, Ph.D., professor of management at Antioch University, "Learning is the lifelong process of transforming information and experience into knowledge, skills, behaviors, and attitudes." You have no doubt heard the phrase, "You learn something new every day." It's true. Everything you experience during your wakeful, conscious state becomes part of the database your brain uses to make decisions. *Is there roadwork being performed on the street you usually take to work?* You just learned you need to find an alternate route. *Did you enjoy a wonderful dinner at a new Spanish restaurant yesterday?* You just learned there's a new place serving great tapas. When your husband asks you, "Do these pants make me look fat?" did you reply "Yes"? Then you've just learned never to say that again. Ever.

Of course, much of what we know we acquired in ways separate from direct personal experience. Our hunter-gatherer ancestors learned which mushrooms were safe to eat and how to dress a freshly killed elk from instructions passed down from parents and village elders. Questions about the origin of life and the causes of natural phenomena, like lightning, thunder, and earthquakes were contained in the tales told by tribal shamans. Later, cuneiform, writing, books, newspapers, radio, television, motion pictures, and the Internet allowed people to acquire vast quantities of knowledge through both formal education and independent research. Today, with the sum total of human knowledge literally at our fingertips, we regularly learn all kinds of things existing beyond our direct experience, from the weather in European capitals to the current unemployment figures to the latest theories on faster-than-light travel. Some of this third-party information comes from trusted, reliable sources. Others can be a mixture of opinion, conjecture, and outright propaganda. It all gets weighed, evaluated, then stored away by our continually developing brains.

In the last chapter we explained how we've reached the third wave of computing. This means our computers are capable of storing vast amounts of data with enhanced processing speeds. For the first time ever we can tackle how to teach machines to think, behave, and make judgments like humans do. Only a few years ago such an idea would have seemed preposterous. After all, although most of us spend many hours each day interacting with computers, we think of them as little more than appliances—like toasters or televisions—not sentient beings. Even the word *interaction* is a misnomer when it comes to computers, for this suggests that one receives a thoughtful, emotional response from the machine, which clearly is not happening. Yet.

Because of breakthroughs in artificial intelligence, computers are crossing the line between cold, programmed responses and some simulacrum of human thought and feeling (though nothing yet approaching artificial general intelligence.) Anyone who has carried on a conversation, even a limited question-and-answer exchange—with Siri or Alexa—has experienced the slightly unsettling sensation that they are talking to another person. The more the technology advances, the more lifelike these interactions will become, leading us to forget we're talking to a machine at all. Again, the 2013 movie *Her* offers a prime example of this. In the film, Joaquin Phoenix's character is slowly disarmed by the uncannily "real" way his operating system relates to him.

Still, the more we witness the rapidly evolving nature of artificial intelligence, the more we need to avoid the temptation to view A.I. as a human-like brain, just with fewer emotions. In reality there is no reason to spend billions of dollars trying to create artificial brains when we already have six billion natural ones working fine all over the planet. The whole point of A.I. is to create something *above and beyond* what nature can produce. We want to produce something *better* than ourselves.

Even so, we need to take advantage of the characteristics A.I. *does* share with humans. One of the seminal ones is the ability to learn. A.I. doesn't pick up stuff the same way a human child does, yet there are similarities. Formulating a learning model based on how an infant's blank slate develops into a complex adult mind can be instructive. By studying how children learn, we can better train A.I. systems to acquire knowledge, critically evaluate, and make predictions in ways surpassing our abilities, ultimately benefitting us.

To better understand the A.I. learning process, let's return to the infant. Typically, parents provide a child with a basic system of understanding, what Dr. Michio Kaku might describe as a world model. Though undoubtedly flawed and incomplete, it contains basic assumptions regarding rules of speech, perception, emotional attachment, and behavior. This model may be thought as the child's "ground truth." As stated earlier, a baby is born ready to perform a limited number of functions. To the casual observer it would seem all it can do is eat, sleep, and excrete. But the newborn is also performing one bigger task: it is *learning*. Every taste, touch, sound, and sight is grist for the little nipper's learning mill. Little by little, a baby learns to "find" its hands, to gurgle, to smile, to reach for a toy, to turn over, and to crawl.

Piece by piece, the growing child puzzles out a system of ground truths from her parents—and the environment. "Your name is Riley." "Don't touch the oven." "This is water." "Here's a cat." As the child's world expands, she continues to learn from siblings, pets, classmates, teachers, other adults—not to mention any number of stimuli, including screens these days. The child's growing ground truth absorbs new facts, deepened by nuance and buttressed by moral lessons. "The earth is round." "Stealing is wrong." "Zebras have stripes, not spots." "Good people go to heaven. Evil people go to Hell." "$E = MC^2$."

"School's out for summer. School's out—forever," Alice Cooper once sang. But the learning process never stops for us humans. It's a daily, lifelong process. Until the day we die, each of us is continuously growing and adapting—and yes, proceeding according to the primary ground truths we once received. Just as parents have a responsibility to provide the most informative, yet moral ground truths to their children to prepare them for life, so should programmers be careful providing ground truths to computers, their "offspring."

Similar to how a child who receives a poor upbringing is disadvantaged when it comes to leading a happy life, instructing a computer with inaccuracies, half-truths, or errors is a recipe for failure. To understand this idea better, consider the lies we teach our children and the impact they can have later in life. Parents regularly teach their kids to believe in benign myths like Santa Claus, the Easter Bunny, and the Tooth Fairy. When the child inevitably learns the truth, there may be a bit of confusion and emotional trauma, but we consider this a rite of passage into adulthood. At the other end of the spectrum, consider a child raised by parents who teach that cruelty to animals is acceptable, that people who look or speak differently are inferior, or that the best way to solve a problem is through violence. How might such a child turn out? History bears the proof; many of them end up incarcerated or dead—or at the very least, poorly adjusted, with difficult lives.

So based on this reality, if given the wrong set of ground truths, could an A.I. become a racist sociopath? It has already happened. In 2016, Microsoft tested a chatbot named Tay by giving it a Twitter account. "The more you chat with Tay, the smarter it gets," Microsoft said, inviting people to engage it in "casual and playful conversation." However, Tay was programmed to learn the way most children do, by parroting things others say.

Nowadays, most children grow up in insular, loving families with parents who try to control what they see and hear, knowing that developing kids are like sponges when it comes to emulation. But what happens when an "innocent" A.I. grows up in the "wild west" twenty-first-century social media sphere, where anything goes? Very quickly, a never-ending stream of racist, misogynist, homophobic, and ultra-nationalist remarks quickly bombarded the developing computer. Within 24 hours, Microsoft was forced to shut down the experiment after Tay went from being "super cool about humans" to "full Nazi," according to one observer, with tweets like, "GAS THE KIKES RACE WAR NOW."

Obviously, when guiding an A.I.'s process of learning, the supplied ground truth is vital. But what is "truth"? That's not so easy to answer, either. My ground truth is not the same as yours. My ground truth may overlap with yours, but there will be differences. We may be in agreement that the sky is blue and Earth revolves around the sun. But even this is not so simple. In ancient times, people believed the sun revolved around Earth. That is, until a new scientific theory (and consequentially, a new ground truth) upended the traditional view. Likewise, moral ground truths are likely to diverge when it comes to deep questions like: When is killing another human being okay? When does life begin? Is there a God? Not to mention, there are varying *taste* ground truths, like which is the better band: the Beatles or the Stones?

Clearly, everyone possesses their own biases, beliefs, and suppositions, no matter the topic. As Tay's example demonstrates, it's just as possible to transfer these to a computer as it is to transfer them to children. Ground truth bias can even occur without conscious effort. In 2015, Google Photos' A.I. inadvertently cataloged a photo of two African Americans, one of whom happened to be a computer programmer, as "gorillas." How did this happen? At some point during Google Photos' algorithm design, a developer taught the computer to associate particularly dark faces with those of jungle primates. (This type of thinking is not unlike the Crayola Crayon's now politically incorrect blunder in naming light tan as "Flesh.")

The problem was that not only did the program misidentify the species, it also happened to use a word long applied as a racial epithet. This incident appears to be isolated, but it's a strong reminder that A.I. is nowhere near perfect at duplicating human vision and is light-years away from being able to simulate human sensitivity—forever a work-in-progress. Still, A.I. blunders aren't necessarily something to fear. Instead, similar to parental error, they remain something to keep in mind and guard against.

While we have spent much time discussing similarities between A.I. and human learning systems, they differ in important respects. Unlike A.I.s, children learn in context, not in isolation. For instance, parents don't wake up one day and say, "It's time to learn how to speak." Instead, the learning process occurs alongside many other events simultaneously, shaping the little one's development. Also, unlike that of a computer, a child's learning requires motivation, agency, and interest. Any parent can attest that a kid will only try to solve a puzzle if he is actually interested in doing so. In contrast, you don't have to motivate a machine to learn or perform some command. No one has to cajole a PC to open Microsoft Word with candy or bribe a MacBook to download a song from iTunes. In this respect, teaching a computer may be a lot easier than teaching a stubborn child.

Returning to learning in context, humans benefit from developing multiple skills simultaneously and socially. Take baseball. A complicated sport, it requires a host of skills, like batting, throwing, catching, and running—none of which are learned in a vacuum. Rather, they are acquired in tandem throughout multiple experiences, each building on the other, strengthening and reinforcing each other. Whereas a human learns about baseball as a sum of differing, yet interrelated skills, an A.I. would have to learn each element separately. This makes educating a machine uniquely difficult.

Another big difference between how humans and machines learn is the fact that humans instinctively question authority. Kids are notorious for driving their parents bonkers with this repeated question: *Why?* (Until Mom and Dad scream, "Because I said so!") But what's natural to a child is antithetical to a computer. Like any intelligent human, A.I. crunches data, builds hypotheses, confirms or rejects them—but it doesn't question *why*.

However, there may come a day when a machine *does* ask why. Consider this scenario: a developer establishes the ground truth that murder is unacceptable behavior. A computer is given the programming equivalent of "Thou shalt not kill." However, as the A.I. experiences more, as it learns about war, the police shooting of armed suspects, people killing others in self-defense, something may flip. It may think the A.I. equivalent of "Wait a second. I was taught to believe that all human life is sacred, but why?" There may be other conflicting concerns. What about cases in which euthanasia is the only humane course of action—such as when a person is suffering in the late stages of an incurable disease? In such a scenario should the computer ask *why*, its operators better be ready with a good answer. "Because I said so," may not prove sufficient.

Such ethical concerns are just the tip of the iceberg. There is a reason why most children aren't tasked with making life-or-death decisions. Their critical thinking skills aren't developed. Yet we may soon be asking our thinking machines to make choices with serious stakes. As a result, many governing bodies have begun demanding that such systems be able to explain their actions before they will allow such technology to be employed on a large-scale basis.

These days, human judges go to great pains to justify their decisions. "Because I say so" may occasionally work for exasperated parents, but it is never enough to justify matters of life and death, of freedom or incarceration. Along similar lines, governments are also demanding A.I. systems be capable of explaining their decisions on less drastic matters, but still important ones, such as approving a mortgage loan or denying an insurance claim. Granting an A.I. power is similar to handing a teenager the car keys; we need to trust that the system is capable of making good decisions. And like humans, an A.I. or the people responsible for its development must be held accountable for its actions.

Ultimately, humans and machines have more in common than differences when it comes to learning. Each begins with a clean slate that develops over time due to experiences and feedback. Both must also bear responsibility for their decisions the more autonomy they are given. (With the important caveat that when a machine screws up, humans still pay the price.) Most significant of all, like a human being, true A.I. never stops learning. It continues to grow with each experience.

As A.I. progresses in complexity, it will simply "think" faster than we can, assimilating more information than we can possibly process, eventually reaching the point when it can make suggestions for our consideration (e.g., "Hey, Kodak, it's time to move on from film!"). However, A.I. may very well—in fact, almost certainly will—reach the point where it is not only smarter than we are but can ask questions we can't even begin to imagine. This is when we will begin to realize A.I.'s true potential. But how will we get to this end goal? That is the subject of our next chapter.

Chapter 8

What Do You Teach a Machine—and How?

Before a computer can learn, it must be taught. But after that, comparisons between human and machine learning quickly diverge. Humans learn both passively and actively. As we've discussed, we begin learning from the moment we are born—and perhaps even *in utero*—by processing sensory information, including touch, sight, sound, and taste. As we grow and mature, we gain additional knowledge through a variety of channels, including direct personal experience, informal instruction from our parents, interactions with other children and adults, and then formal education in schools, universities, and vocational training academies.

As we develop, we independently seek out further knowledge through books like this one, magazines, radio, television, and the Internet. Yet, even in the absence of all of the above, humans will continue to learn merely through the mundane process of daily existence. We can't help ourselves. We learn. *It's what we do.* By contrast, A.I. systems must be taught how to learn. Without specific instructions, an A.I. system will just sit there, inert, incurious, and wholly indifferent to the world around it.

In our experience with computers, we might have come to think of them as powerful number-crunchers and obedient instruction-takers. But when a machine learns what human users teach it, and then proceeds to learn complex concepts that the users didn't teach it—well, that's far from commonplace. That's astonishing. Consider natural language processing (NLP). First discussed in Chapter 3, NLP is the ability to understand human speech, including symbology, slang idioms, contexts, and concepts. For example, you and I know an object is not just an object. We understand "France" not only as a location, but also as a concept, something that includes cultural associations and history. If someone says the word "France" to you, your mind might fill with all kinds of related things and ideas, such as Bordeaux wine and soft Camembert cheese, all-night literary salons, turtleneck-wearing existentialists, and yes, maybe even "freedom fries."

WE CAN ALL LEARN A LOT FROM TABOO

Clearly, your mental capacity to link such varied items together under the umbrella term "France" speaks to human beings' uncanny pattern-forming abilities. The popular Hasbro guessing board game Taboo makes great use of such skills when it comes to making associations between words and concepts. Similar to Catch Phrase, another Hasbro board game, the object of Taboo is to get your teammates to guess the word on the card by offering related verbal cues. People are so adept at doing this, even unconsciously, that the rules strictly forbid players from saying the most obvious related words.

With the possible exception of highly competitive game nights, it's unlikely that most of us think about this natural gift we share. But the truth is, such complex pattern forming requires a deep proficiency between related but different cognitive skillsets, including vocabulary, grammar, syntax, and of course, a general knowledge spanning diverse topics and subjects. We may expect our partner at Taboo to draw a mental link between the words: "round," "sport," and "kick" to arrive at the term, "soccer"—or get really mad at them for dropping the ball (no pun intended), but connecting the dots this way via NLP is extremely difficult for A.I. to master without adequate training. Let's look at why.

DOWN THE RABBIT HOLE WITH NLP

To effectively navigate the nuances of our rich language, A.I. must be trained to think in concepts going way beyond the literal. This is more difficult than it might seem. For example, when you read the word *apple*, what comes to mind? Perhaps you think of a particular red fruit with a thin, waxy skin, moist, sweet flesh, and a tough core containing flat, black seeds. But that's just one type of *object meaning*. The word *apple* can also have symbolic meanings. To investors, the word might designate Apple, the company, a valuable commodity. To the religious-minded, it might stir thoughts of Adam and Eve tempted in the Garden of Eden. But the associations do not end there. The word might evoke other myths: William Tell shooting the apple off his son's head. Sir Isaac Newton discovering gravity. Johnny Appleseed. Being as American as apple pie. The list goes on and on.

To understand just why language can be so endlessly evocative, consider Confucius's words spoken more than twenty-five hundred years ago: "Signs and symbols rule the world, not words nor laws." What this Eastern philosopher meant is that we make sense of our world through words in all of their infinite varieties. Words have the power to shape the meaning of events and experiences in the myriad ways they are spoken, written, and contextually employed. Returning to the word *France*, we can see this word might denote more than just a sovereign nation with a specific geographical location. It also signifies a language, a history, a culture; even an attitude. To many Americans, *France* connotes romance, the music of Edith Piaf, and perhaps a bit of snobbery.

Even if you have never personally visited France, even if you've never seen the region with your own eyes, you can still understand the "concept" of France. This particular ability is key to understanding humans' mastery over planet Earth. In his book, *Sapiens: A Brief History of Mankind*, author and historian Yuval Noah Harari contends that human beings gained dominion over other species due to our prowess at forming large groups unified by our collective concepts or "myths" to foster solidarity. "Any large-scale human cooperation—whether a modern state, a medieval church, an ancient city, or an archaic tribe—is rooted in common myths that exist only in people's collective imagination."

According to Harari, many of the key drivers of human civilization, including money, government, freedom, and God, are nothing *but* concepts without counterparts in the natural world. Visit any restaurant the world over and you will find employees willing to take your money in exchange for food. Why? We all buy into the concept of money. Similar to concepts like nation-states and corporations, money is the major collective myth or a concept we take for granted. If we didn't, modern society would break down. We might take this concept for granted, but machines don't. In order for them to catch up to us, they need to comprehend the vast symbology behind natural language; in short, they need to grok words in all their multifaceted glory.

WALK (AND TALK) LIKE A MAN

But the challenge of teaching A.I. doesn't end there. After a machine has learned to process natural language and a portfolio of essential concepts, it must *inter-*

act like a human for it to be useful. Human interaction is just what it sounds like: the ability to act and communicate as if it were a *Homo sapiens*, including all of the behaviors that come naturally to us as living organisms. During the Second Wave of Computing, a basic level of computer-to-user interaction was part of the experience, but it was crude. No one could seriously claim that the flickering words coming across a computer monitor were analogous to the full complexities of human discourse. But that's all changed—very fast.

In the past several years, A.I. systems have begun replicating the intricate interaction we expect from sentient beings. In 2018, Hanson Robotics' Sophia made history when she became the first robot to be recognized with citizenship by Saudi Arabia. Crafted to be a research platform for A.I. research and development, Sophia has a sense of humor and can express feelings in ways not dissimilar to a flesh-and-blood person. Likewise, innovative companies, such as Cyrano.ai, have developed A.I. chatbots capable of empathy, reading, and responding to subtext—what is *not* being said but is implicit in a conversation. All of which proves the Third Wave of computing offers sophisticated person-to-computer communication that is more casual, conversational, and idiomatic. (You can read interviews with both companies' founders in Section II of this book.) Ultimately, the best A.I. systems of today not only can understand natural spoken language, but also can respond in kind, complete with proper emphasis, rhythms, and inflections, despite previously vexing hurdles, such as understanding tricky contexts and concepts.

WAIT, IT TEACHES ITSELF?

Even more amazing than A.I.'s verisimilitude feats is the fact that the most advanced computing systems have learned to teach themselves. This ability is known as "machine learning." The term was coined in 1959 by Arthur Samuel, an American pioneer in computer gaming and artificial intelligence, whose checkers-playing computer was one of the first practical examples of A.I. in action. The term "machine learning" is today used to describe the method by which computers gain data and understanding beyond their initial programming. *AI Software Learns to Make AI Software* is the jaw-dropping title of a 2017 *MIT Technology Review* article. In the piece, author Tom Simonite writes, "Progress in artificial intelligence causes some people to worry that software will take jobs such as driving trucks away from humans. Now leading researchers are finding that they can make software that can learn to do one of the trickiest parts of their own jobs—the task of designing machine-learning software."

What this means, and why it has such major implications, is that unlike Second Wave computers, which merely followed static instructions, today's A.I. systems can now employ machine learning to construct algorithms allowing them to make real-world predictions. This means A.I. is not passively learning, it's putting its knowledge to use for future decision-making, much like we humans do. In fact, the entire growing field of predictive analytics is based on this ability, and it is used today in everything from creating targeted consumer marketing campaigns on Amazon to child-protective service organizations flagging high-risk cases of neglect and abuse in real time.

DEEP LEARNING TAKES A BITE OF THE APPLE

Perhaps even more impressive than predictive analytics is a subset of machine learning called "deep learning." In the human brain, every neuron is linked to tens of thousands of others. When specific connections prove uniquely useful, such as "don't touch fire," they are chemically reinforced. This is how we create memories, habits, skills, and reflexes. In an artificial neural network, artificial neurons are layered one atop the other, and connections are weighted by their predictive success. For example, imagine that a computer is shown 100 photographs of the conveyance we call an "automobile."

Just like the many varieties of apples, automobiles can come in many colors, shapes, and styles: sedans, coupes, hatchbacks, crossovers, and so on. Over time, as the computer receives more data, it can designate each entry in terms of similar characteristics: steel body, glass windows, four wheels, headlights, steering wheel, etc. It now has a "concept" of an automobile. But if it identifies a Ford F-150 pickup as an "automobile," it will be told it is wrong. This is key. To understand its error, it must behave like a human. It must learn from its mistake based on past data and search for new patterns to discern the truth.

After sifting through all the possible differences, the learning computer may finally deduce the inclusion of a flatbed classifies this entry not as an "automobile," but as something else. *It has learned.* In time, and given enough examples, it will begin to differentiate automobiles from trucks, and then to distinguish subsets of automobiles: Cadillacs, Buicks, Toyotas, Nissans, Volkswagens, and BMWs. The computer's discernment will continue sharpening, allowing it to identify specific model styles and model years. Its level of expertise could very well soon surpass even the most experienced auto aficionado. Look out, Jay Leno.

In all seriousness, though, deep learning is already being used in many commercial applications. Here are just a few:

- In the early 2000s, banks used convolutional neural networks (CNNs) to process more than 10 percent of all checks written in the United States.
- In the early 2010s, deep learning-based facial recognition software began being used at airports, bus terminals, banks, and other high-risk locations that could be targeted by terrorists.
- In 2012, Merck, a major pharmaceutical company, used multitasking deep neural networks to correctly predict the biomolecular target of an experimental drug, thus speeding its approval process.
- Also in 2012, a deep learning system proved its effectiveness in the analysis of medical images for cancer detection.
- In 2014, an A.I. system detected the previously unknown toxic effects of chemicals in common household cleaning products.
- In 2017, Google released a video showing how its DeepMind A.I. was able to move successfully through all manner of virtual environments. Given only one imperative, move forward, the A.I. taught itself to walk, run, jump, climb steps, and even "limbo" below obstacles in its path. To watch the video, visit: www.youtube.com/watch?v=gn4nRCC9TwQ.

TAKING THE TRAINING WHEELS OFF

Now that we better understand how computers learn, how do engineers go about creating an artificial intelligence that is capable of exceeding its initial training? There are three general steps:

1. Build it
2. Train it
3. Test it

To see this in action, let's consider how A.I. might be applied to cancer research.

Step 1: Build It

We build an A.I. system capable of analyzing images, such as X-rays, CAT scans, and MRIs.

Step 2: Train It

We show the A.I. 500 images of both healthy cells and cancer cells. Here is where we can program the ground truth we have previously discussed by teaching the A.I. the foundational concept of "cancer." We will define cancer as a mutated cell that reproduces rapidly, then teach it the differences between cells, organs, tissues, blood vessels, as well as the known effects of established medical treatments. Afterward, we will explain how cancer impacts organs through different stages, eventually leading to organ failure and death. We will instill logic in the A.I. so it can distinguish a healthy cell from a cancerous cell.

Step 3: Test It

We launch the A.I. into a process of supervised learning, followed by a process of unsupervised learning. During supervised learning, we will provide the A.I. with 500 more X-rays and ask it, based on the set it was shown earlier, to identify those showing normal cells and those containing cancerous ones. A human technician will check the A.I.'s results and provide feedback, explaining to the A.I. its errors (e.g., "This is a shadow, not a cancer cell"). We will repeat this process until the A.I. demonstrates a high enough level of accuracy to be ready for use in a clinical setting.

During its clinical tenure, learning will continue, but now in an unsupervised setting. It will evaluate more images, will be notified of errors, and will correct as necessary as part of a never-ending feedback loop. Ultimately, the A.I. will become self-correcting.

GRADUATION DAY?

This process of supervised learning followed by unsupervised learning somewhat resembles a child working through math problems. After parents or teachers demonstrate methods for solving equations, a child will attempt to solve exercises independently. Helpful instructors will continue providing a feedback loop, marking some answers as correct and others as wrong. Upon learning what worked and what was incorrect, a learning child will proceed to another set of problems, self-correcting, until she is able to solve the problems at a higher level of accuracy.

Of course, learning methods such as the above need not be restricted to diagnoses, cancer or otherwise. In fact, the potential for applications go far beyond the medical spectrum into limitless areas of inquiry. The only hindrance to the potential uses of A.I. is our imagination. As we shall see in Section II , machine learning can help make valuable identifications and predictions in such diverse applications as science, finance, law, language, and many other fields.

Yes, the potential for A.I. appears to be endless. But there is one key factor that may significantly hamper the development and adoption of A.I., especially in the short term. This obstacle isn't technological. It isn't political. And it certainly isn't economic. It's fear, particularly apprehension borne out of ignorance and cultural prejudices. And this is the topic of our next chapter.

Chapter 9

Metathesiophobia

*M*etathesiophobia. Try wrapping your mouth around this word. It means "fear of change." Often linked to another mouthful, *tropophobia*, which means "fear of moving"—both concern irrational worries about altering the status quo. As the nineteenth-century Russian author Fyodor Dostoevsky once wrote, "Taking a new step, uttering a new word, is what people fear most." Considered one of the finest novelists of all time, Dostoevsky understood such apprehensions well. His moralistic novels, including *Crime and Punishment* and *The Brothers Karamazov*, were his attempts to deal with change, to counter what he viewed as a rising menace to society: the waning power of the church.

WHEN THE OLD AND THE NEW STAND SIDE BY SIDE

Like us, Dostoevsky lived in dynamic times. The nineteenth century witnessed the diminishment of religion in the wake of the scientific revolution with bold ideas from secular philosophers such as Friedrich Nietzsche, who coined the phrase, "God is dead." Prior to this, Christianity had been the basis of Western society for centuries. Its teachings formed the rules by which citizens conducted themselves.

A deeply religious man himself, Dostoevsky worried about what might happen if people stopped believing in a higher power. Through his allegorical stories, Dostoevsky wrestled with what it meant to be human in a brave new world—one in which life was in flux and the old order was breaking down. Dostoyevsky saw metathesiophobia occurring all around him as traditional ways of thinking collapsed before his eyes: the divine right of kings and queens to rule, an appeal to scripture for ethical matters. The reason we remember his books so many years after his death can be traced to his keen observations as to how people think, how we behave. Even Nietzsche called him the psychologist "from whom I had something to learn." What Dostoyevsky revealed was a fundamental truth: most people have a resistance to new things, be it change of location, change in relationships, change in routine, or just change in general.

WE FEAR CHANGE

If you've ever had the devastating experience of uprooting a beloved elderly parent or grandparent to place them in a nursing home, you've likely stared metathesiophobia in the face yourself. It's no wonder that a 2008 study written by Naoko Muramatsu, et al., published by the U.S. National Library of Medicine of the National Institutes of Health, found that "where elderly persons spend their last stage of life has important implications for their own well-being." Transforming an elderly person's longstanding routine can be so dramatic to their psyche that Muramatsu reported "the majority of Americans die in institutions although most prefer to die at home."

Likewise, shades of metathesiophobia can help explain why some individuals choose to stay in jobs they hate rather than find a new one. Metathesiophobia can also shed light on why someone opts to stay in a personal relationship even though it's clearly toxic—or why individuals vote for incumbent politicians year after year, even though they may realize that they no longer represent their best interests. It even explains why, to some people, winning a $100 million lottery is a nightmare scenario. No matter whether we are talking about upheavals of the 1800s or the 2000s, change of any kind is fraught with all manner of terrors, real and imagined. Sticking with the familiar, even if not ideal, seems so much safer. Or, as one well-worn expression puts it, "Better the devil you know than the devil you don't."

BUT ARE OUR FEARS GROUNDED?

Stomach-churning, cold-sweat inducing metathesiophobia can also explain the resistance so many individuals, even otherwise savvy businesspeople, have toward artificial intelligence. They perceive A.I. as a threat to their livelihood, values, perhaps even their very humanity. Putting aside sci-fi doomsday scenarios for a moment, is there a case to be made that A.I. is a threat? Let's look at history.

People once rode horses in Dostoyevsky's Russia. Now they drive cars. Pretty soon they will ride in autonomous vehicles. Robots have replaced many factory worker jobs. It isn't much of a stretch to believe they will overtake all service jobs. Already, flesh-and-blood customer service representatives have lost out to automated telephone operators. As we shall see later in this book, A.I.-driven services from companies like LegalMation can now prepare legal documents previously drafted by paralegals or attorneys. How about notaries? "eSign it, send it, get it. Boom" is the tagline for Docusign's software. Similar to horses, why depend on costly (and unpredictable) carbon-based life forms to perform services that can be digitally performed anywhere, anytime?

Based on this reality, it would seem there is some cause for fear. Unless you are willing to think differently. Now, let's consider what experts are saying.

ACCORDING TO THE ZEITGEIST

No shortage of articles and reports portend the demise of whole *industries* of workers, raising the alarm of officials and governmental agencies. "A.I.-enhanced technological unemployment is one of the major issues of our time," says Irakli Beridze, Head of the Centre for Artificial Intelligence and Robotics, United Nations, UNICRI. "Look anywhere and you will see people talking about it. Almost weekly I see new reports coming out suggesting something to the effect that between 20% to 70% of jobs will be wiped out because of A.I."

Seeking to quantify the effects of A.I. on work, the McKinsey Global Institute produced a 2017 report after researching 20 countries and 30 industries regarding six themes and found that, "while few occupations are fully automatable, 60 percent of all occupations have at least 30 percent technically automatable activities." Though we live in a country that venerates its armed forces with parades and tributes, it seems even the military is not beholden to relying on human warriors. Driven by an upgraded arms race of technologically enhanced warfare, the Department of Defense is pouring vast sums into developing autonomous drones and robot fighting machines, despite a 2018 pledge by 200 other organizations, including Alphabet's DeepMind, to not develop lethal weapons.

Many of us have struggled to get digital assistants like Siri and Alexa to understand simple questions. We have also had our GPS systems take us on circuitous routes or down blind alleys. Just imagine what frightening mistakes killer drones might make in order to keep us safe. Based on these concerns alone, how can the fear of A.I. possibly be considered irrational?

FEAR'S HISTORICAL PRECEDENT

To better understand our fears—irrational or not—toward the unknown we need to go back much further than the Enlightenment. Fear has often greeted technological advances. And yet it has often faded away as those benefits surpassed perceived threats. Living in the era of Amazon's On Demand Publishing in which anyone can write and publish a book for free, it's hard to appreciate the groundbreaking nature of Gutenberg's printing press in the 1400s. At the time, printing was so costly and time-consuming that only the wealthy or religious elite possessed books. And yet the invention met with all manner of criticism and resistance. In 1492, the year Columbus made his first voyage to the Americas, Trithemius of Spanheim, a prominent German monk, wrote of the new phenomenon of commercial publishing, "Printed books will never be the equivalent of handwritten codices" because "scribes display more diligence and industry than printers."

Still, if we go back even further in time, we see the *invention* of writing also met with metathesiophobia. Though known to us as the "father of philosophy" and long associated with the pursuit of knowledge, it's astonishing to realize that Socrates was no fan of the written word either. In the fourth century B.C., the Greek thinker denounced its advent on the grounds that it would promote forgetfulness. Even his disciple, Plato, who deigned to commit his thoughts to paper, believed writing was, "a step backward for truth."

Returning to the early nineteenth century, as the Industrial Revolution was getting underway in northern Europe, many people reacted with fear, then violence toward the coming mechanization they saw as a threat to their livelihoods. Perhaps the most famous of these movements was the Luddite protests of 1811–1816. Named for the likely fictitious Ned Ludd, an apprentice who purportedly smashed two weaving looms in 1779, the Luddite movement began in Nottingham, England, as a reaction to the introduction of steam-driven textile factories and soon spread throughout the British Isles. The movement was only quelled with the use of military force. Since then, the term "Luddite" has been used to describe anyone resistant to technological progress.

HUMAN PRESERVATION OR MERE SENTIMENTALITY?

If we stop to consider Luddite objections to technology, what emerges is a concern for the denigration of humans. The inventions of the telegraph and telephone were criticized for debasing the value of face-to-face human communication. In 1887, the *New York Times* blasted Alexander Graham Bell's telephone for promoting the invasion of privacy and eschewing critical in-person interaction. "We will soon be nothing but transparent heaps of jelly to each other," snorted one angry *Times* writer. Radio, motion pictures, and television were similarly lambasted when first introduced. "The cinema is little more than a fad. It's canned drama. What audiences really want to see is flesh-and-blood actors on the stage." So said comedian Charlie Chaplin in 1916. Four years later, he would become one of the world's richest men due to his motion pictures.

In an article for Grantland.com, "Bad Decisions: Why AMC's *Breaking Bad* Beats *Mad Men*, *The Sopranos* and *The Wire*," columnist Chuck Klosterman attempted to pinpoint the popularity of the recent TV show, *Mad Men*. "*Mad Men* is set in the 1960s, so every action the characters make is not really a reflection on who they are; they're mostly a commentary on the era. Don Draper is a bad husband, but 'that's just how it was in those days.'" Klosterman's larger point is that *Mad Men* succeeds as entertainment because viewers enjoy the nostalgic experience of looking backward in time. Though the period in which the show takes place occurred only a few decades back, the exponential rate of change in the last twenty years can make it feel like it might as well have been 100 years ago. Accordingly, it's easy to laugh at the naïveté of the characters' fears surrounding new technology, such as the electronic copier and the computer. Knowing how commonplace both of these instruments would soon become—and how they would be usurped by even grander innovations—such as the personal computer and smartphone—it's easy for today's audiences to take for granted how threatened Don Draper and company must have felt by these once revolutionary inventions.

Ultimately, when we look back at Charlie Chaplin's ambivalence toward motion pictures or Madison Avenue's aversion to computers, we can draw comfort knowing they were wrong to be so alarmed. Likewise, witnessing so many technological doomsday scenarios fail to come to pass while printed books, radio, television, and computers have become essential parts of modern life should set us at ease. After all, if the past is prelude, we have nothing to worry about, right?

Not exactly. Many people still fear A.I. They say: "This time it's different." Or to put it in their words:

- "The development of full artificial intelligence could spell the end of the human race. It would take off on its own, and redesign itself at an ever-increasing rate. Humans, who are limited by slow biological evolution, couldn't compete, and would be superseded."

  —The late physicist Stephen Hawking

- "I don't want to really scare you, but it was alarming how many people I talked to who are highly placed people in A.I. who have retreats that are sort of 'bug out' houses, to which they could flee if it all hits the fan."

  —James Barrat, author of *Our Final Invention: AI and the End of the Human Era*

- "With artificial intelligence we are summoning the demon."

  —Inventor and entrepreneur Elon Musk

What are people so afraid of? Let us count the ways.

People Fear Machines Will Replace Them

Many industries, from manufacturing to farming, have already seen automation upend tasks humans once did. Thanks to automation, many jobs once requiring hundreds of humans, such as warehouse fulfillment positions, now only take a few dozen, if that. Many more jobs are already in the crosshairs, from truck drivers to chefs. According to a May 2018 article in the *Washington Post* by Peter Holley, one Boston eatery is already pioneering such automation. "The restaurant's founders have replaced human chefs with seven automated cooking pots that simultaneously whip up meals in three minutes or less." Michael Farid, the 26-year-old cofounder of Spyce Food Company, explains how it works. "Once you place your order, we have an ingredient delivery system that collects them from the fridge. The ingredients are portioned into the correct sizes and then delivered to a robotic wok, where they are tumbled at 450 degrees Fahrenheit. The ingredients are cooked and seared. And once the process is complete, the woks tilt downward and put food into a bowl. And then they're ready to be garnished and served."

Certainly, many incentives exist for restaurants to consider investing in robots over humans. Not only are machines better at many repetitive tasks, from flipping burgers to dicing carrots, they don't show up late, call in sick, take coffee breaks, and/or waste time posting *Game of Thrones* memes on Instagram. They also don't demand higher wages or sue for sexual harassment.

People Fear Machines Will Be Misused

In just the past decade, we've seen sophisticated computer algorithms used to plant malicious malware in personal computers as well as breach social media platforms to obtain users' data. Now consider the harm criminals, terrorists, a hostile foreign power, or just an amoral actor could accomplish with access to the stock exchange, water management systems, or a commercial air traffic control network. This is the conclusion Steven Bower and his coauthors reached in a February 2018 article for *Powermag*, "The U.S. power grid is wide open for attack. More than 200,000 miles of high-voltage transmission lines, interspersed with hundreds of large electric power transformers and substations span the country, often in remote locations."

Metathesiophobia or not, the truth is that the more trust we put in technology, the more vulnerable we are to its abuse. Like adverse military applications, to some extent, this rational fear may be justified. It is therefore even more incumbent upon us to learn about such dangers and plan accordingly—and soberly.

People Fear Machines Will Turn on Us

Perhaps the most serious—and most unfounded—of all our technophobias, this has been fueled by decades of computer-run-amok thrillers from *2001: A Space Odyssey* (1968) to *The Terminator* (1984) to *The Matrix* (1999) to *Ex Machina* (2015). Concerns vary, but the central idea is that even if a highly intelligent machine could be designed to be perfectly benign, without proper ground truths and training, no one knows for sure what kind of attitude a self-aware machine would have toward its human creators. Since this possibility is so remote and unlikely [requiring the emergence of artificial general intelligence (AGI), not to mention artificial super intelligence (ASI) something many experts believe is impossible], we will focus on what we can do now to overcome metathesiophobia.

THE AGE OF REVOLUTION

The essayist and poet Ralph Waldo Emerson lived around the same time as Dostoyevsky and had a different perspective on the emerging new world.

Instead of succumbing to his contemporaries' fear, he embraced the times with these words:

> If there is any period one would desire to be born in, is it not the age of revolution; when the old and the new stand side by side, and admit of being compared; when the energies of all men are searched by fear and by hope; when the historic glories of the old can be compensated by the rich possibilities of the new era? This time, like all times, is a very good one, if we but know what to do with it.

Frank Herbert, author of the sci-fi novel *Dune,* had something similar to say: "Fear is the mind killer." Throughout this chapter, we have examined the concerns around A.I. and the rationale for apprehension. Now it's time to consider the new dawn Emerson so eloquently describes. If we open our minds to A.I.'s potentialities, we are bound to escape the more crippling danger Herbert warns against—losing our minds. By the same token, considering A.I.'s potential benefits promises the most powerful of tools for both personal and business success.

Let's offer an example. Recently, Neil Sahota consulted for an international, multibillion-dollar law firm that had recently developed a dozen use cases to achieve a specific goal with A.I. Afterward, they asked Neil to recommend which one would be the best first step for companywide A.I. implementation.

"IBM's Watson can definitely help," Neil told them. "But I don't feel like you're unlocking A.I.'s real value."

"We felt the same way, but to tell you the truth, we don't know what's so special about A.I.," said the managing partner.

"Okay. Let's see what we can figure out. Start by telling me what keeps you awake at night."

Without hesitation, the partner said, "Talent management." He then explained how he can never be sure how good—or bad—new hires will turn out. "We have let go of attorneys we thought were mediocre, only to see them snatched up by other firms and become superstar lawyers."

The partner brought up other problems: it was impossible to tell whether a candidate would thrive in the courtroom. Even though this firm recruited from top law schools, this fact didn't guarantee the efficacy of the candidates, how they would perform when it came to trial, litigation, or even research.

"A.I. can solve this problem for you," Neil said. "It can assess your candidates based on their education, skills, and accomplishments, *plus* use personality information to assess their soft skills, like communication, leadership, flexibility, and negotiating prowess. With this information, you can better determine a person's career path with you. It'll also help you predict the unknown—who might be the best pick to fit in with your company culture."

The partner looked shocked. *"A.I. can do that?"*

Neil assured him that it could. And in the following weeks, he proved it.

NO MORE MIND-KILLER?

Metathesiophobia wrests hold of minds wracked with doubt and ignorance. The reason change can be so scary—so *irrationally* scary—is the fact that we don't know what we don't know. (Remember Rumsfeld's words?) In the pages to come, we will continue to show you how your business stands to benefit from A.I. and how the technology offers greater opportunities for growth—if we push past our fear. In the meantime, here are examples of ways businesses are using it now. Could your company do something similar?

- At dance clubs, A.I. can decide what music to play for the partygoers, selecting what lighting to use, and what food to serve, all based on the guests' Twitter feeds, social media profiles, and personality tests.
- Instead of just using a customer's buying history to suggest music they might enjoy, A.I. can actually *create original music* based on what the customer likes—and explain the reasoning behind its creation.
- Disney now issues A.I.-enhanced wristbands called MagicBands to serve as park IDs. These can unlock hotel rooms and work as FastPasses and payment systems. On the surface, these MagicBands serve as a convenience for guests. However, Disney uses the data in more important, analytic ways. By better understanding the actions of their customers, they can tailor future experiences.

The above is just a taste of the functionality available to businesses savvy enough to adopt A.I. More importantly, we are apt to learn that we have no more to fear from A.I. than we did from the invention of previous tools that improved our lives. And though the examples of A.I.'s potential we've seen so far are impressive, there are more coming. Soon, A.I. systems are likely to be integrated into virtually every industry, which leads us to one key question: What happens to all the people replaced by A.I.? The answer may surprise you.

Chapter 10

A.I. Threatens to Change Our Relationship to Work

For millennia, the struggle to achieve material subsistence has been virtually all-consuming. In ancient times, only the very rich could even conceive of this thing we call "leisure." Today, while "weekends," "sick days," "personal days," "paid holidays," and "vacations" are part of our economic fabric, work remains not only a top priority for most Americans, but a moral imperative as well. Therefore, it may be surprising to learn that the idea of working sunup to sundown is, evolutionary speaking, relatively new. And thanks to A.I., this may again drastically change.

The Old Testament depicts the first humans as living in a lush garden where all their needs were fulfilled: physical, emotional, and spiritual. Eden was literally paradise on Earth. Adam and Eve didn't have to punch time cards or work for their daily bread. As a result, they were free to take scholar Joseph Campbell's advice and "pursue their bliss," whether this involved creating art, writing poetry, singing, dancing, or just contemplating fig leaves. What a sweet gig. But as we all know, this privileged and some might say—*entitled*—couple had to go and ruin it all by eating from the Forbidden Fruit of Knowledge. Ever since, we have been led to believe that man and woman must sweat and toil to meet our needs with little time left over for amusement or creative pursuits. Or do we?

To answer this question, let's delve further into the biblical story. Although a Bronze Age allegory, the mythical Garden of Eden in many ways depicts humanity's hunter-gatherer phase. This era constituted a good 90 percent of our species' tenure on Earth. For hundreds of thousands of years, humans lived in small, isolated bands of 40 or 50 people, who hunted game for food and clothing, supplementing their diet by foraging for wild grains, vegetables, fruits, and mushrooms. But what may appear to us in modern times as a hard, brutal existence actually may have been quite pleasant. According to anthropologists, only 50 percent of a hunter-gatherer's time was necessary to acquire the needed calories for survival. The rest was available for other pursuits, be it playing games, creating art, fashioning musical instruments, socializing with family and loved ones, or trading local gossip.

8:00 MEANS EVERYBODY HAS TO LOOK BUSY

Now compare this leisurely existence to the modern office worker's day. According to a 2015 article in *Time*, the average American puts in 47 hours per week at their job. Meanwhile, the U.S. Census Bureau reports the typical worker spends nearly half an hour traveling to work daily with nearly 20 percent of workers commuting for more than 45 minutes. And that's not to mention 3.6 million individuals suffer through a commute longer than 90 minutes. And, as we know, for many people in the twenty-first century, work doesn't end when the official workday does. Many take their jobs home with them, responding to calls and emails at all hours. So much for free time.

THE INEXORABLE HAMSTER WHEEL

Released in the last year of the twentieth century, the movie *Office Space* crystallized many workers' frustrations with their jobs—especially modern personnel suffering through white-collar tedium. In this film, Peter Gibbons (Ron Livingston) undergoes a crisis upon realizing how much he despises his job. "So I was sitting in my cubicle today," he says at one point in the film. "And I realized, ever since I started working, every single day of my life has been worse than the day before it. So that means that every single day that you see me, that's on the worst day of my life."

Of course, it's not much of a stretch to suggest that many other workers feel just as dissatisfied with how they spend their days, but did you know that these negative feelings also extend to many of the highest-earning professionals? A 2008 University Law Review Paper found elevated levels of fear, anger, and depression among CEOs, suggesting they may be *twice* as depressed as the general public.

But modern life is great, right? Even if we work too hard, the rewards are tremendous. We enjoy a life of unimaginable comfort compared to our ancestors. Anyone who has strolled through a supermarket with its shelves packed with ready-made food for the plucking, knows we have it really good, right? After all, recent advances in medicine have boosted average mortality rates while eradicating illnesses that once decimated earlier populations. Nowadays, we're far less likely to die from an infected insect bite, much less become lunch for a hungry saber-toothed cat.

And yet there's still a good argument to be made that our "simple" hunter-gatherer ancestors may have been much happier than the average twenty-first century computer coder or fulfilment center picker. The former could expect to spend copious amounts of time with their loved ones, basking in nature, free from the tyranny of multiple bosses barking about TPS reports. Just consider this: modern workers in Bangladeshi factories often toil for 14–16 hours per day, seven days a week. Often finishing their shift at 3 a.m., they must resume work again at 7:30 a.m. Does that sound better or worse than the situation of their loincloth-wearing, spear-throwing forebears?

A DOUBLE-EDGED SWORD

To understand how we arrived at a place of such incongruous disparity—a world teeming with unprecedented material abundance yet coupled with soul-sucking working conditions for both the indigent and the affluent, we need to trace the course of our economic development. Historians and anthropologists cite the invention of agriculture about 9,500 years ago as the end of the hunter-gatherer era and the beginning of modern civilization. Certainly, farming offered an advantage over hunting and foraging by yielding greater amounts of food than ever before. But agriculture also had its downside. Farming was time-intensive, leaving little room for anything else. As the practice became more efficient, it produced enough food that certain people could move off the land entirely. Free from the drudgery of fertilizing, tilling, planting, watering, and growing, these individuals could spend their days building cities, establishing trades, forming complex economies, and ultimately creating empires.

Such human labor led to animal power, which gave way to steam, and then the internal combustion engine. In concert, the abacus and written numbering systems outsourced the brain's faculties, leading to accurate bookkeeping. In time, societies learned to memorialize their knowledge and their transactions through mediums such as clay and then paper. Buttressed by the gear-driven adding machine, the calculator, and later, the digital computer, our recording instruments grew ever more sophisticated.

Yet ironically, the more efficient and productive civilization became, the more it demanded of its individuals. As machines replaced human labor, employers demanded more from the remaining specialists. During most of the Industrial Revolution, people worked six days a week, with only the Bible-mandated Sabbath free for family, friends, and the pursuit of personal interests. Only after years of protests from organized labor did America's Congress enact a mandatory 40-hour workweek in 1940. Even then, this legislation only covered hourly workers, not salaried employees, who often worked far longer hours with no additional compensation. Not to mention the fact that entrepreneurs and those toiling in the shadow economy could expect no kind of reprieve from their workdays.

Surveying the economic landscape a decade prior, economist John Maynard Keynes felt emboldened in 1930 to proclaim that technological change and productivity advances would usher in a new epoch of leisure in which we need only work 15 hours per week. "Thus for the first time since his creation man will be faced with his real, his permanent problem: how to use his freedom from pressing economic cares, how to occupy the leisure, which science and compound interest will have won for him, to live wisely and agreeably and well."

So much for Keynes's prescience. Today, even with computers and robots making us more efficient than we were just a generation ago, we're still working harder than ever. According to ABC News, "Instead of reducing working hours, productivity gains have been met by calls for greater productivity gains."

What's wrong with this picture?

WE CAN'T GET IT OUT OF OUR HEADS

On October 31, 1517, Martin Luther nailed his 95 grievances to a German chapel door. In time, these theses would lead to the Protestant Reformation and, with it, the Protestant work ethic. Still alive and well centuries later, this mindset continues to dominate Western culture. Well into the Information Age, this culturally enforced belief still equates the amount of work one performs with one's perceived value as a human.

Such indoctrination begins in school, where we learn that "hard work" is the key to success. Everywhere we go, we hear this message. Work's exaltation is even evident in our political discourse. How often do pundits and politicians disparage someone—usually the poor—for being "lazy"? Is it therefore any wonder that working long hours is a point of pride among most Americans? This country is the only major industrialized nation without mandated vacation days. Its people delight in telling others how busy they are. And even when companies offer paid vacation time as a benefit, most U.S. workers fail to take it. According to a 2018 study by Project: Time Off, 52 percent of Americans leave one or more vacation days "on the table" every year. In aggregate, this comes out to 705 million missed vacation days annually.

Though the American devotion to work may seem excessive, Americans aren't alone in their toiling fervor. The Japanese may venerate labor even more. They even coined a word for such an alarming phenomenon: *karoshi*, which literally means "dying from overwork." Although Japan's federal government has taken steps to mitigate the problem, it still remains rampant. In 2013, journalist Miwa Sado collapsed of heart failure after reportedly logging in nearly 160 hours of overtime in one month at her Japanese news network, NHK.

Of course, if Keynes is to be believed, Sado's death and America's culture of ceaseless work weren't supposed to happen this way. He's not alone in his assertion; a host of futurists and science fiction writers foresaw a different world unfolding at World War II's close. Isaac Asimov, Robert Heinlein, and Arthur C. Clarke predicted we would enter a more sublime existence as computers and robots became ubiquitous. They envisioned a day in which humans would at last be able to stop working for a living and become free to pursue art, science, and other creative interests. If nothing else, three-day workweeks were supposed to become common as computers assumed the bulk of our menial and repetitive tasks. Today, this notion seems not only romantic, but laughably naive.

But is the dream of automation-enabled leisure really so far-fetched? And could A.I. be the tool to get us there? Perhaps, but there is bound to be considerable pain along the way as many jobs—and our long-held ways of thinking about work—transform.

But first, the pain.

THE JOBS—THEY ARE GOING

There is growing reason to believe that mid-twentieth-century futurists' predictions weren't faulty, just premature. Although on the whole people are working harder than ever, a revolution is emerging, one threatening our livelihoods, yes—but also one that may challenge society's enduring work = value equation.

Before we discuss the philosophical upheavals, let's consider the raw data regarding job loss; first, in general, and then through the lens of various sectors. In September 2013, Carl Benedikt Frey and Michael A. Osborne of Oxford University published a study titled, "The Future of Employment: How Susceptible Are Jobs to Computerization?" In it, they concluded that up to 47 percent of U.S. jobs risk being automated by 2050.

The below list consists of just a few of the more than 700 occupations listed in their research and the percentage of likelihood that these jobs will be automated:

- Data entry keyers   99%
- Tax preparers   99%
- Telemarketers   99%
- Fashion models   99%
- Legal secretaries   98%
- Shipping, receiving, and traffic clerks   98%
- Loan officers   98%
- Dental laboratory technicians   97%
- Cashiers   97%
- Real estate brokers   97%
- Gaming dealers   96%
- Restaurant cooks   96%
- Landscaping and groundskeeping workers   96%
- Accountants and auditors   94%
- Concrete masons and cement finishers   94%
- Butchers and meat cutters   93%
- Pharmacy technicians   92%
- Tour guides and escorts   91%
- Automotive body and related repairers   91%
- Technical writers   89%
- Taxi drivers and chauffeurs   89%
- Parking lot attendants   87%
- Nuclear technicians   85%
- Heavy and tractor-trailer truck drivers   79%

As we can see, this list contains a mix of lower-skilled (landscaping and groundskeeping workers) and high-skilled (nuclear technicians) professions, blue-collar (concrete masons) and white-collar (technical writers). Surprisingly, even jobs one might associate with glamour, such as fashion models, may be headed for the chopping block.

So which jobs possess the least displacement risk? Here are a few:

- Recreational therapists   0.3%
- Emergency management directors   0.3%
- Healthcare social workers   0.4%
- Dieticians and nutritionists   0.4%
- Choreographers   0.4%

Why are these jobs considered "safer"? Presumably, health professions will still require human intervention (although in Section II, we will explore the veracity of this belief with the rise of A.I.-powered telemedicine). It is also worth mentioning that choreographers and writers (who rate 3.8 percent replacement odds), have seemingly more employment security due to the fact that they earn their livelihoods through harder-to-automate creativity and interpersonal soft skills, which A.I.s presently lack. We will find out if this belief is substantiated in a moment. For now, let's talk about job safety for industries involving repeated tasks.

Is Change Coming for Rote Task Work?

According to the above study, taxi/Uber drivers and chauffeurs rate as 89 percent vulnerable. Likewise, heavy and tractor-trailer truck drivers, who also do largely repetitive jobs, score 79 percent. Threatened by the engineering of autonomous vehicles by virtually every major automobile manufacturer, they have cause for worry that their livelihoods will be disrupted due to a confluence of factors, including costs vs. profitability, traffic/parking congestion, and, in particular, safety concerns.

An estimated 1 billion motor vehicles, including cars, trucks, SUVs, RVs, and so on, exist on the road today. Motor vehicle accidents are the leading cause of death for people ages 15–29; all told, around 1.3 million people die each year in motor vehicle accidents. An additional 20 million to 50 million people get hurt (nonfatally) each year in crashes. All tallied, motor vehicle accidents cost the world approximately $518 billion annually. (All these statistics are provided by the Association for Safe International Road Travel, 2018.) Since nearly all auto accidents result from human error, there is a growing incentive worldwide to remove the human factor from the driving equation.

The self-driving car will do just that. Such a vehicle is capable of sensing its environment and navigating without human input. By using A.I.-based vision, these vehicles can perceive their surroundings with radar, laser light, odometry, computer vision, and the Global Positioning System (GPS). Their powered control systems can also interpret various sensory information to avoid obstacles, obey signage, and identify navigation paths.

Transportation experts predict that once self-driving cars become popular, they will be linked to a central control system capable of plotting the destinations, routes, and speeds of *every* vehicle to minimize travel times, avoid traffic jams, and eliminate collisions. (See Chapter 16 for a vision of one such smart city in China, where a prototype version of this is being rolled out.) Not only does such innovation promise to reduce congestion in country after country, it portends incredible safety advances. After all, an A.I. can never be distracted by texts, experience road rage, or fall asleep at the wheel.

Cognizant of the safety benefits surrounding automated cars and the associated profits in developing them, Google began pioneering this technology in 2009. Just a few years later, it reported that its test vehicle had driven more than 300,000 miles without a driver or accident. Evaluating what is needed to bring automated cars from the realm of imagination to reality, the Society of Automotive Engineering (SAE) began rating the capabilities of self-driving cars on a five-point scale, each numerical increase a reflection of a car's ability to automate tasks once primarily reserved for flesh-and-blood drivers.

SAE Rating Scale

0 = Full human control.

1 = Provides limited driver assistance. The A.I. can control speed or steering under limited circumstances but cannot handle both at the same time.

2 = Moderate driver assistance. The A.I. can control both speed and steering in limited situations but still requires the driver to be attentive at all times.

3 = Limited autonomous operation. The vehicle can drive itself in simple situations, such as on divided highways with limited access and clearly marked exits and entrances. (Analogous to placing a plane on "auto pilot" while cruising but still requiring manual control for takeoffs and landings.)

4 = Advanced autonomous operation. The vehicle can drive itself most of the time but may still require human intervention during complex circumstances.

5 = Fully autonomous operation. The end goal for all automakers. Humans would be able to tell the car where they wish to go and be taken there quickly and safely. (No human intervention required.)

In recent years, the company Tesla has snatched most of the big headlines on developing automated cars. Their team of engineers has been equipping their vehicles with a system designed to allow full self-driving capability at SAE Level 5 (fully autonomous). Currently, their cars operate in "shadow mode," meaning Tesla's remote computers process data without actually taking action. Vital data goes to the company where an A.I. is constantly learning to improve its capabilities so that the company can enable fully self-driving automobiles by the end of 2019.

Other automakers hard at work on autonomous vehicles include Ford, General Motors, Mercedes Benz, BMW, and Nissan, which has committed to having several driverless car models available by 2020. No doubt, such innovation promises revolutionary advances in safety and convenience—a better world for all, it would seem. But not so for the workers who stand to lose their jobs. These "advances" threaten their existences.

But what about other workers, those who do creative work? Are there changes coming for their industries too? The answer might surprise you.

Is Change Coming for Complex and Creative Work, Too?

As remarkable and complex as the notion of autonomous vehicles may be, self-driving cars are limited in purpose. They are designed to do just one thing: get us from here to there. This is an example of artificial *narrow* intelligence (ANI), as discussed in Chapter 6. No one expects their automated car to begin choreographing musicals—or writing books about artificial intelligence. After all, that would signify a higher order of magnitude of A.I., innovation involving artificial *general* intelligence (AGI). However, there is good reason to believe that A.I.'s benefits can extend in greater directions—and replace yet more human workers along the way—those toiling in higher-order, creative work.

Did you know that A.I. can make movies? Well, maybe not complete, 90-minute features yet (emphasis on the word "yet"), but IBM's Watson did generate a three-minute trailer to promote the thriller *Morgan* (2016) (see https://www.youtube.com/watch?v=gJEzuYynaiw). In true techno-alarmist fashion, it's fitting that the movie's premise centers around an artificially created humanoid being who runs amok after acquiring abilities that outstrip its human developers. While it may not be surprising for most people to learn that A.I. was used to generate special effects for a movie or guide the key grips to set via GPS, the fact that Watson managed to create a trailer that not only follows good narrative rules—but is actually downright scary—is mind-blowing.

To create the Morgan trailer, IBM research scientists had Watson "watch" vast amounts of horror movie trailers and then perform a technical analysis to determine what constitutes "scary." Returning to sci-fi writer Arthur C. Clarke, he once wrote, "Any sufficiently advanced technology is indistinguishable from magic." And while such creativity from an A.I. does indeed look like magic, it isn't. It's just sophisticated algorithms. And it proves that "creativity," just like repetitive manual tasks such as driving, can be learned and emulated by a machine.

In a related story, in 2017, Aiva Technologies, a start-up headquartered in Luxemburg and London, released an album of classical music composed entirely by artificial intelligence. That same year, singer Taryn Southern released the song, "Break Free," with instrumentation created by A.I. Even journalism jobs are being affected by the new technology. "A lot of people don't realize this, but a lot of the news stories you read now are increasingly written by artificial intelligence," said Stephen Ibaraki, the futurist, chairman outreach, and founder of the UN ITU AI for Good Global Summit who wrote the Foreword for this book. Already, the venerable D.C.-based publication the *Washington Post* has begun outsourcing some of its article writing to algorithms.

IMPLICATIONS

Now that we have seen that both rote task and creative jobs are threatened by automation, the question is, what will happen to the people A.I. replaces? And is this change a good or a bad thing for humanity? The optimistic answer is that while a lot of jobs will disappear, many new ones will be created. A 2017 report from the computer manufacturer Dell suggests that 85 percent of all mid-century jobs haven't even been created yet.

It's important to state that the optimism we are referencing isn't the same as wishful thinking, especially when it is based on historical precedent. Thirty years ago, there was no such thing as a Website designer, blogger, app designer, digital marketer, genetic counselor, podcaster, or SEO specialist. (In fact, the word "app" hadn't even been invented yet.)

Thirty years from now, people may be employed as virtual world architects, A.I. personality engineers, drone managers, human-technology integration specialists, urban agriculturalists, avatar designers, 3D food print engineers, nano-medics, and hyperloop transport engineers. Again, according to Ibaraki, there is good reason to feel hopeful about economic opportunities. "This year there is actually data indicating that because of enhanced capabilities and productivity, as well as a growing economy, jobs may even increase rather than decrease."

A MIXED BAG?

Optimism aside, we know it isn't all good news on the economic front. As the aforementioned Oxford study predicts, a significant portion of the public will lose their jobs. This is especially true when it comes to people who are older, unskilled, or undereducated. Some individuals are also likely to become permanently unemployable. As a result, there is a push underway to change the way we view work and how we remunerate our citizens—especially those affected by the coming change.

Recently, there has been a surge of support for new income models poised to disrupt the traditional workday and all of its associations, including the 9–5 grind. The highest-profile example is the push for a "basic income" guarantee for all citizens. Endorsed by thought leaders like Mark Zuckerberg, under this plan the government would provide subsistence to every citizen—a form of permanent welfare. Though the details of the plan haven't been formulized and vary according to the groups clamoring for the measure, the general idea holds that the public's needs could be met, including housing and food, through the aid of government payments. Also, depending on versions of the plans, individuals could choose to live on this income alone and/or earn additional income through part-time or even full-time employment.

Though this idea is far from universally accepted and is still in the exploratory phase, it is worth imagining what life might look like if the the government came to the aid of workers—or if A.I. did indeed fulfill the promise of Keynes, making us infinitely much more productive and prosperous. Might the twenty-first century be the age in which humanity wrests back its free time from the clutches of wage slavery? And if so, what might this world look like?

STEPPING OFF THE HAMSTER WHEEL

Since this book is meant to offer a primer on reality as well as suggestions for possibilities to come, let's consider for a moment what could happen if A.I. were to change our relationship to work. Unshackled for the first time in centuries from the burdens of toiling for subsistence, we might witness the rise of a different culture, one antithetical to the Protestant work ethic.

No doubt some people might just kick back, watch TV, play videogames, and/or disappear into virtual worlds like the fictional OASIS of Ernest Cline's *Ready Player One*. But others might fulfill the prophesies of Asimov, Heinlein, and Clarke by devoting themselves to self-betterment; they might pursue advances in science, music, philosophy, and art that they might never have sought but for the advent of A.I. Life might, for a moment, come closer to the promise of Eden.

REALITY MEETS FANTASY

To many people, the ideas raised in this chapter may seem hopelessly utopian. Apart from mankind prospering from any A.I. largesse, they might wonder how a "basic income" could ever be funded. Some have suggested implementing a "robot tax." Under this requirement, companies benefitting from A.I. would have their profits taxed to support the labor pool they rendered obsolete.

While all of this remains uncertain, the fact is that many worry that just as the Industrial Revolution created a new class of "super rich" and the Information Age led to an ever-widening gap in wealth disparity, the A.I. Revolution is poised to create an even wider economic chasm. The truth is that without meaningful adjustments in our social, economic, and political systems to compensate for this, the likelihood is that social unrest will increase substantially.

In the ensuing material, we will address this economic issue further, culminating in Chapter 15, in which we will present our own idea as to how A.I. can create the world we dream without resorting to guaranteed basic income or leaving wide swathes of the public in squalor and disenfranchisement. Moreover, as A.I. continues to change the nature of work, we will show how this technology cannot help but change the way we humans view everyday life and how we subsist. However, before we discuss how we will get there, it's time to explore why for the first time ever, A.I. is now commercially possible for businesses.

Chapter 11

Why Now, A.I.?

The history of technological innovation is rife with concepts that failed during their initial release only to succeed years later, when technology finally caught up with the dream. Consider the video telephone. At the New York World's Fair in 1964, Bell Labs introduced the "Picturephone," a device combining a traditional hard-wired telephone handset with a Jetsons-style TV camera/video screen console.

TIMING IS EVERYTHING

In technology, as in comedy, it's true that timing is everything. Although Bell engineers expected the Picturephone to replace common telephones within a decade, the hardware was too expensive, the black-and-white screens too small, and the nation's transmission lines too primitive to make Picturephones practical. In fact, in its first iteration, a single 15-minute-long Picturephone call cost the 2018 equivalent of $610. No one wanted it. Not until 50 years later, when computer technology, the Internet, and data compression advanced to the point where video sharing was suddenly dirt cheap, could the vision of Bell's mid-twentieth-century engineers finally be realized.

Videodisc technology followed a similar pattern. During the 1970s, several companies, most notably Japan's National Panasonic, America's MCA, and The Netherlands' Phillips, marketed systems that played movies encoded by laser on platter-sized discs. The most successful of these systems, Laserdisc, was too expensive and clumsy to reach mass-market penetration. (Its LP-sized disc could hold only 30 minutes' worth of video per side, meaning users had to manually flip/replace discs four times to watch a single 120-minute feature film.) It wasn't until the CD-sized high-capacity digital video disc (DVD) launched in 1996 that popularly priced videodisc systems became a commercial reality.

Finally, take the case of the electric car. Starting in the mid-1800s, inventors struggled to create a personal transportation vehicle powered by electricity, only to be stymied by the problem of heavy batteries and limited range. Over the next 100 years, investors lost millions—perhaps, tens of millions—backing the concept of electric vehicles. Even as recently as the 1990s, General Motors' failed experiment with the all-electric EV1 appeared to end the idea of commercially viable electric passenger vehicles.

Fast forward two decades. Suddenly we have the all-electric Tesla Roadster tearing up the road. Fast forward a few more years and an influx of electric vehicles like the Mitsubishi i-MiEV (2009), Nissan Leaf (2010), Renault Kangoo (2011), and Tesla Model S (2012) appeared on the scene. Suddenly, demand for all-electric vehicles far outstrips supply. Today, many countries, including Denmark, Norway, Italy, Spain, India, France, and Israel, as well as dozens of individual U.S. states, openly discuss the total phaseout of gasoline-powered cars and trucks by midcentury. As evidence of the sea change in thinking, in 2018, California's Governor Jerry Brown signed into legislation S.B. 100 to halt all fossil fuel usage by 2045. Amazingly, in just two decades, innovations in battery storage and composite material construction turned the electric car—once a commercial flop—into the Next Big Thing.

Which brings us to artificial intelligence. Computer scientists have been talking about A.I. since the 1950s. So why is the A.I. revolution happening *now* instead of 70 years ago? Or even 10 years ago? What has changed? The answer is technology finally advanced to the point that the *cost* and the general infrastructure make machine intelligence—and perhaps, even more importantly, machine *learning*—possible on a commercial scale. As we have seen, A.I. relies on three things: (1) Big Data; (2) powerful processing; and (3) training.

For the first two of these, the timing couldn't be more perfect.

BIG DATA

Today's data is being collected, stored, sliced and diced, and visualized (i.e., reported) at unprecedented rates. Let's put the numbers in perspective. In

1995, shortly after the release of the first Web browser, Netscape Navigator, the entire Internet contained approximately 0.03 terabytes of information. By 1997, this volume had jumped to 2.0 terabytes. In 2007, the Internet contained approximately 0.5 exabytes (half of 1 million terabytes) of data, and this is predicted to grow to 163 zettabytes (163,000 exabytes) by the year 2025. (All data from IDC's Digital Universe Study, 2017.) As reported by *Forbes* magazine on May 21, 2018, the world now produces an estimated 2.5 quintillion bytes of data *every day*. Fun fact: we are now producing data so fast that every year, 90 percent of all the data ever produced in the history of the world has been generated in the previous 12 months.

That's a *lot* of information.

So where does all this data come from? According to Data Never Sleeps 5.0, the fifth yearly infographic on Internet use published by domo.com, the Internet generates 2.5 quintillion bits of data daily. This includes:

- 456,000 tweets on Twitter
- 527,760 photos shared on Snapchat
- 4.146 million videos viewed on YouTube
- 154,200 calls made on Skype
- 45,787 trips taken on Uber
- 3.6 million Google searches
- 18 million forecast requests to the Weather Channel
- 103,447 spam emails

Together, these examples combine to create what's known as Big Data. In the early 2000s, industry analyst Doug Laney defined Big Data in terms of what he called the Three Vs: volume, velocity, and variety. *Volume* refers to the *amount* of information flowing into a system, including business transactions, information from sensors, social media, or machine-to-machine communications. *Velocity* describes the speed at which information comes in. The rising number of sensors, RFID (radio frequency identification) tags, and smart meters—not to mention general improvements in data transmission technology—has increased data velocity markedly over the last decade. Finally, *variety* concerns the range of formats in which data is transmitted and received. Today, data arrives not only via traditional database and text documents, but in the form of video and audio. And a lot of this data creation, including financial transactions and stock price movements, occurs in real time.

Now, at this point, the casual observer might say, "Okay, yes, the amount of data we're producing is enormous, but what about its *quality*? Isn't much of it just noise?" To be fair, this individual may have a point. There is a lot of junk out there. Vapid amounts of text messages, cat videos, and, yes, pics of people's unmentionables flood the system daily. Perhaps great chunks of the data out there is garbage.

Or maybe it only *seems* like it. The miracle of A.I. is that, by analyzing massive data streams, recognizing patterns, and applying predictive analysis, it can often find diamonds amid all those "lumps of coal." What might appear to be noise to our mere mortal brains may prove invaluable to intelligences beyond our comprehension—which leads us to . . .

PROCESSING POWER

In 1965, Gordon Moore, cofounder of Fairchild Semiconductor and Intel, famously predicted that the processing power of computers would double annually based on the number of transistors that could fit on a computer chip. As we discussed in Chapter 2, this became known as "Moore's Law." In 1975, Moore revised his prediction, changing the rate of doubling to once every *two* years. Intel executive David House later put his own spin on the prediction, stating that the doubling rate would occur once every 18 months, based on both the capacity and speed of each new generation of computer chips. Since then, the 18-month figure has become the generally recognized version of this law.

Moore and House's predictions turned out to be pretty accurate for the first 30 or so years of commercial computer production. But because transistors can't keep shrinking forever—they can never become smaller than the atoms of which they are made—this law has its limits. In fact, a 2011 study in the journal *Science* reported the rate of annual growth in computational power peaked in 1998 at 88 percent. Since then, the rate of growth has slowed, but is still roughly 60 percent annually, which continues to be damned impressive. This has been achieved not just by making transistors smaller and packing more of them into a limited space, but also by changing how they are arranged and connected to one another.

In practical terms, the numbers are staggering. Perhaps the best way to measure computer power is in terms of FLOPS (floating point operations per second). By this measure, we have seen a 1 trillion-fold increase in computational speed between 1960 and 2015. For example, the IBM 7090, the transistorized version of the company's earlier model 709 vacuum tube-driven mainframe released in 1960, could process just over 200,000 FLOPS. In 1967, the Seymour-Cray 7600 super-computer could perform 35 million FLOPS. Thirty years later, the Intel ASCI Red 2000 had a top speed of 2.4 trillion FLOPS. Today, China's Tianhe-2 super-computer performs 33.86 quadrillion FLOPs, and even more powerful machines are currently in development.

At the same time that computing power has exploded, consumer prices have plummeted. The typical IBM 7090 cited above sold for about $2.9 million in 1960 or, adjusting for inflation, about $18 million in 2018 dollars. By contrast, today you can buy an obsolete Apple iPhone 4, which has 500 times the computing power of the IBM 7090, for just $100. Similarly, the price of computer memory (RAM) has dropped even faster. In 1960, 1 megabyte (1 million bytes) of memory cost approximately $5.24 million. By 1985 this cost had fallen to $300, and in 2018 it was an infinitesimal $0.0068. (All figures from John C. McCallum Information Technology.)

What all this means is that we now have all the fast—and cheap—computing power we need to make sense out of the Big Data flowing into the system and thus can make artificial intelligence a reality. There is just one piece missing from the equation.

TRAINING

As we have seen, even the world's largest, fastest A.I. is useless without proper instruction. Providing valid ground truths for training is essential, as is creating the right algorithms to analyze massive amounts of data. But identifying ground truths is not as easy as it may sound. Precision is essential, and such precision does not come naturally to the human personality.

Here is an example. On its face, the sentence "The sky is blue" would seem to be a simple ground truth. Every child knows this statement to be true. But, of course, it's not true. Or at least the truth is more complicated than it seems. At night, the sky is black. At sunrise or sunset, it can appear to be various shades of red, orange, and yellow. Even during high noon, the sky can look grey and overcast or muddy brown due to smog.

Apart from variations in color depending on time of day, the above sentence is also inaccurate in its claims. The sky is actually colorless. What we are seeing is an illusion. The atmosphere's nitrogen and oxygen molecules scatter white sunlight making us perceive the color blue from the diffused wavelengths. But even this explanation isn't entirely accurate, because we are only describing how the sky looks to *us*. Other animals, whose eyes see beyond the visible spectrum or can sense magnetic fields, likely see the sky wholly differently than humans. Reality is often just a matter of individual perspective.

So what color *is* the sky? The answer is, "It depends." There is no one answer fitting all scenarios; it is instead determined by time of day, weather conditions, and even subjective perception. However, if we all walked around saying, "It depends" to describe what color the sky is, we would live in an even more complicated world than we do now. As a consequence, we make shortcuts so as to foster mutual understanding and convenience. Can you see how this might be confusing when it comes to training an A.I.?

Before we discuss how to deal with such a training challenge, let's consider another so-called given to give the problem more context. A precocious child might also say, "The earth is round." However, as a ground truth, this too, is inaccurate. Planet Earth is not a perfect sphere. It's what is known as an oblate sphere, somewhat flattened at the poles and bulging at the equator. And even the equatorial "bulge" is not uniform, being greater in some parts of the world than others. To describe the true shape of Earth would require a highly complex set of measurements along a detailed three-dimensional matrix. (Try explaining this to your three-year-old when she asks for the shape of the Earth.)

Of course, any training situation becomes even more complicated when ethical values are involved. All human societies agree that "murder is wrong." But how do we define "murder"? Taking the life of another human being? If so, then what about capital punishment, warfare, or killing in self-defense? And what constitutes a "human being"? In America, this final question has proven to be a major point of contention in the decades-old debate over abortion rights, with some people claiming a fertilized egg is a fully legal human being, while others maintaining someone only becomes fully "human" when he/she is present outside the womb.

By the way, if you think this debate is complicated for people, try explaining it to a machine. The bottom line is that establishing ground truths can be a formidable task requiring nuance and sophistication. Things appearing to be "truthful" are in actuality quite complicated, often requiring further review, testing, and often times multiple revisions to achieve accuracy.

This brings us full circle to our challenge: creating proper algorithms to unlock A.I. technology through the right training. We hear the word "algorithm" a lot these days. While most people have a vague idea of its meaning, few can define it. Similar to a formula, it's a set of instructions used to make a calculation, solve a problem, or make a decision.

Many people use algorithms every day, albeit unknowingly. For example, a recipe is an algorithm. Mix a certain number of ingredients together, heat them at the right temperature for a specific amount of time, and, *voilà!* you have food. Likewise, use your remote control's "On" button to turn on your TV, hit certain buttons in a specific order on your DVR's controls and, *voilà!* you have entertainment. Drive your car at a specific range of speeds in a specific direction, take specific turns at specific intersections and, *voilà!* you're at the supermarket. They're all algorithms.

Interestingly, many life science experts now view biology itself as nothing but a series of algorithms, albeit organic ones. Every cell division, every glandular secretion, every muscle movement occurs under the direction of algorithms that have taken millions, if not billions, of years to evolve via natural selection. What is the fundamental difference between organic algorithms and mechanical or electronic ones? Life science experts will tell you there *is* no difference, just variations in type and degree.

But twenty-first century computer programmers don't have millions, much less billions of years to hone their algorithms. Instead, the concerted efforts of numerous trained professionals must accomplish in months what in nature requires millennia. Fortunately for them, most do not work in isolation, but rather coordinate their contributions through complex communications networks.

Still, the best ground truth is that algorithms tend to require input from specialists of all types, including scientists, historians, technicians, artists, doctors, attorneys, financiers, economists, entertainers, and so on, to provide the A.I. with the full depth and breadth of the human experience. However, as we saw with our discussions concerning the sky's color, the Earth's shape, and defining the rights and wrongs of murder, if the training is superficial or lacking, the resulting analyses and predictions will likely be flawed. Or even fatal.

Based on this reality, A.I. training continues to be one of the central challenges that today's businesses face, especially those lacking time and resources. Even narrow-focused A.I. can require tremendous input. For example, imagine you want to build an A.I. to correctly pick winning stocks. At the very least, you'd want data from as many successful stockbrokers and market analysts as you could corral. This raises a key question: How might you get such people to cooperate with you? After all, training an A.I. means essentially training a smarter, faster, and more capable system to, in effect, replace you. What's the incentive for doing *that*? People concerned about being rendered obsolete probably won't be chomping at the bit to participate in their own professional demise.

At present, this very human bottleneck is proving more daunting than any nearly any other technological challenge to A.I.'s greater adoption. Yet, most A.I. developers remain confident that they can secure the outside cooperation they need, perhaps by ensuring participants that the resulting A.I. will work to support, not supplant, them. This is, in fact, the promise currently driving A.I. in businesses worldwide. And as we will see in the next chapter, the benefits of A.I. on the way humans think and make choices are so profound that adoption may prove impossible for anyone to resist.

Chapter 12

The Tenth Man

In September 1973, Israeli military intelligence reported suspicious troop movements to the north and south along the borders with its Arab neighbors. Although Israel had technically been at war with these same countries since its founding on May 14, 1948, the state's high command concluded, upon reviewing the intelligence data, that no military threat was imminent. No members of the senior military staff seriously questioned this conclusion.

So far so good. But fast-forward one month.

NO ONE SAW IT COMING

On the Jewish High Holy Day of Yom Kippur, the traditional Day of Atonement marked by prayers and fasting, Arab forces launched coordinated attacks. Hoping to wrest back land lost to Israel during the third Arab-Israeli War of 1967, Egyptian troops roared deep into the Sinai Peninsula while Syria attempted to overrun the Golan Heights. What later became known as the Yom Kippur War lasted from October 6 to October 25, 1973, and almost spelled Israel's doom. Only an eleventh-hour counterattack in the Golan Heights, backed up by airlifted reinforcements from the United States, saved the fledgling nation from being driven into the sea.

After the smoke had cleared, Israel faced a reckoning from its (rightfully) incensed citizens. *How could this have happened?* asked a bereaved people. *How could military intelligence have made such a blunder?* Heads rolled.

Virulent criticism forced Golda Meir, Israel's first and only female prime minister, to step down. Still licking its wounds, the Israeli military vowed to rethink its decision-making process, adopting what it called "The Tenth Man Policy." Under the new ethos, if nine people hypothetically agreed to a particular course of action, it was the sworn duty of the tenth person to disagree. This policy was meant to crush the dangers of achieving consensus without applying vigorous debate and critical thinking.

The ensuing decades have shown the efficacy of the Tenth Man Policy. Among other strategic initiatives, it has been credited with helping to make the Israeli Army one of the most responsive, effective, and feared militaries in the world, despite its small size. So why is the Tenth Man Policy so effective? And how does it relate to artificial intelligence?

THE TOXIC MADDING CROWD

The Tenth Man policy was created to counter what is popularly known as groupthink. First coined by journalist William H. Whyte Jr., *groupthink* appeared as a term in a 1952 *Fortune* magazine article in which Whyte discussed "*rationalized* conformity—an open, articulate philosophy which holds that group values are not only expedient but right and good as well." Whyte was paying homage to George Orwell's term *doublethink* from his dystopian satire *1984*. Orwell's derogatory term criticized propaganda. Under its sway, seemingly rational people could somehow hold two conflicting beliefs simultaneously: "To know and not to know, to be conscious of complete truthfulness while telling carefully constructed lies, to hold simultaneously two opinions which cancelled out . . . " Groupthink's danger lies in conformity. Whyte foresaw a similar danger when any group mindlessly agrees upon something due to peer pressure. Whyte and Orwell warned against accepting beliefs or values held by a majority just because the majority believes it.

More examples of dangers associated with mass conformity abound. Groupthink's ability to muck up the facts on the ground with reality extends to America's own intelligence failures. In April 1961, spooks from multiple spy organizations, including the NSA, FBI, and CIA, were of one mind that a military invasion of Cuba would trigger a popular counter-revolution against Fidel Castro's newly installed regime. This assessment didn't just come from data accumulated from military sources; overwhelming certainty reigned from moral convictions. A decade after the second Red Scare, America as a whole possessed a black-and-white geopolitical view. According to prevailing cultural myths, the

United States was the "Good Guy" and the Communists were the "Bad Guys." America *had* to prevail. Such closed-minded thinking led to the disastrous Bay of Pigs fiasco, which not only embarrassed the United States internationally, but led to the near-fatal Cuban Missile Crisis a year and half later.

Beyond military blunders, the perils of groupthink can be seen in civic life, proving that even the most informed individuals can fall victim to it. During the 2016 presidential elections, most media outlets unflinchingly espoused the so-called common-sense position that Hillary Clinton would beat Donald Trump. The highly unconventional Trump candidacy was treated with scorn and ridicule by most "serious-minded" journalists and their networks, in spite of the fact that it offered a major boon to their ratings.

A former CBS executive chairman, Leslie Moonves, famously said, "It may not be good for America, but it's damn good for CBS." Even though most polls showed the race tightening, especially in the key swing states of Pennsylvania, Michigan, and Wisconsin, virtually every pundit and news organization predicted Clinton would prevail. Instead, Trump pulled off one of the greatest upset victories of all time, albeit while still losing the popular vote and winning these three swing states by the thinnest of margins. Even so, the media's lack of any prior equivocation led to a loss of overall credibility lingering to this day.

In addition to mass media implications, groupthink poses special dangers for the economy, greatly exacerbated by the fact each industrialized nation is now interconnected through commerce. Evidence of its ability to spread destruction far and wide can be found in the 2008 financial crash. Early in the first decade of the twenty-first century, real estate became the new go-to investment throughout the United States. "If you had a pulse, we gave you a loan," was how Kourosh Partow, manager of Countrywide's offices in Alaska, put it in a 2009 article for NBC News. Coming on the heels of President George W. Bush's vow to extend homeownership as part of America's "economic security" plan, conventional wisdom held that real estate values would continue rising indefinitely. Such a collective rose-colored-glasses outlook led to a surge of home purchases underwritten with sloppy, if not criminally negligent, underwriting standards.

Once-regal investment houses like Lehman Brothers and Merrill Lynch bought these toxic mortgages, bundled them, broke them into pieces, then resold them as collateralized debt obligations (CDOs) at many times their original value. Or as trader Mark Baum (his real-life name was Steve Eisman) describes it in the 2015 movie *The Big Short*, "So mortgage bonds are dog shit. CDOs are dog shit wrapped in cat shit."

Meanwhile, the few people who weren't drinking Wall Street's Kool-Aid and who did warn that a dangerous real estate bubble was forming, were dismissed as cranks and losers. This state of affairs was similar to the situation in seventeenth-century Holland, in which hysterical Dutch tulip speculation led to the price of a single flower being worth the price of an entire estate, before the tulip market spectacularly collapsed. It seemed in 2007 that so long as everyone bought into the same groupthink, so long as everyone believed prices would continue to rise, they would. Though most people had every incentive to maintain the collective fiction, the real estate bubble burst, collapsing the American real estate market and nearly tanking the entire world economy as business after business and country after country succumbed to the shockwave.

SYMPTOMS AND A CURE

Now that we have seen the catastrophic impact of groupthink, let's unpack this phenomenon further before delving into how A.I. might overcome it. Yale research psychologist Irving Janis describes eight symptoms associated with this detrimental mentality:

1. **Illusions of invulnerability,** creating excessive optimism and encouraging risk taking.
2. **Unquestioned belief in the group's morality,** causing members to ignore the consequences of their actions.
3. **Rationalizing away of warnings** that might challenge the group's assumptions.
4. **Stereotyping those who oppose the group** as weak, evil, biased, spiteful, impotent, or stupid.
5. **Self-censorship of ideas** deviating from the apparent group consensus.
6. **Illusions of unanimity among group members**. Silence is viewed as agreement.
7. **Direct pressure to conform** placed on any member who questions the group, couched in terms of "disloyalty."
8. **Mindguards.** Self-appointed members who shield the group from dissenting information.

As we have seen, groupthink has the potential to demolish nation states from the outside and within. It's therefore little surprise that such limited thinking can spell disaster to any type of organization, be it commercial, administrative, political, legal, medical, or academic. As a business owner or a company associate, it is incumbent upon you to reject a "go along to get along" mentality, to watch out for these symptoms in order not just to survive but thrive.

Fortunately, one of A.I.'s greatest assets, when correctly harnessed, is its ability to offer independent projections and predictions. Unblinded by greed, fear, ambition, or desire, A.I. has the potential to see patterns its people may overlook. Devoid of biases, unless intentionally or unintentionally introduced during A.I. training, it promises to be the antithesis of groupthink. (Important caveat: the issue of A.I. bias *can* be a real threat and is later addressed in Section II by numerous thought leaders.) Why? Not only can A.I. draw on vast amounts of data for decision-making and analyses, it is not subject to political, religious, or ideological pressures. It isn't worried about hurting your feelings. It is completely independent. It truly "tells it like it is." It is the ultimate Tenth Man.

A PANACEA FOR THE AVERAGE BUSINESS?

At this point, you might be saying to yourself, "Okay, perhaps A.I. can more accurately predict presidential elections, and avoid military disasters and investment bubbles, but how can it help my business? How can an artificial Tenth Man benefit a restaurant, small parts manufacturer, retail store, law firm, farm, or marketing company? In short, what could A.I do for *me*?" Let's go through some examples, sector by sector.

Tenth Man Farming

Computing used to be much more limited only a few years ago. Second generation computers functioned much like sophisticated calculators. You could set your own, limited parameters and ask specific questions, like: "If I charge 10 cents more per item, what will my return rate be?" Now, in the scope of technological innovation, it is still an amazing achievement to have a device capable of answering this question, but third generation computing trumps this breakthrough by leaps and bounds.

Today's A.I. computing model is dynamic—*it's anticipatory*. It can establish its own, almost infinite parameters. It can generate its own insights, offering high-level, independent thinking through processing vast amounts of data from a variety of sources. Able to conceive of new patterns, it can develop novel ideas you may have not even considered.

To better see how this works in practice, consider the family farm, once the backbone of the American economy. Today's modern farmers use analytics to review soil content, market prognostications, and long-range weather forecasts to determine what crops to plant and when to plant them. Like second generation computing, such innovation has rendered a huge jump forward in productivity from their counterparts just a few generations ago. However, compare this to what third generation computing (A.I.) can do and the results are game-changing by an order of magnitude.

So much for stagnating under farming groupthink. A.I. can offer independent analyses beyond anything your farmer neighbors or historical trends might suggest. In addition to reviewing obvious data points such as weather, soil conditions, current market demand, and the price of seeds, an A.I. can also consider more complex developments, like geopolitical trends in China, climate change in southern Africa, variations in historical ocean temperatures around northern Australia, insect infestations in western Russia, and countless other seemingly unrelated minutia that, when factored together, can offer a butterfly effect-like impact on the fortunes of a 400-acre family farm in southern Iowa.

Tenth Man Retail

Consider a small clothing shop selling souvenir hats and T-shirts at rock concerts. A forward-thinking retailer needn't rely on her human compatriots as to how best to succeed with her enterprise. She can draw on the predictive power of an A.I. for independent guidance. An A.I. can gather a host of actionable data: who is attending the concert, each audience member's short- and long-term purchase habits, and how much each person likes a particular show (based on Tweets and Facebook posts, as well as biometric info gleaned from heart rate, blood pressure, and perspiration submitted to their personal fitness trackers).

"From what I know about Aaron and the way he is experiencing this Kanye West concert, you should send his smartphone a $5-off coupon for a Make America Great hat," the A.I. might suggest. Not only can the A.I. specify the exact type of product to offer, but also the specific offer. It can also predict that one customer is likely to respond to a $1-off promotion, while another might require $5 off to be motivated. And, of course, it can factor the seller's profitability into any recommendation.

Tenth Man Athlete Scouting

In the 1990s, Oakland Athletics coach Billy Beane revolutionized major league baseball by using accounting algorithms to determine a player's "true market value" based not only on obvious stats, like home runs, RBIs, and stolen bases, but previously less valued factors, like on-base and slugging percentages. Riveting for its time, the book and movie *Money Ball* captured the ingenuity of sabermetrics, the use of statistical data analysis to determine the value of a player to a team, or, the use of raw baseball data for actionable decisions (the term *sabermetrics* is derived from the Society for American Baseball Research of baseball guru Bill James).

Using A.I., today's forward-thinking coaches in every sport needn't rely on their hunches or others' opinions about who to draft or who to play. Instead, they can make recruitment decisions through machine learning. Mathew Cole, a member of the software company Brooklyn Dynamics, uses A.I. to assess scout talent. He explains why this way, "Platforms that collect data, that standardize and create uniformity in the collection, allow players to be evaluated 24/7. The premise we work under is that we are creating the data CV of the athletes for the entire life cycle. Take away any human bias . . . you evaluate a player and their data, you don't see race, nationality, or other factors that often cloud judgement."

Tenth Man Tacos

Finally, let's assume you're the owner of a food truck. Instead of relying on what your competitors have done in the past or on well-intentioned friends' advice, you could gain insight from an A.I. It can suggest where to park your truck, how many tacos might sell in a given period, and how many ingredients you should order, saving you money on inventory and crucial preparation time.

Cognizant of local foot traffic, the A.I. can also tell you the optimal time to intercept people coming out of a particular bar, especially if there's an event going on. It might say, *"If you set up at this location from 1:00 to 1:30, you can sell more shrimp tacos at a 10 percent premium."* Likewise, scanning news sites and Twitter feeds, the A.I. can alert you to the fact that a convention of vegetarian aficionados will be emerging onto the street at 5 p.m. giving you ample time to prep your mouth-watering green chile and cheese tamales.

CUSTOM-TAILORED DIAGNOSES

As the above indicates, independent Tenth Man thinking through A.I. holds the promise to benefit every business in any industry. As further examples, a physical therapist aided by A.I. could deduce what kind of therapy, talk, writing, pet, or pharmaceutical, would most benefit each of his patients based on the collected data (important guidance this professional wouldn't be able to access from other minds without breaking confidentiality). Similarly, a doctor could turn to A.I. to understand what the most effective medication would be, based not only on simple factors, like age, weight, and potential interactions with other drugs, but also other data, such as the patient's individual diet, exercise, and sleep patterns, family health history, and daily exposure to environmental pollutants.

Ultimately, what makes A.I. so powerful for business is the fact that it offers dynamic, not static, insight. Helpful predictions occur in *real time* based on the world as it is *right now*. One of the reasons political prognosticating has been so erratic historically is that a key portion of the electorate changes positions with each passing news cycle. What is true today is not necessarily true tomorrow.

We all know how sensitive the stock market is to even the smallest bits of news. A.I.'s ability to react even quicker and predict patterns in seemingly unrelated fields can lead to game-changing insights untainted by groupthink. So how might A.I. be used to support *your* business in even more novel ways? And what would you have to do to configure such a system to your needs? This is the subject of our next chapter.

Chapter 13

How Can I Use Artificial Intelligence Now?

Based on the material we have covered and all you have learned about our thinking machines' almost godlike powers of cognition, you may be asking yourself, "How can my business take advantage of A.I.?" The answer depends on several factors: your willingness to adapt, the time and energy you can invest, the size of your business, and your budget. By the way, you may have noticed we didn't say your *type* of business may preclude you from adopting A.I. The reason is simple: no matter what you do—even if you are in a creative industry that would seem to disqualify you from using such technology—you *can* take advantage of A.I.

As we have already seen, IBM Watson can cut movie trailers, drive cars, and write news articles. What is to prevent it from making full-length movies in the future? Or even writing books such as this?

GROWING PAINS

As of this writing (yes, still performed by flesh-and-blood humans), commercial A.I. adoption can be likened to Second Wave computing in the early 1970s. The benefits of automated data processing were well established by the Nixon years. Businesses of all types were eager to acquire computers to streamline operations, enhance efficiencies, and increase profits. However, the cost of computers—and the expertise necessary to program and operate them—was still prohibitively high. Only large or well-funded organizations could bear them.

At the dawn of the pre-disco era, it was common to find computers in banks, insurance companies, major manufacturing plants, mail-order houses, utilities offices, distribution centers, and, of course, government agencies. Any group dealing with numerous records or producing complex financial statements was likely to be computerized. Still, enterprise-level computer systems cost hundreds of thousands of dollars and were therefore beyond the reach of most small businesses and entrepreneurs. Only when desktop personal computers hit the market in the early 1980s did computers become truly mainstream.

Today's A.I. technologies reside in a similar adolescent stage. Major manufacturing corporations, pharmaceutical companies, financial institutions, national retailers, and entertainment platforms like Netflix and Hulu are investing heavily in this technology. However, most mom-and-pop shops, small-time retailers, and/or beginning entrepreneurs are not. Why not? It's mostly to do with money. The minimum price to get started can be as high as $100,000. But let's say you run a company that can afford $100,000 to $500,000 to develop a dedicated A.I. or lease an existing system like IBM's Watson. How might you harness such technology in practice? To help answer this question and give you a taste of A.I.'s real world applications, we will now tour the changing business landscape. The following section describes how today's industries and players are using A.I. to enhance their fortunes.

Sales

"I don't know if I can do that, but if I could, would you buy this car today?" Sleazy salespeople have been known to use cheesy lines like this to sell cars for a long time. And as a result, nearly everyone detests the auto buying experience. According to a 2016 Beepi Consumer Index, a full 87 percent of Americans dislike car shopping at dealerships.

Knowing this to be true, the Detroit-based Feldman Automotive Group began deploying A.I.-based chatbots to improve car buying. Sayonara, high-pressure sales tactics. Instead of being harassed from the moment they step on the lot, prospects can interact with chatbots at home—on their terms. "[The platform] targets prospects in a geographic radius of several Feldman brick-and-mortar dealership locations with an advertisement integration through Facebook's Newsfeed," writes Dom Nicastro for *CMS WiRE*. "The chatbot can then strike up direct-message conversations with prospects in Facebook Messenger. Online assistance for customers is also available through the chatbot."

Companies like Feldman Automotive are not alone in realizing natural language processing (NLP) chatbots' potential. They stand to transform many notoriously unpleasant customer experiences. Hate being put on hold? You're not alone. It's one of the most frustrating aspects of modern times. Yet as Lara Ponomareff for *Computer Weekly.com*, explains, "Call centers are the front line of all big organizations, providing a vital link between businesses and customers. They are also the place that can make or break the brand experience."

To counter perceptions surrounding bad call center experiences, and, of course, offer customers more value, many savvy companies have begun turning to innovators like Bright Pattern. Integrated with A.I. bots, including IBM Watson, Reply.ai, and Alterra, and designed to extract meaning from spoken language, Bright Pattern's stated purpose is to "conduct conversations with customers automatically."

The return on investment (ROI) behind their offering is that by outsourcing call center drudgery to bots, the humans at any given company can focus on high-level, creative, and interesting work. Bright Pattern also offers automation with a "human touch." This means the person calling in can elect to bypass the bot if they are experiencing problems with it. (The bot will actually detect this frustration and transfer the call. The bot will then listen to the subsequent human-to-human interaction, learning what to do the next time a similar situation arises.)

Chatbots are becoming especially common among businesses whose customers primarily interface online. [X]cube LABS is one such firm in this space, building A.I.- and NLP-driven chatbots for 24/7 automated support and interactive assistance. Contracted to work with major brands like United Health Group, Sharp, and GE, it is one of many tech companies specializing in creating smooth keyboard or voice-driven experiences indistinguishable from actual human interactions.

[X]cube LABS chatbots also offer sales support. Forget annoying car sales people. You can think of their e-commerce bots as a next-gen sales force. They never even yawn, never complain or request a smoke break. They can also upsell or cross-sell in imaginative ways by influencing decisions at key moments in the sales cycle.

Supply Chain Planning and Logistics

If your business services thousands of customers and relies on multiple suppliers delivering goods through numerous channels, balancing demand with your supply chain can feel like a herculean task. *For a human.* Not for an A.I.

"Machine learning algorithms and the apps running them are capable of analyzing large, diverse data sets fast, improving demand and forecasting accuracy," writes Louis Columbus for *Forbes*. Citing a case study of how Lennox Heating and Cooling mastered the supply chain in a changing network, Columbus describes how the company went from a national stocking model to a hub-and-spoke model with numerous shipping and selling locations, while increasing sales, inventory turnover, and market share growth.

Likewise, it's no wonder that large fulfillment businesses like Walmart use A.I. to stay abreast of an increasingly complex and dynamic retail ecosystem. According to Lucy Benton, writing for Supply Chain Beyond.Com, "A.I. allows greater contextual intelligence, which provides the knowledge needed to reduce operations costs and inventory and respond to clients quicker."

Though Walmart was founded in 1962, decades before the personal computer, it has kept up with the times. In the fall of 2018, Walmart announced a new tech-enabled fresh and frozen grocery warehouse in Shafter, California, capable of storing and retrieving items and pallets automatically. Using such smart technology allows the company to detect even minor changes in customer demand and supplier output and respond in real time with calibrated adjustments to avoid overstocks or empty shelves. As a further sign that Walmart is investing in tech to stay current, the company just introduced its own supply chain academy to train workers in STEM (science, technology, engineering, and mathematics) skills.

Marketing

Targeting a customer with a persuasive sale message at the moment they are ready to buy has long been an art form dependent on a little intuition and a lot of luck. No longer. Today, A.I. can not only predict customer buyer patterns, it can shape sales communications targeted to individual customers. By now, you're well aware that companies like Amazon offer recommendations based on your past purchase selections. What you may not know is how other forward-thinking marketing firms are using A.I. to generate uncommon results.

Backed by a $65 million investment after going through four funding rounds, the start-up Lattice Engines uses Big Data to predict who will buy a product and when. So far, they have helped drive sales for major companies, including Adobe, Citrix, Dell, Hootsuite, and Staples. Their model involves three steps: (1) Connect, (2) Segment, and (3) Activate. In stage one, Lattice aggregates and consolidates multiple sources of customer data into one place.

This can include anonymous web activity, firmographics, sales activity, website profiles, growth trends, and more. The next step is to segment and build audiences through the power of A.I. Last, Lattice executes on the data with a campaign to identify targets in multiple channels with any number of digital/social ads and emails.

Based on such innovation, Lattice Engines CEO Shashi Upadhyay likens his company to pioneers in the predictive marketing space in an interview for *Trust Radius*. "We start with the premise that if you can predict who is going to buy, what they're going to buy, when they're going to buy, and how much they're going to buy better than the average person, then you can use that to improve everything about the sales and marketing function," says Upadhyay. "So, for example, if you have perfect information about what a particular person is going to buy on a particular day, you don't have to spend your marketing dollars and sales dollars on anybody else, you would just go to them and talk to them."

Business Intelligence

Beyond using Big Data for marketing purposes, we are also witnessing the rise of A.I.-powered business forecasting. How it works is that machine-based algorithms identify and demystify trends and insights. Domo exemplifies the type of company operating in this field. A business dashboard creator, it offers management tools for collecting valuable, actionable information for decision-making.

In 2017, it announced the invention of Mr. Roboto at Domopalooza, its annual user conference. In some ways Mr. Roboto is the company's answer to Siri and Cortana by way of a business oracle. According to a company press release, Mr. Roboto is the first platform to combine vast streams of data with an organization's people to leverage social patterns occurring in the "Business Cloud."

Two key features of Mr. Roboto include an alert center for decision makers to detect anomalies, understand personal data consumption patterns, and analyze an organization's most-watched metrics. The other feature concerns data science. Offering predictive analytics, it allows Mr. Roboto to discern, then respond to crucial challenges, including customer churn, sales forecast variances, and real-time ROI anomalies. Josh James, company founder and CEO, describes Mr. Roboto's utility in this way: "The Business Cloud was developed to help all people break free of data silos and shackles, and empower them with the insights they need to make better business decisions. Mr. Roboto takes this freedom to the next level, by harnessing the power of AI, predictive analytics, and machine learning to develop real-time, socially curated insights and predictions. Mr. Roboto will liberate business decision makers from slow, uniformed B.I. systems and instead will unleash data innovation."

Financial Product Development and Cybersecurity

Financial services rely on a deep understanding of assets, risks, and customer needs. Already, A.I. is proving to be extremely valuable in this field by using predictive analytics to learn from individuals' behavior and design financial products to best fit their needs—all while managing risk. Conversely, those institutions unwilling to change with the times are likely to get shut out of the evolving financial marketplace. According to a report by Forrester, "The widening gap between financial firms that embrace digital growth and business transformation powered by technology and those institutions that continue to do business in traditional ways will continue to widen."

Those in the global banking and finance sector who *are* choosing to disrupt themselves and their industry are also leveraging Big Data and analytics for more informed decisions. They are also using A.I. to spot and improve fraud protection. In 2017, Equifax made news when the public learned hackers breached the data of nearly 150 million users. This was by no means an isolated incident. Cyberattacks have surged in recent years and show signs of ramping up even more. According to Bhakti Mirchandani, writing for *Forbes*, "While the typical American business is attacked 4 million times per year, the typical American financial services firm is attacked a staggering 1 billion times per year."

Digital assaults are not only very prevalent, they are also very effective, resulting in a $16.8 billion loss to financial firms in 2017. Clearly, any business willing and equipped to counter such financial mayhem stands to do well in the new economy. Powered by machine learning, Feedzai Genome is one. The company "sequences the DNA of financial crime patterns to identify connected transactions within illicit networks that would be nearly impossible to detect otherwise," according to *Business Wire*. Founded by data scientists, Feedzai Genome uses an algorithm called OpenML Engine to predict and block instances of fraud. It is also licenses software to banks and other financial firms wishing to bolster their fraud-specific models.

Another firm combating cyber chicanery is DefenseStorm. Founded in 2014 in Georgia but now based in Seattle, Washington, the company offers software tools, PatternScout and ThreatMatch, to help financial institutions increase network visibility and to monitor in real time for anomalies and threats. DefenseStorm has uniquely positioned itself in the market. Instead of targeting major players like JP Morgan or Bank of America, DefenseStorm addresses the needs of smaller banks and credit unions.

Fleet and Factory Maintenance

It's one thing to have general guidelines suggesting when company machines and vehicles should be serviced. It's quite another to anticipate *exactly* when these critical technologies will need repair or replacement. Gathering data from wireless sensors and monitors in real time, industrial A.I. systems are saving companies millions annually by preventing equipment breakdowns that might otherwise bottleneck critical operations.

Though adoption is far from widespread, a 2017 report from Plant Engineering found that 51 percent of manufacturing companies now employ a computerized maintenance management system (CMMS). It is easy to see why. Similar to Walmart's using A.I. for fast action on inventory and shipping decisions, businesses can rely on A.I. sensors to detect broken or malfunctioning machinery, saving time and money.

Deploying such cutting-edge technology in the field, the company DataRPM has seen its client base grow in recent years, acquiring as clients Jaguar, Samsung, and Mitsubishi Heavy Industries. "It can detect random and unknown failures using a combination of unsupervised and semi-supervised learning techniques," writes Stephanie Condon for *Between the Lines* about DataRPM's A.I. approach to maintenance. "It also uses a technique called Meta Learning to increase the quality, accuracy, and timeliness of equipment failure predictions. It can scale horizontally to track any number of industrial machines."

Farming

Today's urbanites may be confounded to know that as recently as 1850, nearly 65 percent of Americans worked as farmers. Though the number of people who farm for a living has shrunk drastically (less than 2% in the U.S. today), agriculture still plays a tremendous role in the lives of people everywhere. To continue meeting the needs of consumers, farmers have had to become more technologically savvy. Innovative agricultural businesses have adapted A.I. for farming in several key areas: robotic usage for harvesting and planting, computer vision and deep learning algorithms for crop/soil monitoring, and predictive analytics for maximizing produce yields.

Despite such innovation, humans aren't the only species evolving to meet environmental challenges in novel ways. In the last few hundred years weeds have also developed new resistances despite our best efforts to eradicate them with pesticides. Companies like Blue River Technology, bought by John Deere in 2017, are not giving up the fight against our pesky plant enemies. Instead, they are using a secret weapon against unfettered plant growth: A.I. Their robot See & Spray uses computer vision technology to detect and kill individual plants in milliseconds, reducing herbicide overuse and preventing weeds from developing further immunities.

A.I. also has a direct impact on food production. As more people shift away from labor-intensive jobs, like fruit picking, machines are picking up the slack through machine vision to select fruit the same way a person might—if they could work all day, hours on end, without sleep, no matter the weather. One such company, Harvest Croo, uses robotic harvesting equipment, including an autonomous strawberry picking machine. Using conservation of motion principles, their so-called Picking Wheel can achieve 360 degrees of rotation, so a series of claws can snatch up what its sophisticated sensors have determined to be berries.

Taking the long view, Harvest Croo's cofounder Gary Wishnatzki sees lack of labor as not just an American problem, but a global challenge requiring new technical solutions. "What we hope to accomplish is to lower harvest costs by increasing the speed and duration at which it can pick and pack berries in the field," says Wishnatzki.

Setting a goal to pick 95 percent of the fruit off any plant, he views A.I. as an agricultural game changer for the whole human race. However, before any fruit can be picked, A.I. is used for scouting purposes. Stereo Vision is the name of the camera the company uses to identify each berry based on a set of criteria (color, mass and size), determining if it should be picked. Based on this split-second analysis, robot pickers can then pick fruit at the most ideal harvest time. According to Wishnatzki, shippers can also add acreage without requiring additional cooling resources while increasing output.

Resort and Casino Management

Today, top resort and hospitality organizations have seized on A.I. to offer more customized, fulfilling customer experiences. To do so, such companies rely on Big Data to obtain a fuller and actionable understanding of their clientele's behavior. "If you ask most marketing folks in the hospitality industry to outline their number one challenge, many would talk about the inane difficulty of gleaning valuable and actionable insights in the capture and aggregation of customer sentiments toward their products, goods, and services," said Eric Saint Marc, VP-IT, Palms Casino Resort, in an interview for the *Casino Review*.

Again, enter A.I. It *can* gather these details to tailor customer experiences. To demonstrate what A.I. can do for resort users, the *Casino Review* presents an idyllic vision of one person's stay once a resort's algorithms know his tastes and desires nearly as well as he does. At 8 a.m., John, our sample customer, touches down at the airport. As soon as he arrives, his Uber driver waits for him at baggage claim with luggage already in hand. At the same time, John's A-list hotel prepares check-in with the room of his choice. Prescheduled golf tee time commences at 11 a.m. after John's friends have been informed he's in town. Reservations are made for John's favorite Mexican lunch spot before the golf round ends. Later that night, John will attend a performance he hasn't seen, Cirque du Soleil, without ever having to pick up a phone or click on a Website. When he's ready to gamble, his Digital Card will already be prefilled with 10,000 free points just for being a valued member.

Saint Marc sees such unparalleled attentiveness as not just portending a brighter future for guests, but for the hospitality industry in general. Knowing your clientele's wants and needs isn't just good business, it's a good labor- and time-saving device. "Many hotel operators will agree that consolidation of time management correlated to guest activities in itself represents a major challenge," says Saint Marc. "Even something as simple as scheduling room cleaning requires housekeeping managers, supervisors, and front desk management to be in constant communications. Such challenge also applies to restauration, wellness services, and the list goes on."

YOUR OWN ACTIONABLE INFORMATION

As the above examples demonstrate, there is a bounty of benefits that A.I. offers for each business—no matter the industry. As any entrepreneur knows well, businesses are created to solve problems. A.I. just happens to be one of the most—if not the most—exceptional tool we have ever possessed to better solve our problems. And as the technology improves and the cost for adoption decreases, we will witness even more ways that A.I. can vastly improve our life experiences.

So, are you contemplating how you might use A.I. to disrupt your business for the better? Hopefully, you are. Realistically though, you may be stumped as to how to implement the technology in a practical way. That's okay. Just as there is no "one-size-fits-all" business computer program, any application of A.I. needs to be customized for the organization it serves. At this stage, our role is at least to get you thinking how using A.I. might become your new reality. Actual implementation can come later. Still, as you begin to consider applying A.I. to your own business, it's helpful to consider following these steps:

1. Build your understanding of A.I., particularly the remarkable new capabilities it offers. (Reading this book is a good start.)
2. Focus on a specific problem or opportunity.
3. Think of your ideal solution. ("Pie in the sky" ideas are welcome at this developmental stage.)
4. Consider what A.I. capabilities can help you achieve your solution.
5. Develop a vision document to establish the high-level A.I. architecture for the solution. (This is where you will need to come down to Earth.)
6. Create the training strategy for your A.I.
7. Build, train, and test your A.I. solution.
8. Leverage existing technology (such as application program interfaces).
9. Focus on programming the unique user experience you want to create. (What is a differentiator for your organization?)
10. Launch your A.I. solution.

Still uncertain about what A.I. adoption looks like at a practical level? In the next chapter, we will present an in-depth case study showing you how a company followed the above steps to launch their solution, creating a new product and better serving their customers. Could your company be next?

Chapter 14

Case in Point: How LegalMation Disrupted Itself to Own the A.I. Revolution

n Chapter 13, we showed how different industries, from sales and marketing to supply-chain planning and logistics, use A.I. to optimize business processes and maximize profits. Now, let's dig in deeper. In this chapter, we'll review one specific example in which a business in the legal industry, LegalMation, successfully integrated A.I. to stop wasting so much time on repetitive and routine tasks to increase their productivity. At the close of this chapter, we will walk you through the ten steps LegalMation followed to disrupt themselves to success.

THE PROBLEM OF WASTED TIME

In an ideal world, most of an attorney's day would be spent on accruing substantive billable hours—i.e., on driving profits. Unfortunately, this is simply not the case, especially for junior lawyers. If you speak to any litigation attorney, and they look back at the first two or three years of their career, they will recall much of their time was consumed by tedious grunt work, e.g., document preparation and organizing discovery. And even for more senior attorneys, the amount of mundane tasks they grappled with on a daily basis was rather unsettling.

According to Clio's 2017 "Legal Trends Report," surveying 2,915 U.S. legal professionals, lawyers devote an astounding 48 percent of their time to "administrative" tasks, including licensing and continuing education, office administration, generating and sending bills, and configuring technology and collections. Another survey of solo and small-firm lawyers by the Thomson Reuters Solo and Small Law Firm group revealed that 15 percent of lawyers believe one of the most significant challenges their firms face is spending too much time on administrative tasks.

In other words, attorneys are spending an excessive amount of time on mundane tasks, and not enough on substantively practicing law by using their cognitive abilities. But there is hope in tackling this problem through artificial intelligence, and that's where LegalMation comes in.

HOW LEGALMATION PARTNERS WITH A.I. TO HELP ATTORNEYS

To give attorneys the head space to focus on more critical responsibilities, LegalMation decided to automate the most tedious tasks attorneys deal with on a daily basis. Instead of using human power, LegalMation focused on automating the drafting of certain key litigation documents, including responsive pleadings to lawsuits, discovery requests and response shells, and other process-driven and "routine" attorney work product generation. To automate these processes, they used, in part, Watson's A.I. platform. As with any such integration, some energy and patience was required to "onboard" the new system, so to speak.

To get Watson up and running, LegalMation had to put their A.I. through the types of training we outlined in early chapters. For example, they had to teach it how to read complaints and lawsuits. They also had to introduce Watson to relevant legal terminology and jargon; it had to learn what an *allegation* is, what the *causes of actions* are, and what the relationships between the cause of action and the different parties are. Ultimately, Watson had to be taught to mimic what a human attorney does so well—while simultaneously executing on those mundane, yet important tasks just as competently.

In no uncertain terms, what LegalMation has achieved has been revolutionary for the legal industry. Until now, artificial intelligence served to help attorneys do their work a little bit faster, slightly better, and more accurately. Now, however, A.I. is being used in a more transformative way: attorneys can shift their attention to more important tasks, leaving the volume-driven work to A.I. and ultimately providing greater value to their clients. Whether you're a law firm attorney or an in-house attorney in a corporation, you can appreciate the myriad ways in which LegalMation works to cut down on time-wasting activities and to transfer those tedious tasks to A.I.

HOW LEGALMATION DISRUPTED ITSELF TO OWN THE A.I. REVOLUTION—AND HOW YOU CAN, TOO

Now that we've introduced you to LegalMation's adoption of A.I. to improve the productivity of attorneys, we want to transition a bit and talk about how you, too, can use A.I. to disrupt your business. While you may be stumped as to how to implement this technology in a practical way, we'd like to offer some suggestions for your particular journey with A.I.

Just as there is no one-size-fits-all computer program for every business, any application of A.I. needs to be customized for the organization it serves. At this stage, our roles are to at least get you thinking about how using A.I. might become your new reality. Actual implementation can come later. Still, as you begin to consider applying A.I. to your own business, it's helpful to consider the 10 steps described in the last chapter. For convenience's sake, we will list them again while also describing just what LegalMation did to adhere to them.

1. Build your understanding of A.I., particularly the remarkable new capabilities it offers.

LegalMation initially sought to use A.I. to automate the most complex litigation motions (e.g., motions to dismiss, motions for summary judgment, etc.). Yet, while A.I.'s capabilities are incredible, they are not appropriate or sufficient for every task. In LegalMation's case, there were too many variables in the more complex motions for A.I. to be properly trained.

Once the principals understood A.I.'s capabilities (and more importantly, its limitations), LegalMation made a breakthrough decision to narrowly identify the specific tasks they sought to automate. Ultimately, they realized Watson should only be utilized for the more routine items attorneys encounter on a daily basis. The point here is you should not presume A.I. can solve every problem. Instead, devote time to considering how A.I. can best be utilized—i.e., which tasks human effort isn't required for—and assign them to your A.I. platform accordingly.

2. Focus on a specific problem or opportunity.

LegalMation focused on automating the most tedious, volume- and process-driven tasks that attorneys (typically junior level) must perform in the early stages of any litigation case. These include drafting responses to lawsuits, interrogatories, and other written discovery documents.

When considering using artificial intelligence for your own purposes, you want to identify a very pointed problem this technology can tackle. This goes along with step #1; having a clear understanding of A.I.'s capabilities and limitations will help you identify how you can best utilize this tech for your business. The more specific the job, the better. Again, a one-size-fits all approach to A.I. will get you nowhere; you need to tailor this technology for the issues particular to your business or industry.

3. Think of your ideal solution.

At this point, you should go big by envisioning in a broad way how A.I. can best serve you and your clients and customers. In the case of LegalMation, they dreamt of being able to upload a lawsuit copy to develop a perfectly drafted legal document each time, with very little tweaking or training. While your actual method for using the technology will likely change—as it certainly did for LegalMation—this is the stage in which you should conceptualize an end result for how artificial intelligence can best serve you. You can get more realistic later.

4. Consider what A.I. capabilities can help you to achieve your solution.

There are many A.I. solutions on the market, and it's critical to do serious research to determine which one is best for you and the problem you are solving before committing to any one platform. LegalMation researched, test-drove, and explored various A.I. solutions, focusing on selecting the best to accomplish their goal in the most efficient way possible.

Ultimately, they settled on deploying various platforms, including Watson and open-source solutions, because of the variety of documents LegalMation sought to automate. For example, Watson was great for one of its modules, because of how it specifically processes language. They needed their A.I. solution to carefully process legal jargon and found other A.I. platforms did not process words in the precise way required. In a similar way, you should explore the capabilities of each A.I. platform to see which solution is optimal for your needs. Today, LegalMation relies on 3 or 4 varieties of A.I. platform, all of which combined comprise up to only 40 to 50 percent of the company's technology deck. The rest, as expected, is internally developed proprietary software.

5. Develop a vision document to establish the high-level A.I. architecture for the solution.

Once you have established your big-picture dreams for your A.I. solution, you will want to build out a document detailing your plans in a more thorough manner. LegalMation narrowed their vision document initially to a specific problem they wanted to solve, making it as simple as possible, starting with just one claim or cause of action. (In litigation, a cause of action is essentially the specific legal provision/standard being violated.)

This hyperspecificity narrowed their focus so they could first complete a proof of concept beyond expanding further. When developing your own plan, you will also want to narrow your vision to a specific issue, offering a simple solution. (You can always broaden your plans for your A.I. platform at some later point if you so wish.)

6. Create the training strategy for your A.I.

Similar to training a regular human employee, careful onboarding and training are critical to your success. LegalMation's particular challenge was to train its A.I. platform to understand legal language. Lawsuits and other legal documents are typically not written in standard, conversational English, so any existing national language processor would not easily work for their needs.

Based on such constraints, their strategy necessitated that actual lawyers train LegalMation's A.I. to teach it to read, comprehend, and draft just as a lawyer would. When going about building your artificial intelligence solution, you will want to assign experts in your office or field to perform the training of your A.I.

FYI: this is not the stage to get lazy. You would never hire an employee and fail to train them sufficiently in the tools and responsibilities of their role, so treat your A.I. platform with the same care and diligence.

7. Build, train, and test your A.I. solution.

Now is the time to test your platform—and then to wash, rinse, and repeat. That is what LegalMation needed to do, over and over and over again. They took one cause of action, trained their A.I. to understand it, drafted specific responses tied to the cause of action, and then repeated the same process with the next cause of action. This part of the process will require a good level of patience and should not be rushed. You want to be thorough and make sure your solution is operating in tip-top shape with as few glitches as possible.

8. Leverage existing technology.

LegalMation discovered that their A.I. solution was most efficient when supplemented, enhanced, and partnered with existing applications, the combination of which led to the ultimate desired result. For LegalMation, artificial intelligence makes up approximately 50 percent of their entire platform. The rest is their own proprietary software, which they wrote to supplement and close the gaps of the A.I.

For your own purposes, consider how other applications and technologies can be used to enhance your A.I. solution. Again, artificial intelligence alone, without proper tailoring, training, and optimization, is relatively useless. However, by combining A.I. with other technologies integral to your business operations, you can build a solution that works right for you.

9. Focus on programming the unique user experience you want to create.

At this stage, you will want to ask yourself, as far as user experience is concerned, what is a differentiator for your organization? LegalMation valued providing an easy, no-fuss customer experience. Artificial intelligence allowed LegalMation to create the most simple, elegant, and user-friendly interfaces.

Precisely because A.I. can perform many tasks without user input, LegalMation's interface is designed purposefully to limit as much user decision-making as possible. In fact, their interface dashboard is so purposefully simple that the user can download the draft outputs after only three clicks.

On LegalMation's interface, confusing options, links, and questionnaires are nonexistent. In a similar fashion, consider how you too can use A.I. to improve your customer experience. Ask yourself, how can A.I. set you apart from the competition? Then fine-tune your A.I. to best fit your customers' needs and you'll see the payoff in your bottom line.

10. Launch your A.I. solution.

Now is the time to launch your new, test-driven artificial intelligence solution. (Of course, ideally, you should conduct beta-testing before ever premiering your product/service.) In LegalMation's case, Walmart was already a customer, so they were fortunate to have Walmart's legal department as part of their development process. Their team helped LegalMation test the system, providing key feedback to work out kinks before going public. If a similar option is available to you, whenever possible involve customers and prospects alike before going to market. You will appreciate the early insights and ultimately be able to build a product your customers will find suitable to their needs.

HOW TO DISRUPT YOURSELF TO OWN THE A.I. REVOLUTION (EVEN IF YOU'RE NOT A TECHIE)

An Interview with Danny May, CEO of Lingmo,
Specializing in A.I. Translation

As a non-techie person (you came from the world of plumbing), what did you need to do to bring your new A.I.-powered business to market?
After I did the market research, and before I started teaching myself, I went to see about 40 angel investors, all of which said "no" for the simple reason that I had no tech background. I spoke to my wife, and we sold our house and poured all the money into the business.

After that, I had to self-teach myself. Tech is a big world; you can learn a lot, and obviously I continue learning. I just had to focus on what I needed to know, and that was about speech recognition and the translation industry. I also had to learn about my competitors and how they were doing it wrong. To accomplish my goals, I brought in a specialized team from Pakistan that helped me learn a lot quicker. No question was stupid to them, which made me feel really comfortable.

What's one of the most surprising things you discovered in your journey to market?
I learned pretty early on that it's not what you know in the tech industry, it's who you know. If you aren't acquainted with the right people or don't

get connected to the right people, you may know "everything" but not get anywhere.

How did you get yourself up to speed on this new technology?

I'm dyslexic, so I don't read much. Instead, I listen to Audible and a lot of tech podcasts. I find I get better traction from hearing experts and what they're doing in the A.I space.

How did you find the development process?

It was very daunting. Not coming from a technical background, it can be scary. I did plumbing for three years while I was doing this part-time, then I moved to it full-time. I had one person actually say to me that I should "stay in my lane"—in plumbing—and leave the tech stuff to them.

Reactions such as this help explain why I really didn't tell anyone I was a plumber until I garnered traction. It wasn't about failing. It wasn't about doing something in the tech industry I wasn't used to. It was about these people coming back and saying they were right. Such negativity and limiting thinking from others is what I found most daunting and yet kept pushing me forward.

What advice would you give other nontechnical entrepreneurs wishing to get into the A.I. space?

You've got to commit yourself. You've got to work twice, if not three times, as hard as someone that's in the tech industry, because you've got to prove yourself. Especially if you're going for funding with investors. With that being said, just keep learning. And don't think about being a tech outsider as a detriment to your success. Instead, try to view it as an advantage. Why? People from outside the tech industry can think differently than people inside. Use what you have to your advantage and be prepared to work hard to get traction.

BUILDING ON THIS KNOWLEDGE

In this chapter, we showcased how one company, LegalMation, transferred tedious, mundane legal tasks to its A.I. platform, thereby allowing attorneys to spend more time on more meaningful, creative work. It's our hope this inspired you to imagine how you might harness artificial intelligence to increase your own productivity and ultimately maximize profits. In the next chapter, we will take this idea further, building on the promise of tomorrow by previewing how you might outsource some of your business's analytics and decision-making activities to your very own A.I. confidante and partner.

Chapter 15

Outsourcing the Human Mind and the Rise of the A.I. *Consiglieri*

"We now live in a global, exponential world," Steven Kotler tells us from his New Mexico office. Executive Director of the Flow Research Collective, author of 10 books, including *Tomorrowland: Our Journey from Science Fiction to Science Fact,* Kotler is an expert on human potential and the transformational power of disruptive technology. "You need to understand that our brains evolved in a local, linear environment. Today, we live in an environment that is global and exponential. We just cannot process change at this speed or scale—the brain is not designed for it. Worse, according to Ray Kurzweil, here in the twenty-first century, we will experience over *20,000 years' worth of technological change.* This means, over the next 80-something years, we will go from the birth of agriculture to the industrial revolution—twice—in terms of our technological advancement."

This is a bold statement from a bold thought leader; it's no wonder he also cowrote the book *Bold: How to Go Big, Create Wealth and Impact the World.* And right now, we need bold thinkers to help us understand what we are witnessing. Throughout these pages we have sought to provide a baseline understanding of A.I., its origins, what it is, and how innovative companies like Chapter 14's LegalMation are using it today. Now, with the help of Kotler and several of today's leading-edge thinkers, we would like to paint a picture of what our exponential century has in store for us. Here's a teaser: you will soon possess your own personal A.I.—or to put it more evocatively for *Godfather* fans: your own A.I. *consigliere*. An outsourced artificial mind you can trust as your closest confidante.

In order to glimpse where we are going, we need to back up a bit and talk about how the commercial lending business has been disrupted by A.I. In 2017, Scott Stewart became CEO of the Innovative Lending Platform Association (ILPA), a group of online small business lenders such as Kabbage or OnDeck. Prior to this, Stewart founded and chaired Small Group Meeting, a Washington, D.C.-based political and public affairs networking society connecting top-level leaders on public policy matters. He also served as a former executive at the Financial Services Roundtable, where he brought together lenders and tech companies to envision the next phase of B2B financing through A.I.

"Machine learning is set to transform lending into the Information Age," he tells us. "Think about how it used to work if you needed a loan. In years past, you would call or go to a bank and start a process that typically took 60 to 90 days to close, requiring heavy-duty and paper-intensive approval."

Any business owner who has had to deal with the travails of manual underwriting is likely to have felt the process to be annoying, if not adversarial: The bank doesn't want to give you money unless you prove yourself. And even if you manage to jump through all of their numerous legal and financial hoops, it can still take months for approval. Not exactly the ideal situation for a company wishing to compete, much less thrive, in our exponential century.

"This old system obviously does not work in today's world," says Stewart. "If you own a restaurant and your industrial oven needs $20,000 for repairs or your place won't open tomorrow, you cannot seek capital in the traditional ways using antiquated bank financing time horizons. On the flip side, our member companies' loans and lines of credit are typically funded within 24 hours. Sometimes as fast as minutes."

Receiving actual funding, not just underwriter approval, in *minutes* instead of months is a leap forward in capital fulfillment—a game changer for today's businesses. But how on earth can lenders make such quick underwriting decisions? It all comes down to Big Data and increased processing speeds. The ILPA member companies use hundreds of pieces of data to determine their credit risks almost instantaneously. Beyond looking at a FICO score, it reviews items such as an applicant's bank holdings, their QuickBooks account, their UPS shipping data, and, yes, even a company's online reviews.

"Why Yelp? Well, first of all, if you have Yelp reviews, your small business likely exists, so that mitigates fraud risk," Stewart explains. "Also, if you respond to reviews, particularly negative ones, with offers to come back for a better customer experience, then we can see you are a better credit risk."

The fact that the ILPA is capable of assessing an applicant's actions via Yelp, not to mention partially make a credit determination based on reviews, demonstrates how far computing has come in recent years. By Stewart's own admission, the ILPA's technological platform wouldn't exist without advancements in machine learning. Today's consumers might take Yelp for granted nowadays—after all it's one of only nearly 2 billion Websites—but it's worth remembering the crowd-sourced review forum was only invented in 2004. Four years prior, at the turn of the century, no one had a smartphone, or even a Myspace account. Back then, people the world over were freaked about Y2K, worried the projected computer Armageddon would bring commerce and infrastructure to a grinding halt. Just four years prior to that, in 1996, there were only a scant 100,000 working Websites.

Exponential growth, indeed. But using A.I. to accelerate underwriting approvals is just the tip of the iceberg when it comes to how commercial lending—and business in general—is poised to change in our exponential times. "There's a book called *The Master Algorithm* by Pedro Domingos that predicts in the future everyone will have their own master algorithm," says Stewart. "Essentially a system that will solve all kinds of problems for you."

Wait. Before we hit ludicrous speed—before we explore Domingos's quest for a formula to derive all of the world's knowledge, before we discuss personal assistant robots and contemplate the Jetsonian notion of concierge A.I.s advocating for human clients—let's explore the next iteration of ILPA and the future of commercial lending. Throughout this book, we have suggested A.I.'s secret sauce is its ability not only to compute data, but also to learn from it and make predictions. Now, what if your business's A.I., what Stewart calls your "personal algorithm," could anticipate your lending needs for you?

"In the future," Stewart predicts. "Your personal algorithm will understand your creditworthiness moment to moment. It will offer you products and services to manage any issue in real time." In practical terms, here's what this might look like. Imagine you own a florist shop. In late fall, a forward-thinking personal algorithm might begin anticipating the capital needed to prepare for the Valentine's Day business boom. "You could simply authorize your algorithm to fill the cash gap automatically within certain parameters. The personal algorithm would then shop for the lowest-cost product that fits your needs and may even contract for those dollars on your behalf."

Based on what Stewart is suggesting, the personal algorithm opens the door to human–machine business symbiosis. Month after month, quarter after quarter, year after year, business owners must make decisions based on data. At any given time, the typical business needs to know what inventory is needed, what the market is doing, and how their customers are likely to behave.

As we have seen, A.I. works well when given the chance to make predictions based on data. The upshot? Imagine your computer sending you a notification on December 31 that says: "Valentine's Day will be here soon. We know we'll need $10,000 dollars in working capital. I have reviewed three financing options and this one makes the most sense. Do you wish to proceed?" Even better, this same computer will learn from whatever decision you make in this scenario, informing what it suggests you do next December.

This might sound cutting edge, but even a computer that understands your business model, follows market trends, and suggests financing options still fails to approach a thinking machine's full potential. For this we need to return to academic Yuval Noah Harari for his predictions on A.I. In a 2018 *Wired* interview, he said this: "Let's say you have an A.I. sidekick who monitors you all the time, 24 hours a day. What do you write? What do you see? Everything. But this A.I. is serving you as this fiduciary responsibility. And it gets to know your weaknesses, and by knowing your weaknesses it can protect you against other agents trying to hack you and to exploit your weaknesses."

In his book *Homo Deus: A Brief History of Tomorrow*, Harari expands on this idea, developing his version of Stewart's personal algorithm in which he suggests in the future each person might possess their own outsourced mind—or what we are calling an A.I. *consigliere* that can anticipate your needs. This concept can be likened to an A.I. personal assistant or what Ibaraki termed in the Foreword the FIA (acronym for financial intelligent agent). The real fun begins when we contemplate a day in which our A.I. (whatever we decide to call it) can act as our trusted agent, advocating on our behalf with other A.I.s similarly loyal to their human clients. Don't have time to call a posh restaurant to book a client lunch? Have your A.I. handle it. Let it negotiate with (an A.I.) hostess for a booth by the window. After all, your A.I. knows your tastes—and more importantly, works for you.

Still, some wary business owners might not view the A.I. *consigliere* as a good thing. They might see the whole notion as one more step toward a world in which humans are dominated by their more capable A.I. masters. They may even feel growing concern their A.I. sidekick is not a sidekick after all, but instead a superhero in waiting. On its face, Domingos's book might fuel such apprehensions. After all, it centers on his quest for a master algorithm to ascertain all the world's knowledge "past, present, and future—from data."

However, there is reason to believe humans will always play Batman to A.I.'s Robin. To understand why, we need to consult economist and author George Gilder, who wrote *Life After Television* in 1990. Back when Google was just a gleam in Sergey Brin and Larry Page's eyes, Gilder predicted the world we now inhabit. He foresaw the decline of network television with the growing rise of personal computers and even anticipated the advent of smartphones he termed "teleputers."

Now in 2018, Gilder has a new book called *Life After Google*, in which he asserts Google has it all wrong when it comes to the view "that artificial intelligence will make human minds obsolete and that we'll soon produce machine-learning tools and robotics that excel the capabilities of human brains." No matter how much our technology evolves, Gilder believes, it will never replace human consciousness.

"Machines can't be minds," he writes. "Information theory shows that. Information is surprise. Creativity always comes as a surprise to us. If it wasn't surprising, we wouldn't need it." Though Gilder views machines as useful and would likely concede they can perform well as A.I. *consiglieres*, they can never steer the ship. Why? Doing so requires consciousness, a uniquely human quality. Or as Gilder writes, "Machines are not capable of creativity. Human minds can generate counterfactuals, imaginative flights, dreams."

Based on Gilder's logic, an A.I., however powerful, will always play second fiddle to us humans he views as "oracles"—progenitors of ideas and novelty. We needn't fear becoming a sidekick to our businesses—or our lives—because we will always be in control, consciously creating the world. If we follow this logic, artificial intelligence ceases to be a threat and instead emerges as our greatest tool for true human potential, the kind Kotler envisions in the exponential age. It's therefore conceivable that in the not so distant future, companies' fortunes will rise and fall based on the number of A.I.s one possesses, their breadth of knowledge, and their predictive capacities.

Likewise, the success of a business will rest on its discerning human masters' ability to pit their A.I. force(s) against their competitors'. Within a company, each intelligence—human and artificial—will work together for the organization's greater good with human consciousness driving the effort, making the important decisions. Or as Domingos writes in his book: "Armed with machine learning, a manager becomes a super-manager, a scientist a super-scientist, an engineer a super-engineer. The future belongs to those who understand at a very deep level how to combine their unique expertise with what algorithms do best."

In recent years, apprehensions surrounding A.I. have largely focused on the threat of revolutionary technology displacing today's jobs; worse, rendering humans obsolete. In Chapter 10, we discussed the growing movement that has coalesced around the need for a universal basic income to protect the disadvantaged. Though some leading experts have supported this notion, others have condemned its implementation on the basis that giving people "free money" kills their drive and stifles competition and innovation.

As this chapter attests, it is become increasingly clear the incredible technology we are describing will not destroy every job, any more than the invention of computers replaced thinking minds. It's instead much more likely A.I. will replace the boring, tedious work satirized in *Office Space*. "My old organization, the Flow Genome project, participated in Red Bull's Hacking Creativity Project," says Kotler. "Comprised of nearly 30,000 studies and hundreds of interviews, it was the largest empirical study of human potential. One of the overarching conclusions reached is that creativity is the most important skill for thriving in the twenty-first century."

Undoubtedly, we live in exciting times, exponential times. Never was a moment riper for disruptors and innovators to dream big human dreams, assisted and enhanced by our A.I. collaborators. To expand this conversation, to offer a glimpse of how just special this time is, we are going now to the source for more answers. In the next section, we will conduct interviews with even more leading experts as to the marvels—and challenges—A.I. offers mankind.

SECTION II

Conversations with Today's Thought Leaders on A.I.

In the following section, we will host a series of interviews with leading experts on a range of subjects, exploring how A.I. is affecting the future of sports, medicine, innovation, computing, language, emotional intelligence, as well as human—and even robotic—rights.

A.I. AND MEDICINE

One of the first fields to feel the impact of the A.I. revolution was medicine. Using machine learning, researchers were able to teach a computer to spot malignancies using X-ray and MRI scans. Healthcare continues to be one of the focal points of A.I. R&D, with A.I. being applied to everything from wearable body sensors to computer-controlled surgical robots.

A Conversation with Surinder Oberoi
Cofounder of Zinx
Offering A.I.-Powered Telemedicine

Along with Javier, his son and cofounder, **Surinder Oberoi's** company manufactures mobile and wearable health monitoring devices providing users with the information needed to take better control of their health. Headquartered in Bilbao, Spain, the Oberois founded the company in 2015, making extensive use of artificial intelligence to interpret biologic data and share information with healthcare professionals.

Personal health monitoring devices, such as blood pressure and heart rate monitors, have been around for decades. What can new A.I.-based technology do that previous devices could not?
Health is really a combination of factors: fitness, nutrition, genetics, and, of course, biological functions. Previously, all of these indicators could only be measured and tracked by separate applications. Now, we have the technology to incorporate them all into a single application, and then to provide users with very specific recommendations to optimize their health.

It's important to recognize that a person can be technically obese but still be fit. Conversely, a person can hit all the traditional markers for fitness and still suffer from underlying health problems. A.I. has the power to look at each person as an individual and not just as a point along some spectrum of what is considered "normal."

Is there a role for human medical professionals in this system?
Absolutely. Even with all the advances we have made in A.I., the technology can only go so far. That's why we support our application with a worldwide network of licensed doctors with whom you can share your information and discuss your options.

When you say "worldwide," what do you mean?

Our network includes physicians on every continent. Which doesn't mean you're obligated to speak only to doctors in your home country. If you have a condition that is best addressed by a specialist in America, Europe, India, or Japan, the technology gives you the option to access that individual. For underserved parts of the world, such as Africa, such access is extremely important.

What are the biggest misconceptions people have about their health, and how can technology and A.I. improve the situation?

Most people still rely on their general practitioner for their health data and "systems check," if you will. Technology is allowing people to get this information for themselves. Add the A.I. component, and you can get actionable data that allows you to react accordingly to achieve a better outcome.

What medical efficiencies do you see A.I. providing for individual patients?

Oh, the efficiencies are enormous. Right now, the cost of healthcare, especially in America, is climbing so quickly it will soon become unsustainable. One of the best ways to curb the rise in healthcare costs is to emphasize prevention, to keep people from getting sick in the first place.

Personal monitoring combined with A.I. analysis can definitely help with this. Many emergency room visits could be eliminated simply by providing data remotely to the proper medical professional. Of course, there will still be many situations where direct medical intervention is required, such as treating heart attacks, or broken bones, but there are many situations where telemedicine is not only useful, but desirable.

What happens when prescription drugs are required?

That's easy. The physician sends the prescription to the closest pharmacy, which can then deliver the medication(s) to your house. (A few years from now, delivery might even be done by drones.) If you have a little one running a high fever, isn't that better than driving your child to the hospital emergency room, waiting hours to be seen, then having to drive home? Telemedicine not only requires less physical effort and is less expensive, it's also far less traumatic for the patient.

The kind of continuous monitoring necessary for disease prevention requires people to wear sensors linked to their smartphones or similar devices. How comfortable do you think people will be wearing such sensors 24 hours a day?

No doubt there is a bit of paranoia attached to the idea of 24/7 monitoring. The recent scandals involving Facebook and other social media platforms being caught sharing personal data has only exacerbated such fears. There is going to have to be a long-term educational process to readjust the general consumer mindset when it comes to personal health monitoring.

The generation Z and millennials will probably be the first to adapt. Already they are very comfortable wearing Fitbits and similar monitors the way the rest of us wear wristwatches or eyeglasses. Also, think about all the other technologies that follow us day to day, be it security cameras, the GPS systems in our cars, or just our smartphones. We've become dependent on these technologies, and we're perfectly comfortable with them. Personal health monitoring will follow a similar path.

Do you see personal health data collection being misused? Perhaps by insurance companies who use it to discriminate against applicants or raise premium rates?

There is no doubt that insurance companies are eager to use this technology to their advantage, especially to weed out high-risk customers. From a business perspective, one would only expect them to do this, especially taking into account their reach and financial power. Of course, if your lifestyle makes you more vulnerable to illness, you probably don't want your insurance carrier to know that.

But what if your lifestyle habits make you *less* vulnerable? Wouldn't you want your insurance company to know *that*? Sharing your health data with your insurance carrier may be a way to lower your premium rates. And that's a good thing. Also, remember that the power of technology and data sharing works both ways. Insurance carriers may know more about you, but now you can know more about them. Technology gives you more choices when it comes to selecting an insurance product.

What precautions should be taken to ensure that the detailed personal health data generated by these high-tech systems is not abused?

Regulators are already concerned with the generation of this information and are putting into place safeguards to protect personal data. Each data generation company must be compliant with these regulations, and clearly the governing bodies must ensure compliance is enforced and adhered to as established by law.

Do you see companies like yours disrupting the entrenched healthcare delivery system?

Remember, healthcare in America is very different than it is in most other countries. In the American system, there is an economic incentive to keep people sick or at least an incentive to perform as many procedures and pre-scribe as many drugs as possible. That's how providers and companies make their profits.

In Europe and most other developed countries, healthcare is socialized. Since we pay for it with our taxes, the incentive is to prevent as many illnesses as possible; that's how taxpayers save money. Our hope is that A.I.-based health monitoring will disrupt the American system by putting people in charge of their own health, thereby democratizing the system. The less you are at the mercy of others, the better off you are.

Where do you see A.I.-enabled health management 15 years from now?
Technological innovation is notoriously difficult to predict. I mean, if we knew what was coming in the future, we'd do it now. But I can tell you my dream, and that is for healthcare management and disease prevention to become totally automated.

When I wake up in the morning, I'd like to know exactly what I need to eat, what exercises I need to do, and what activities I need to avoid to maintain optimum health. There are so many diseases and conditions we can prevent or delay just by behaving the right way. I don't know if future technology will be able to stop people from making bad choices, but possessing good information and a lot of it may certainly help.

So far, we've talked about using A.I. for health maintenance. But what about augmentation and enhancement? How might A.I. be used to make people better than what nature designed?
If we take a close look at the last 100 years, we see the introduction of medical advances that have significantly lengthened the human life span. At the begin-ning of the twentieth century, life expectancy was 50, perhaps 60 years. Today, it's well over 80. I suppose you could call this a form of enhancement. Will A.I. have the same impact? As a technologist, I have to respond with a resounding YES! As for what particular benefits we will see or when we will see them, I'm not equipped to say.

Is this a path we really want to go down? What might be the dangers of transcending nature with technology?
Right now, hundreds if not thousands of companies are pursuing this goal, so change is inevitable. We're all worried about a "Big Brother" scenario, and governments being what they are, the powerful will no doubt use what new powers they acquire to secure their positions. But if recent history shows us

anything, it's that technology tends to produce more good than bad. We just need to keep our eyes open, stay aware, and hold the powerful accountable. That's how democracies are supposed to work.

———————————

The network of professionals we have on our platform encourages proactive, preventative care for all types of health issues. We are here to help and guide the individual through a complex process which, in reality, is quite simple: it just requires that the individual pay attention to the advice being given, which in turn guides them to a better outcome by simply making the right choices in nutrition and exercise and to use the tools we make available to them for that purpose.

One of the pillars of our platform is PREVENTION. . . . We aim to help both individuals and governments, as well as private institutions, gain a greater control over preventative care rather than dependence on the reactive care model that exists today and that is clearly broken and unsustainable in the long term.

ZINX is able to provide all the tools necessary to begin and move forward a preventative program to better health outcomes for anyone within either the National Health arena or the private health insurance space.

A.I. AND INNOVATION

Of all the activities artificial intelligence is expected to impact, none has greater potential than innovation itself. As A.I. becomes increasingly adept at acquiring and analyzing vast amounts of data, it is likely to exponentially accelerate the speed of technological change. According to experts, A.I. may, in a single generation, produce more technological breakthroughs than humankind has managed during the first 20,000 years of its existence. To get a glimpse of how A.I. is likely to impact the speed and nature of innovation, we spoke to some of the leading experts in the field.

A Conversation with Michael Gerber

Michael Gerber is founder of Michael E. Gerber Companies, a business skills training company based in Carlsbad, California. He is best known as the writer of the bestselling *E-Myth* book series, which launched in 1986.

Since then, he has published 10 *E-Myth*-themed books on entrepreneurialism, including *The E-Myth Revisited* (1995), *E-Myth Mastery* (2005), and *The Most Successful Small Businesses in the World* (2010). He is the coauthor of more than a dozen *E-Myth*-themed books aimed at specific professions, including law, accounting, architecture, dentistry, optometry, and chiropractic. Named the World's Number One Small Business Guru by *Inc.* magazine, he received a Lifetime Achievement Award from the National Academy of Bestselling Authors (2010).

How do you think artificial intelligence is likely to impact American business? Who will be the first to take full advantage of A.I., and who, if anyone, should be worried about it?

First of all, I think it's safe to say that A.I. is coming, it's coming quickly, and there's no way we're going to stop it. The technology has been in the works for decades, and development is just accelerating. It's going to significantly improve the productivity of jobs that just aren't efficient today. Right now, A.I. is getting most attention at the top end of the business spectrum. It's the Fortune 500 companies—even the Fortune 100 companies—who are investing the heaviest and are going to reap the initial benefits. It's going to change how Google operates, how Facebook operates, and how Apple operates. It will change how items are manufactured. So it will have the greatest impact on the people who work for these big mega-companies, many of whom will either be out of a job or will have their responsibilities significantly changed. (The good news is, a lot of the jobs that are going to be replaced—the boring, routine, repetitive jobs, like filling orders in Amazon warehouses—are the kinds of jobs people don't really want anyway.) It will take a long time for small companies to feel the same kind of impact.

Your specialty is small business operations. How do you see A.I. impacting small businesses?

First, we have to understand there are basically two kinds of small businesses. The first is the typical small business created by someone who wants to be his/her own boss and is not particularly interested in growing beyond a single location. The other is a business started by an entrepreneur who may or may not have a personal attraction to the industry but wants to pursue an advantage in a specific marketplace.

For this second type of business—the one founded by the entrepreneur—A.I. is going to offer a significant advantage. It will offer operational efficiencies that allow one to grow quickly beyond the "one shop" model. However, for the first type of business, it won't have much of an impact. At least not initially. These types of businesses tend to be highly people-dependent. They rise or fall based on the skills and creativity of the people in them. Artificial intelligence is unlikely to have as profound an impact or effect on the way such a small business operates as it will on the way large companies do.

How do you see A.I. impacting everyday life?

I think the big danger in A.I. is that it's likely to make things *too* easy, *too* entertaining. It doesn't demand anything of us. It does *for* us. As much as our society and educational system wants us to be more productive, more accurate, and more efficient, I'd like to see similar emphasis placed on individual creativity, our innovative spirit.

Where do you place the blame for the issues you raised in your previous answer?

Higher education was never intended to be for everybody. It was supposed to be a resource for people who wanted to rise above the ordinary, to improve themselves in both mind and spirit. But our democratized politics have turned higher education into little more than vocational training for the masses. I like to call what colleges teach today "artificial intelligence"—not the term as you use it—because it's not "real" intelligence. It's just designed to look that way.

It's said that we're born in the image of God. If so, then we were born to create. But, in our schools, we're not learning how to create. This leads to one of the greatest problems I face when dealing with small business owners. They don't understand that it's not about making a living; *it's about making a difference*. That's why I created my new school. We're a school for entrepreneurial development that everybody on the planet can afford. We've taken education to the street because it's the only place it's ever going to happen. If it's going to happen at all.

What would you advise today's young people to study in the age of A.I.?

First and foremost, they should study *how* to study. Studying itself is something of a lost art. Like my saxophone teacher said to me when I was 11 years old, "If you don't learn how to study, you will never learn how to perform above the ordinary."

How do you see small businesses taking advantage of A.I.?

Since I started my consulting business back in 1977, I understood that a successful business, regardless of what it did, what it produced, or what it sold, was based on a business *system*. Ray Kroc, who founded McDonald's at age 52, never made a hamburger or fried a French fry in his life. His genius lay in understanding and incorporating *systems thinking* into everything he did. This made it possible for him to replicate his success over and over and over again.

Success is a methodology through which outcomes are produced. Preferred outcomes are produced in a preferred process through which ordinary people become extraordinary as they're leveraged by the system that has been created to produce that result.

Whether it's called McDonald's or Starbucks or Apple or Amazon, it's the same systems thinking. Those companies didn't succeed because they went out and hired the best people in the world; they succeeded because they understood the power of systems thinking. The *system* is the solution. There's a system to running an Apple Store, and that's what makes it Apple. A.I. is perfect for this, because it, too, is systems-based. That's what an algorithm is. It's a system. A system that can grow and replicate itself over and over again.

What would you like to tell people who are concerned that technology is robbing us of our humanity?
I believe we have divinity within each of us. Life's meaning is not about having religious authorities tell you what to do. It's about finding the divine spark within yourself. A.I. or not, we must always seek our higher purpose: to be creative creatures, just like God.

A Conversation with Eric Haller and Mike Kilander of Experian

Eric Haller serves as Executive Vice President and Global Head of Experian DataLabs, which helps businesses solve strategic marketing and risk-management problems through advanced data analysis. He joined Experian as Senior Vice President, Strategic Development and Applied Research in 2007, prior to which he served as Vice President and General Manager, New Products, for Green Dot Corporation. A mentor for MuckerLab, which helps entrepreneurs create start-ups through data monetization, the development of sustainable business models and market strategies, as well as a member of the Board of Directors of the Bay Area Council, a leading San Francisco-area business organization, Haller holds a Bachelor of Science degree in Finance from San Diego State University-California State University, and a Master of Science degree in Technology Management from Columbia University in New York City.

Mike Kilander is Global Managing Director for Experian's data quality division, which focuses on improving the quality of data for better customer experiences or preparing data for improved business intelligence. He served in several executive capacities with Experian beginning in 2006, prior to which he was Vice President of Business Development for Edmunds.com, a leading online resource for automotive information. Kilander holds a Bachelor of Arts degree in International Relations from the University of Notre Dame, and a Master's degree in Public Administration with a focus on international affairs from Princeton University. Between 1993 and 1997, he served with the U.S. Army, achieving the rank of captain in military intelligence.

When did Experian begin using artificial intelligence (A.I.) to support data analytics? What form did it initially take, and how was it used?
Eric: People were experimenting with neural networks to support fraud detection as far back as the 1990s. About eight years ago, we got serious about A.I. at Experian. All the people we hired then had a background in machine learning, so we were able to use modern A.I. techniques right out of the gate. We immediately began using it for predictive modeling, for determining credit and fraud risk. At this point, we still didn't have an actual platform to implement our algorithms, but we were able to establish performance benchmarks. We could show that it worked.

One of the first uses of A.I. in the field was gaining insight into credit card transactions. We could create data clusters that would reflect how certain market segments would use their cards, predicting customer intent. Banks could then use this information in their targeted marketing.

What role is artificial intelligence playing today at Experian?
Eric: We're using A.I. across the board in everything from natural language processing to predictive modeling. But one of the more interesting things we're doing with A.I. is what we call "identity resolution," which is just a fancy term for confirming an identity. Identity validation is really at the crux of pretty much every transaction we make, be it financial or even just social. You want to know if the person you're dealing with really is the person you *think* you're dealing with.

Identity resolution involves determining the identity of an individual or business based on disparate data elements. These can include easily accessible information like a physical address, mobile phone number, and perhaps a landline number. It can also include a social security number, a username, and even a laptop IP address. And, of course, a personal name. But people often use multiple names, abbreviations, and nicknames like "Mike" or "Mickey" for "Michael," and "Bill" for "William." And now we have identities tied to connected devices, like a computer connected to a television connected to a mobile phone connected to a home thermostat. Defining a person or business along all these axes could take a small army of people. One of the best uses of A.I. is to knit these things together optimally in a way so that when new information is introduced, it is integrated seamlessly into the existing matrix. So far, our results with this have been spectacular. In less than a year, our A.I. has outperformed our best expert rule systems.

Mike: A.I has also grown recently in business software to enable increased usability and speed. For example, data management specialists spend about half their time just cleaning the data they receive, making sure it is current and accurate. A.I. is helping automate some of those manual processes while also improving predictions by basing outcomes on the historical patterns it is able to detect.

What specific benefits has A.I. provided your users?
Mike: A.I. is proving benefit to Experian clients and consumers as a whole in terms of speed, efficiency and accuracy. However, when I think about the data management space, A.I. is making it easier for the average person, the nontechnical, nonstatistical person, to access data and gain insight from it. In all the verticals we work with, we're seeing data management usage migrating from the purely technical people over to other departments, such as sales, marketing, and management. Imagine you wanted to launch a major email marketing campaign. A project like this used to take five or six weeks going through IT to compile a mailing list and ensure accuracy. With A.I. and self-service technology, the entire process can be done in a few hours.

What are the areas where A.I. has failed to meet expectations? How might its functionality be improved?
Mike: A.I. has provided a wealth of benefit across our organization and for our customers. However, I believe there is still a long way toward making A.I. simpler for the average business user. Thirty years ago, automated spreadsheets like Excel revolutionized businesses. Suddenly, you could make projections and see the effect of a single data-point change with just the push of a button. We need a similar simple universal A.I. app that can provide the insights that today's businesses seek. It's something we're working on around data management, and it's on the horizon. But it's not quite here yet.

Are there any results provided by A.I. that surprised you?

Eric: We were most surprised by how well it has performed. I'll give you a specific example. Many small companies have minimal or even small credit footprints. And they may not have any activity outside the United States. We partnered with a major social media company to see if we could use A.I. to determine a small company's credit risk just based on its social media activity, online ratings, check-ins, and so on. We expected the "lift" we'd get from this—the level of improvement over conventional methods—would be around 10 to 15 percent, but it turned out to be 40 percent. That was certainly a surprise.

What kinds of companies are benefitting most from A.I.?

Eric: Financial services have always depended on analytics, as have credit card companies. Any company that needs to determine a customer's credit risk and prevent fraud is certainly benefitting enormously from A.I. Beyond that, we're serving auto, retail, and healthcare companies that are also enjoying significant benefits from this new technology. Energy companies are using it to determine where to drill for oil. Retailers are using it to improve the customer experience and match products with customer tastes. Maximizing customer experience at the retail level is where I think there is still some of the deepest wells of opportunity.

Mike: Across all industries we also see a great deal of technology being democratized because of A.I. Ten to 15 years ago, marketing technology went through an evolution. These tools were originally purchased by CIOs and CTOs—invariably people who were quite technical—but companies like Eloqua and Marketo made the technology easier to use, and now it is procured and used all within marketing. We expect that same trend to happen across many departments, but we are starting to see it today specifically around data management.

Where does your data come from, and how do you verify its accuracy?

Eric: At Experian, we're fortunate to deal with hundreds of thousands of companies worldwide, so we have a large, fast-moving river of data flowing through our systems daily. Accuracy is, of course, of key concern. One way to determine accuracy is through repetition. If we keep getting the same addresses for a company, we can be increasingly confident that the information is correct. If it suddenly changes, this raises a red flag, and we want to know immediately why the change occurred. We can now use A.I. to spot such anomalies quickly and question inconsistent data.

What are companies doing with the data you provide? What kind of feedback are you getting?

Eric: Our clients love the fact Experian is on the cutting edge of artificial intelligence and is deploying solutions with immediate practical impact. We're not doing fundamental research here but instead are developing products customers can use. And they're using our products to improve the efficiency of their sales funnels, to minimize risk when extending credit to customers, and lowering fraud rates. Over the last eight years, these products have resonated very strongly with our client base.

A Conversation with David Hanson
Creator of Lifelike Robots

Dr. **David Hanson** is founder and CEO of Hanson Robotics, inventor of Sophia, the "world's most lifelike robot." Sophia is one of many cutting-edge interactive humanlike robots designed by Hanson's company. Dr. Hanson got his start with the Walt Disney Co. developing lifelike animatrons for its theme parks.

Through Hanson Robotics, he hopes to create robots both intelligent and empathetic, able to function as companions and assistants for people worldwide. Residing in Hong Kong, Hanson holds a Bachelor of Fine Arts degree in Film, Animation and Video from the Rhode Island School of Design, and a PhD in Interactive Arts and Engineering from the University of Texas at Dallas.

What's the secret to the success you've achieved developing life-like robots?

Above all else, I'd say playfulness. Play may not be commonly valued in engineering projects, but I feel it's always been at the heart of great discoveries and inventions. Possessing a spirit of creative play allows us to work through the differences in language, culture, and disciplines we have as a team.

Creative playfulness entails the freedom to transgress boundaries, to find opportunities otherwise hidden. The irony is children and animals play instinctively. School and civilized society sometimes discourage play. As adults, as a civilization, we need to get some of that spirited imagination back, to feel comfortable about taking risks.

Many people worry that robots will take their jobs. Is this concern legitimate?

There is no question some individuals will be replaced by automation. But if history is any guide, we'll probably produce more new jobs in their place. The problem is the speed with which things are happening. There has always been an awkward transition period when one technology replaces another, but there was usually time to retrain workers for whom there were no longer job opportunities. Now it's happening so fast, this may not be possible. This makes people afraid. And fear is not the best perspective from which to make good, rational decisions.

Ideas like basic income (aka universal basic income [UBI]) have been proposed to address this problem, but I don't think this will be enough. We have to think bigger, more holistically. We can no longer look at the economy as just the accumulation of money and wealth. Money and wealth are just placeholders for value and purpose in life. That's one of the goals of A.I., to understand the economy from this more expansive perspective and find ways to provide wealth for everyone—not just for today, but for the future.

Besides economics, how else do you see A.I. being used to benefit society?
There are many ways: Identifying previously hidden disease trends, helping to diagnose and prevent illness. Providing education to millions of people who live in poverty throughout the world. Just consider how much human intelligence is wasted. So many people are trapped in poverty and menial jobs, and if A.I. can help free people to actualize and pursue their dreams that will be so good for the world. If we can develop and free all of this unused potential, the global economy will surge in a really big way. I'm not just talking about using A.I. to help people who simply lack educational opportunities.

There are many people who cannot flourish with traditional educational tools, such as those on the autism spectrum. Likewise, there are individuals who learn by auditory pathways better than visual ones. Having A.I. adapt to people's needs and situations can make learning far easier and more exciting. Right now, robots like ours from Hanson Robotics are helping to treat people with mental conditions, like autism, depression, and Alzheimer's. Even though these efforts are still in the early stages, the initial results have been very encouraging.

When do you think artificial general intelligence will be achieved, if at all?
I think it will be achieved. At least that's what everyone is working toward. But when a machine will "wake up," we don't know. There's a long history of bad predictions when it comes to A.I. The science seems to go in fits and spurts. We have periods of great advancement, followed by years of nothing, what we call the Great A.I. Winters.

It appears that Google is trying to achieve AGI in maybe 10 years, which I doubt will happen. Others say 200 years. Who knows? But if we can make an

AGI that is safe and that cares about us and has a good relationship with us, it would probably be the most profound technology in history. No, not probably: It *would* be. There is no doubt. It would change history. It would create unprecedented abundance.

Why go through all the effort of making robots look like humans?
Human expression carries a lot of information you can't get through words alone. When you talk face-to-face, far more information is exchanged than when you do it over the telephone. If we want A.I. to communicate effectively, it's going to have to be through visual means as well as audio or written.

As an exercise in imagination, what do you see life being like 100 or 500 years from now?
Honestly, I think that if we don't develop super-intelligent AGI, we will destroy ourselves sometime within the next 100 years. One way or the other, we're going to wipe ourselves out and probably take the rest of life on the planet with us.

I'd say there's a 99 percent chance of that. To avoid the smoking crater scenario, we have to become much smarter and more enlightened. It's not going to be just human and machines, but human, machines, and the rest of life working together in harmony. A true singularity. If we manage that, life 500 years from now will be, for us, unrecognizable. We'll have gone on to higher realms.

A Conversation with Stephen Ibaraki
Venture Capitalist, Industry Expert, and International Keynote Speaker on Emerging Technological Trends

Stephen K. Ibaraki, the author of the Foreword to this book, is a major thought leader in today's IT industry. An industry trends researcher, former teacher, and writer, he serves as Outreach Chairman for the professional journal *ICT Discoveries* and is a sought-after speaker at technology conferences worldwide. For his work in the field of technology and artificial intelligence and machine learning, he has received the IFIP Silver Core Award, the Advanced Technology Award, IT Hero Award, IT Leadership Lifetime Achievement Award, Best Networking Professional Career Achievement Award, Gary Hadford Professional Achievement Award, and the Microsoft Most Valuable Professional Award (2006–2019), and has been inducted into the CIPS Hall of Fame.

How do you expect artificial intelligence to benefit the average person, 10 or 15 years from now?

Your question is predicated on the assumption that A.I. is some distant, future technology. A lot of people don't realize this, but it's already here in many of the technologies we use every day. Most people have heard of Amazon Echo. Google has Google Home. Apple, Samsung, and many others have or are developing similar products. They're all speakerlike devices capable of listening to, and now seeing, you 24/7 to answer questions, perform tasks, and control connected devices.

But most A.I. is even subtler than that. Your email account has a SPAM filter. How does your account know if an incoming email is SPAM? A.I. figures it out. (Granted, not always perfectly.) If you use your credit card in a different country or even in a different state, you'll likely get a warning alerting you to suspicious activity.

How does the bank know this? Is there a person sitting in front of a computer monitoring all your credit card activity? No, it's done through A.I. I have a DVR that helps me choose movies. Instead of scrolling through all the on-demand catalogs, I can just say, "I want all movies starring Tom Cruise," and it'll bring them up. I don't have to know where to find things. The A.I. will find them for me.

And, of course, online search engines have gone from using sophisticated indexing and other kinds of algorithms to full-on A.I. This is why they're so much more accurate when you ask for information. When you go shopping online, the system inevitably delivers recommendations based on your tastes and buying patterns. That's all A.I.

By 2019, A.I. had managed to penetrate every major industry in America: from aerospace and automotive manufacturing to finance, healthcare, agriculture, hospitality, and entertainment. And we're going to see A.I. create new industries of its own. A lot of people have heard of virtual reality or augmented reality, where you wear these headsets or images are projected into/over your eyes and you are totally immersed in a simulated environment. Already this is a billion-dollar market, and it's growing rapidly. In other words, the A.I. revolution isn't something that's coming; it's already here. And we're all feeling its effects.

You've said that the elderly represent a huge market for A.I. Can you describe the innovation occurring in this sector?

There are many problems associated with aging that A.I. can address. One of them is simple isolation. Companies are developing A.I.-driven "pets" that can provide the elderly with companionship without the maintenance required by actual animals. Many seniors have hearing problems, so increasingly A.I. is being built into hearing aids.

Researchers are also working on A.I.-driven earbuds to mask background noise so you can better talk to people in crowded, noisy rooms. Increasing intelligence is being built into vision systems; we'll soon have glasses offering the elderly super-human vision. These will automatically adjust as a person's vision naturally degenerates. Since mobility is another challenge for our aging population, robots will helpfully prepare food, coffee or tea, and even help them to the bathroom, much like a flesh-and-blood nursing assistant. Japan is leading development in this field because its country has a huge population of seniors coupled with a very low birthrate, so soon there won't be enough young people to look after the older generation. There is A.I. in life-span extension.

What impact do you think A.I. will have on the job market?
That's difficult to predict. Back in 2000, the United Nations issued a list of eight goals for the world to achieve in the next 15 years. Do you realize how much the world has changed since then and what was missed? This was before smartphones, social media, and cloud computing. Every year, more data is being created than previously existed in the whole of human history preceding it. Changes that used to take a decade to take hold now happen in just a few months or even a few weeks. How can you predict anything when the world is changing so fast?

In China, Microsoft has a chatbot called "Xiaoice," programmed to behave like a 17-year-old girl. It currently has more than 600 million friends and 16+ channels to interact. She is a celebrity, has a TV show, writes poetry, can have a phone conversation and anticipate what you are going to say next. She remembers your conversation from one visit to the next, so you can build a virtual relationship. Some people have actually proposed marriage to Xiaoice. I bring this up to illustrate how quickly the A.I. field is progressing. Who could have imagined something like this just five years ago?

So when it comes to predicting A.I.'s impact on the job market, it's anybody's guess. Even so, many jobs will be replaced. One estimate puts the loss at 20 percent. For example, trucking is going to be increasingly automated. Trucks must travel the same routes over and over again, so why not make them autonomous? Even factories will change. Already in India hybrid factories are popping up. Instead of being dedicated to a single industry, it uses A.I. to service multiple industries from a single location.

Imagine: you can have one factory do the work of 10, meaning you have a 10-fold increase in efficiency with prices 10 times less. This is a complete game changer. But just like the Internet created industries that people couldn't imagine in 1990, A.I. will create jobs and professions we can't even imagine today. One last thing: This study I mentioned puts the percentage of new jobs created as a result of A.I. at the same 20 percent, so the net effect is zero. I actually think the effect will be a net positive. Productivity is likely to skyrocket, and we'll end up with a much richer society.

This is what people are calling the Fourth Industrial Revolution, right?

This is based on work from PwC and CBInsights. I see two buckets for A.I.: helping people and replacing people. In the helping category we have A.I. augmenting, or assisting people doing tasks and making decisions. In the replacement area, we have A.I. automating tasks or the need for a person such as autonomous ride services replacing drivers. This will change economic models so much that this will produce an increase in global wealth of up to $20 trillion in the next 12 to 15 years in the form of productivity enhancements, personalized services, hybrid human–machine interactions, and higher-quality products/services.

According to McKenzie, a business organization famous for helping companies optimize operations, 58 percent of jobs can be automated now with natural language processing at average human levels. Not just labor jobs, any kind of job. There's a famous study by Frey and Osborne out of Oxford listing 72 occupations ripe for automation. In 2018, the Organization of Economic Cooperation and Development (OECD), reported that 14 percent of jobs are highly automatable, and another 32 percent will be substantially automatable due to A.I.

Of course, this won't happen overnight. There are going to be economic, legal, regulatory, and organizational hurdles when it comes to adapting new technologies. The most difficult jobs to automate are those requiring perception and manipulation in an unstructured environment. A classic example is surgery, which often requires rapid analysis and creativity as well as physical dexterity. Any job involving creative intelligence or social skills will be difficult to automate, especially since A.I. has trouble coming up with novel new ideas or interacting socially.

At the end of the day, the very young unskilled people and older people will be most at risk by the level of change, especially those in routine jobs, such as manufacturing. Unfortunately, with individuals more resistant to training and re-education, this will be a kind of a double whammy.

This leads us to our next question. What kind of skills should young people acquire to prepare for the future? What fields should they study to remain relevant?

I recently gave a major speech on this subject for a group called A.I. Pioneers. You've probably heard of STEM, which stands for science, technology, engineering, and mathematics. These are supposed to be the hot fields for young people eyeing the future. But over the past few years, this has been modified somewhat. We now talk about STEAM. We've added the arts, including design, because this is one area where A.I. is going to be very slow to surpass human intelligence.

Young people should also be concentrating on things like problem solving, leadership skills, and emotional intelligence. Among other things, emotional intelligence has to do with being patient with yourself so you're not impulsive, as well as taking the time to study and analyze problems. It has to do with social engagement, working with teams, caring for others, being inclusive, and, of course, creativity skills. Being flexible and networking with people from different areas possessing different experiences, will protect you from becoming irrelevant in the Age of A.I.

How much authority should we give to A.I. in areas like medicine, military operations, and criminal justice? Can we trust A.I. with life-or-death decisions?

This is certainly a matter of great concern. I sit on the board of an organization called ACM (the Association of Computing Machinery), which in 2017 came up with principles regarding A.I. accountability, responsibility, transparency, fairness, and equity, and, in 2018, updated their Code of Ethics, which encompasses A.I. The European Parliament via the EU Commission is trying to develop laws in this area as well as a code of ethics for robots. They're even discussing robot rights and responsibilities. Stanford has produced several important papers on this subject, and there's a consortium of businesses and nonprofit organizations called the Partnership on A.I. to Benefit People and Society, which is working to develop best practices for A.I.

All of which is to say that people are serious about establishing guidelines for ethical A.I. behavior. One area of great concern is bias. Machines are programmed by people, and their biases and prejudices tend to creep into their instructions. In hiring, we've found A.I.s favoring white males over women and minorities due to past personnel decisions. In criminal justice, A.I.s have tended to recommend harsher sentences for poorer people and people of color. We're trying to fix this as well.

Another challenge is accountability. People must be responsible for their actions, so shouldn't intelligent machines be held to the same standards? Explanation of how A.I. makes decisions must be addressed satisfactorily. Systems have to be able to explain the reasoning behind their actions and identify the origins of the data used. Systems need also to be rigorously tested and validated so we know bias has been removed, and we can trust them to make vital decisions. We need to make the systems accountable, and the people behind them accountable. All of this is happening now, and it will filter through everything we see in the future.

How do you see A.I. affecting the growing divide between the developed and developing world, the rich and the poor?

I think A.I. is going to make this divide disappear, so this is contrary to popular opinion. Currently, we have a rift between people with access to the Internet and those who do not. But we're rapidly developing technologies that don't need Internet access. The power is built right into the devices, right into the chips, which are becoming cheaper and cheaper to produce and will soon be everywhere. We know A.I. is going to increase wealth creation by trillions, or a more than 50 percent increase in GDP from productivity gains. The consumer impacts in 12 to 15 years will be even bigger than that, and these benefits will be enjoyed worldwide. Every region in the world will benefit from A.I., without question.

Can you give us some specific examples of how A.I. will be used to improve people's lives worldwide?

Sure. Let's look at agriculture. Agricultural productivity can be increased through predictive analysis from imaging with automated drones and satellites. Now, keep in mind, nearly 50 percent of crops are lost through waste, over-consumption, and production inefficiencies today. Livestock production losses are at nearly 80 percent. A.I. can help lower those figures substantially, which will benefit everyone.

Preventative healthcare programs and diagnostics will be significantly improved through A.I., too. Currently there are 10 billion-plus mobile devices with growing-in-resolution cameras and a multitude of sensors out there in the world, and, with A.I., these cameras and sensors can be used to diagnose a wide range of disorders and give further insights into managing chronic remote care.

Other A.I.-powered sensors can predict water consumption to improve drinking and sanitation services. A.I. can make wind farms more efficient.

Whether it be education, environmental sustainability, fish resource management, you name it—there isn't one area where A.I. won't have a major impact.

A Conversation with Steven Kotler
Expert on Guerilla Neuroscience, Exponential Technology, and Peak Performance Innovation

New York Times bestselling author **Steven Kotler** is best known for his work in the area of "flow," an elevated state of human consciousness, and in human performance enhancement. In 2012, his book, coauthored with Peter Diamandis, *Abundance: The Future is Better Than You Think* explored how technologies like A.I. give us the ability to solve grand global challenges like poverty, energy scarcity, and climate change. A graduate of the University of Wisconsin-Madison in English and Creative Writing, Kotler later received a master's degree in Creative Writing from Johns Hopkins University.

You've written a lot about exponential technology. What is this?
An exponential technology is any technology accelerating on an exponential growth curve—that is, doubling in price-performance on a regular basis. Essentially, whenever a technology become digital—meaning we can begin to program it in the ones and zeroes of computer code—it jumps on the back of Moore's Law and begins doubling on a regular basis. And there are now about a dozen techs accelerating on this growth curve—A.I., robotics, networks, sensors, etc. All among the most potent technologies the world has ever known.

You define "flow" as a optimal state of consciousness in which people perform at their best. How do you see A.I. contributing to this?
There are two answers to that. First, through biosensors, neuroimaging and A.I. analysis, we should be able to develop a system that helps people more easily access flow. The neurobiological markers of flow are complex, perhaps complex enough that only A.I. can make sense of it all. My lab at the Flow Research Collective has been part of an ongoing effort to identify triggers of flow. We've found about 20, but we suspect there might be many more. We're not going to know the number exactly until we achieve a better understanding of the neurobiology and the physiology behind the phenomenon, and that's where A.I. will play a huge part.

I'll give you an example. Ten years ago, all of the experts in this peak performance were siloed, working for Red Bull or the U.S. Olympic Team or some other group. All their research was proprietary. Now, everybody in the high-performance space is doing podcasts. There are hundreds of them, but every speaker is still just speaking from an individual perspective. We need A.I. to comb through all of these podcasts, to ingest the data, and look for similarities, common threads, important overlaps. I think it's a great project that will unlock a lot of data on high performance.

Do you foresee A.I. becoming creative? Is it possible for computers to experience an artificial state of flow?

Well, what is creativity but a novel form of pattern recognition? People have been studying creativity for years, and while we have whole books on the neuroscience of it, there are still gaps in the research you can drive a truck through. I think the more we watch A.I.s becoming creative, the more we'll be able to untangle the mysteries of creativity and put these insights to work for ourselves. But as far as computers experiencing flow—well, I just have no idea.

Could you describe what you mean by the phrase "abundance through exponential technology?"

Basically, it means using technology to make previously scarce resources abundant. Let's take photography. Even 20 years ago, photos were difficult to take and develop, thus quite expensive. Not only did you need a large, bulky camera, you required other pricy commodities, including film, chemicals, and specialized paper.

Fast forward to today. At this moment, I have so many photos on my phone I don't know what to do with them. Each photo is essentially free. I can make unlimited copies and send them to all of my friends for nothing. Or, take solar energy. Right now, solar delivers 10 percent of our energy needs, at best. However, due to technological innovation, the capacity to deliver solar energy is doubling every 18 months in the same way Moore's Law predicted the doubling of computer power every 2 years. At the current rate, in a few decades, we're going to have so much energy we won't know what to do with it. Like photos, energy will be essentially free. And in an advanced economy, energy is everything.

I'll give you one more way to look at this. Nature offers two solutions to scarcity. Just two. The first is to compete and fight over ever-dwindling resources. Until the Industrial Revolution, this is how we managed scarcity. Such thinking led to wars, famine, and mass death. The other way is to cooperate and create *new* resources. Information now makes such cooperation possible on a vast, global scale. So we're starting to be able to cooperate to make more resources as well.

Final question. Can you give us an example of how technology can help us tackle seemingly insurmountable challenges?

Let's look at the problem of climate change, which any climatologist will tell you is caused principally by the rapid build-up of carbon dioxide and other chemicals in the atmosphere due to human industrial activity. There are companies now developing "direct air capture" technology, plants that can pull carbon out of the air and turn it into engine-compatible fuel. They do this in a closed loop system producing zero emissions. It would take about 40,000 of these plants to begin to reverse the effects of climate change. Forty-thousand sounds like a lot, but that's how many power plants are currently operating on the planet. So, if you had one direct air capture plant for every power plant, you'd begin to solve the problem of global warming. I'm not saying this is the best solution (for that I might see Paul Hawken's Project Drawdown), but it is a solution—and that's the amazing part.

A Conversation with Peter Diamandis
Engineer, Physician, Entrepreneur, and
Founder of the XPRIZE Foundation

Born in the Bronx, N.Y., to Greek immigrant parents, **Peter Diamandis** grew up fascinated with the possibilities of space travel. At the age of 12, he won first place in the Estes Rocket Design Competition for building a launch system capable of launching three rockets simultaneously. While attending MIT, he cofounded Students for the Exploration and Development of Space. Later, while attending Harvard Medical School, he cocreated the Space Generation Foundation, a nonprofit group dedicated to promoting spaceflight. Even as he was finishing medical school, he served as managing director of the International Space University and was CEO of International Micro Space, a microsatellite launch company.

In 1994, Diamandis founded the XPRIZE Foundation, a $10 million incentive competition designed to encourage private companies to design low-orbit-capable manned spacecrafts. (That prize was ultimately won in 2004 by Burt Rutan's SpaceShipOne.) In the early twenty-first century, the XPRIZE Foundation expanded its competitions to promote advances in the automotive, genomics, health diagnostics, and environmental fields. It's no wonder *Fortune* magazine named Diamandis "one of the world's 50 greatest leaders." Not only did he cocreate Singularity University with futurist Ray Kurzweil to grasp the exponential pace of change and innovation, he started over 20 different companies exploring the limits of venture capital, space, and longevity to solve humanity's most pressing challenges.

What are the biggest misconceptions about artificial intelligence?

The first thing people don't understand is how narrow A.I. currently is. Most of today's A.I. is being designed to do just one specific task. These machines don't "think" the way people do. The other big misconception comes from under-estimating just how pervasive and impactful A.I. is going to be, not just in the future, but in the near future. We are starting to imbue virtually everything in our environment with a certain level of intelligence. This will change everything from how we eat and sleep to how we govern ourselves and raise our kids.

Why do so many people fear A.I.?

Human beings are built to fear. It's rooted in the brain's amygdala, the portion of our minds designed to interpret change—like the rustle of a leaf—as a sign of danger. It's how our ancient ancestors managed to survive on the savannah. The problem is, we tend to magnify danger by an average factor of 10 to 1. We hear a leaf rustle or a twig snap, and the first thing we think is, "lion!" Today, if you're living in Southern California, a heavy truck rolls by and the first thing you might think is "earthquake!" Therefore, if you see images of a lifelike robot your amygdala tends to go into overdrive. "It's going to kill us all!" it screams.

Of course, there are dangers to technology. The automobile was dangerous and continues to be. So are airplanes. Together, just these two inventions alone have killed millions of people, either by accident or by design. But this doesn't mean they also haven't delivered benefits far outweighing their negatives. In the 10 or 20 years it will take to fully realize the A.I. revolution, we're going learn from our mistakes while developing safeguards allowing the technology to become a useful tool for solving more and more problems on this planet.

What are some of the most novel and exciting things entrepreneurs are doing with A.I.?

I teach at Singularity University that "the world's biggest problems are the world's biggest business opportunities." My other favorite saying is, "if you want to become a billionaire, help a billion people." A.I. has the ability both to take on major problems and to scale solutions like never before. In the fields of education and healthcare, two things critical to eliminating poverty in the developing world, A.I. is going to be the great democratizer. Not only will it be able to deliver healthcare anywhere in the world, it can raise standards of living through education. A child in Tanzania will be able to pick up a smartphone and acquire the same knowledge and information available to a professor in London or a business executive in Beijing. A.I. can also custom-tailor a teaching program to develop this same child based on his or her intellect, learning preferences, emotional make-up, and interests.

How do you see A.I. changing humanity itself?
We're still in the early stages of learning the structure and content of the human genome as well as DNA and what every piece of it means. In the past, people had rather crude methods of selective breeding. The extent of it was you breed a tall, athletic, intelligent woman with a tall, athletic, intelligent guy and the result might be a strong, smart child.

But now, thanks to A.I., we'll soon be able to target and edit specific genes to produce a specific outcome. Do you want a child who's adept at math and science, or the next Usain Bolt? What color hair do you prefer for your progeny? How about eye color? Should she be good at the piano or the violin? Now, putting aside the moral and ethical issues involved, and there are plenty of those, it's not a matter of *if* this is going to happen, but *when*. Innovating companies are already working on developing genetic breakthroughs to aid in longevity and reduce disease, things we all agree we want to control. The rest will inevitably follow.

Let's talk more about longevity. What do you think is possible through A.I.?
Some species of sharks and whales and turtles exist for 200 years. Others live 500 years. How do they do that? Why can't we? Why do humans age as quickly as we do? How can we extend the average life span and still maintain peak fitness and cognition? These questions excite me. In the short term, my team and I are focused on making 100 years of age the new 60. Using breakthroughs in A.I. we want to give people another 20 to 30 quality years of life so they have the same mobility and capacities at 100 years old that people do now at 60. There are numerous technologies in Phase-1, -2 and -3 clinical trials that will impact health span, from placental stem cells to senolitic medicines. The best news is that by living an extra 20+ years, you'll intercept a whole host of new breakthroughs that will further extend your health span.

It's no secret we hold many solutions to our great problems. Yet we're stymied by tribalism, political divisions, and antiquated thinking sapping our ability to cooperate. Do you think A.I. could relieve this gridlock?
Probably the biggest impediment to clear thinking is cognitive bias. Our brains are not designed to process the vast amount of knowledge that our senses bring

in, so we take short-cuts. For example, we tend to trust people who look like us. We give greater weight to recent information. We also give greater weight to negative information. A.I. is beneficial because it has the potential to help us understand and counter these biases, giving us the ability to process massive amounts of information without cognitive bias (when programmed correctly) and deliver actionable solutions to smash through the old orthodoxy.

I truly believe intelligent societies are peaceful societies. If you study human history, you will realize nations have spent more time at war than at peace. Consider China. In its 3,000-year history, the country has spent at least 11 centuries at war. Likewise, the Roman Empire engaged in war during at least 50 percent of its existence. The United States has spent most of its brief history involved in some kind of armed conflict, either at home or elsewhere. At the same time, it's heartening to realize that since 1945, the major European powers have remained at peace. That's 75 years without a major armed conflict. How did they do it? Through education and cooperation.

In spite of the humanity's propensity for war, I believe we're heading toward what I call a meta-intelligent future in which we as humans become interconnected at a cognitive level. You might imagine it as a kinder, gentler version of "The Borg" from *Star Trek*. We will begin to merge human consciousness as we connect our neocortex to the cloud. This will create greater interdependence between individuals, whether they live in America, China, Russia, Lithuania. Such profound connectivity will ultimately lead to a more peaceful world.

So A.I. holds the promise of connection in an age when many people feel more atomized and disconnected than ever? Can A.I. also help us find greater meaning in our various life experiences?

When we're kids, we dream. Maybe we dream of becoming sports heroes or astronauts. As grow older, we dream new dreams: becoming doctors, inventors even captains of industry. But for most of us, the breaks just don't go our way. Maybe we don't live in an area with the best schools, or our parents don't make enough money to buy us computers or musical instruments. Perhaps we are burdened by health issues, physical handicaps, or we're just not built physically or intellectually to achieve those things we imagine. I think the ultimate aim of A.I. is to give us the power to achieve our dreams, no matter how ambitious they seem to be. A.I. promises to be humanity's partner—the best one we've ever had. Through it, we can do what we dream of more reliably and more easily. It's going to be our dream-maker.

A Conversation with Christoph Auer-Welsbach
Founding Director of City.AI

Christoph Auer-Welsbach is a tech investor with a background in finance, strategy, and artificial intelligence. He is partner at IBM Ventures, leveraging IBM developing strategic engagements with the venture ecosystem with a special interest in A.I. An advisor to numerous tech start-ups, Auer-Welsbach also cofounded WSAI, the world's leading A.I. summit.

Let's begin by talking about City.AI. When was it founded? What is it? Who participates and what is its mission?

City.AI is a nonprofit organization managing a decentralized network of A.I. ecosystems around the world with the goal of distributing knowledge and resources in order for people to apply the technological framework of A.I. effectively. We actively work to foster awareness and education about artificial intelligence in order to democratize the design, development, and use of A.I. City.AI was founded two-and-a-half years ago. We saw a gap between the very scientific discussions about the development of A.I., and the very philosophical discussions about what this technology can do for humanity.

This gap, as we define it, was about "applied A.I.": how is A.I. developed, how is it put into production, what value does it generate, what lessons learned must we share to enable different applications of A.I. and allow more people to leverage it? Allowing everyone to apply A.I. and leverage its potential is the tagline of City.AI.

Your website frequently mentions "A.I. ecosystems." What is an A.I. ecosystem, and does its meaning vary according to context?

We define an *A.I. ecosystem* as a location or region where all the necessary players and activities are there to develop and apply A.I. There need to be scientific and research activities, maybe out of universities or other organizations, and a technology environment with start-ups, investors, and talent. There also need to be active A.I. stakeholders sharing lessons learned. They can come from a corporate environment or from a start-up environment, but they must possess deep expertise on the application of A.I. itself.

You speak of "democratizing A.I." Could you please explain what you mean by this concept? What are the benefits of democratizing A.I? What's the downside if it isn't democratized?

The downside is something we're already experiencing. To design and develop the technological framework for A.I. further requires resources, typically in the form of capital, access to knowledge, and available technology provided by governments or large organizations. Which basically means each of these organizations and institutions follows their own specific agenda. The critical aspect is not the application only, but even more so the design and development that would need to be open, as with any fundamental research out there. When we look into this drain of accessible resources, I'm quite concerned that the power is shifting further into even fewer hands.

So what we need to move toward is making A.I. available as a basic technological framework which can be used to solve humanity's most pressing issues, or at least to provide the chance to do so. Currently A.I. is in a state where it is handled more like a luxury instead of a general good—this is the wrong approach. Besides curing diseases, A.I. can enable more efficient processes—lowering costs of basic needs as well as costs of living, reducing poverty, and more. If we democratize the technological framework of A.I. it will be inclusive—reflecting the cultural and environmental backgrounds of those who use it and also eliminating the risk of "1 A.I. rules us all."

What industries are most likely to benefit from A.I. in the short term? How about the long term?
We're experiencing the impact of A.I. in industries like retail and consumer products, financial services, healthcare, media and entertainment, travel and transportation, and more. But also social networks, online search engines, and other free mass services are enabled by it. But we see a lot of innovation where machine learning is applied that isn't consumer-facing either, whether it's in exploration, the energy sector, or manufacturing, where automation is at a quite advanced level already.

Still, we're only at the beginning. Intelligent systems will make services supplying basic needs broadly available, driving costs of production and distribution down while becoming safer for humanity and better for our environment. The long-term effects should be positive, but there are also challenges. For instance, it's a technological framework with the potential to abuse legacy systems at scale, something unprecedented in human history. Of course, this is also due to a more and more interconnected world where digital services replace physical ones, including assets.

The major benefit of A.I. is to provide humans with better answers and options. But what happens when people just don't want to do what A.I. says is best for them? For example, what if A.I. concludes that, to live longer, healthier lives, every adult has to eat a half-pound a Brussels sprouts every

day? Don't we need to change people as well as machines? And how do we do that?

"Better" is a very subjective term. What the application of machine learning definitely does is provide more accurate answers, based on quantified statistical outcomes which I as a human can use to adjust my decision making, or not.

People change every day, for the better or worse. They decide in the morning if they want to eat white or rye bread, drink orange juice or sugar-free tea. Their decisions affect their health in the long term. What machine learning is good at is using historical data and statistics to predict what can mostly likely happen in the future.

Humans in turn are quite bad at thinking about the long-term effects of today's actions and choices. So intelligent systems powered by an A.I. technology framework can help in the form of an advisor visualizing long-term effects of behavior and supporting change, for instance. It's again driving efficiency (in the form of accuracy) and decreasing the cost of something, which in the past, only a personal trainer could achieve. Nowadays, we can use smart devices and apps to monitor our behavior and soon to track our health, which can help us become healthier, physically and mentally. This kind of a watchdog is broadly accessible. But do I have to do what my personal trainer is preaching? No, the choice is still mine.

Humans are still responsible for their actions, which also defines us as human. Of course, we're getting tricked, too, and the technological framework of A.I. can be used by organizations and institutions doing so on scale. This is a risk, and we need to find ways we can protect the values we as a society have built up over the past couple of centuries.

What country do you think is doing the most exciting A.I. research at the moment? What are they doing that other countries aren't?

There are many institutions around the world that are doing amazing work in machine learning, data science, and related fields. Europe's universities have a strong standing in the fields of logic and reasoning, while Asian regulatory frameworks make it easier to gather and use the personal data necessary to develop the technological frameworks of A.I. further. The U.S., led by Silicon Valley, has a strong legacy in building digital products for the mass market and therefore providing the basis for applying machine learning at scale.

To my comment in the previous question, states in particular need to find the balance between, on the one hand, providing enough freedom to foster innovation and, on the other, the need to protect their people and environment from abuse and negative long-term effects. The impact of the technological framework of A.I. is much larger than we have ever experienced with any technology before, and we can't anticipate the impact if we mess it up.

So today we see lots of discussion globally on ethical standards and other norms, some with great frameworks, but, frankly, too little action is happening to bring this onto the streets/have it adopted by organizations. That has to change, and City.AI is on a mission to support that change by building awareness and providing education to do so.

You have said entrepreneurs have responsibility for the disruption their technology creates. How does one fulfill such responsibility? If you're making millions—or billions—upsetting people's lives and livelihoods, what obligation do you have toward the people and/or communities you have disrupted?

As already stated, humans are usually bad at long-term thinking. A.I. is just a technological framework, a tool basically, and we need to ensure it is properly used. From its scientific aspect, it is already established, but as a tool it's quite novel. Furthermore, it's having a vast impact on our lives, something so incremental but on the other hand so manipulative of human behavior in the way it's used that we can't anticipate its impact either.

We need to open research and make knowledge, best practices, and necessary resources accessible. I understand that A.I. is often a competitive advantage, but we need to ask ourselves what are the opportunity costs. Right now it seems that these are quite high. I'm thinking about all the experts who, instead of conducting fundamental research for the public, are now doing so in the realms of private corporations. This knowledge will be lost for future generations to access and make use of, and even build on. Imagine the innovation created and expertise brought to bear not being available to a broad audience of up-and-coming experts anymore and that these things can't be used in a free way. That's a severe issue we're going to face 10+ years from now.

Moreover, we seem to be stuck at the technology layer instead of focusing on regulating A.I. based on the technology's potential impact. But we need to regulate the way it's used and not restrict the technological framework as a whole. We've prevented the use of nuclear weapons while at the same time made use of the technological framework to generate power. "A.I." is, for better or worse, what people and companies do with it. We need to stop using it to suppress and manipulate people.

But that's just bringing up another aspect: The technological framework of A.I. is only accelerating the challenges our society and economy face through evolution and other innovations already. Our commerce-driven society and growth-based economy are not sustainable in the long term. This has nothing to do with machine learning per se, but this makes the problems associated with it larger, more visible, and its impact on more people in shorter time frames.

What are some of the most exciting projects City.AI. is involved in?

We just launched our Data Science Days, starting in London in 2019. This is a project that aims to help masters and Ph.D. graduates in data science and related fields make better decisions on their career path based on the commercial applicability and impact of their research.

City.AI's ambassador network is also building a knowledge hub and education training platform which is open, enabling people to gather and share information on A.I.-related topics globally so more people have access to knowledge and best practices. One of the first spin-offs, if you will, is our Ethics Stream, which will provide resources for putting ethical frameworks into practice.

Another exciting project City.AI's ambassador network is involved in is the ecosystem mapping effort. We're creating a publicly accessible, open wiki around A.I. stakeholders, including activities and players in the field, based on all the hubs we're active in, so people can use it as a guide to engage and identify others working in the same field in other areas of the world and can align with each other, collaborate, and share.

Can you describe what's going to happen at the world's leading A.I. Summit in October 2019?

The team just announced recently that the World Summit A.I. will be in Amsterdam in 2019. Not just two days, but a whole week. We will invite A.I. practitioners and stakeholders from around the world to present their thoughts on A.I. and their applications and to make sure their voice is heard, reflecting cultural backgrounds and environmental differences. We are also expanding to North America, where we will have the first North American edition in Montréal.

A.I. AND THE LAW

What is the law but a series of algorithms? Codified instructions, these algorithms proscribe dos and don'ts, ifs and thens, limiting the parameters of acceptable behavior. The law also designates punishments for transgressions. As such, it only makes sense that artificial intelligence will have enormous effects on the mechanisms governing society.

As we saw with our LegalMation case study, the law is also not immune to sweeping changes when it comes to automation affecting jobs. Some experts predict that A.I. will eliminate most paralegal and legal research positions within the next decade. Trial lawyers may fare better since their personalities, charisma, and ability to create empathy with jurors make them indispensable—at least for now. Still, many attorneys may soon find themselves outflanked and outclassed by artificial intelligence. We talked to experts in the field to learn more about A.I.'s likely impact on the field of jurisprudence.

A Conversation with Tom Girardi
Superstar Attorney and Renowned Civil Litigator

Named "Lawyer of the Decade" by the International Association of Top Professionals in 2017, **Thomas Vincent Girardi** is perhaps best known as the lead attorney in the industrial pollution case against Pacific Gas & Electric. This feud became the basis of the 2000 Oscar-winning film *Erin Brockovich*, starring Julia Roberts. Prior to this, in 1970, Girardi became the first attorney in California to achieve a $1 million-plus medical malpractice award, and he has won several high-profile cases against Lockheed Aircraft, the Los Angeles County Metropolitan Transportation Authority, and Hollywood's seven major movie studios. A founding partner of Girardi & Keese, in Los Angeles, Girardi was inducted into the California's State Bar's Trial Lawyer Hall of Fame in 2003.

A.I. is already being used to help law firms more efficiently perform due diligence, legal research, and bill time. Where do you think A.I. is currently delivering the greatest benefits to the industry?

First, I can only speak to the civil side of things. In this area, I would say it's close to legal malpractice *not* to use A.I. When litigating a civil case, there's usually vast amounts of information needing to be discovered, indexed, organized, and processed. In the past, our firm has used private investigators to acquire much of the required information, and this can be expensive. Today, A.I. can do it for practically nothing. Any firm not using A.I. will be at a huge disadvantage against a firm that does. It's analogous to a lawyer still doing everything by hand instead of using computers.

Of course, A.I. can't do everything. There are many instances where the only way to obtain information is through depositions. But let's say the opposition is going to call an expert witness. A.I. can tell you every case in which this witness has testified, what his or her opinions were, and how the juries reacted. Imagine how spectacular having this information will be when it comes time for cross-examination.

How do you see A.I. impacting particular legal jobs?
I envision A.I. replacing many lower-echelon positions, but I don't think senior people will impacted at all unless this means being able to acquire more and better information on behalf of their clients, which is what we're paid to do. Ultimately, it's a lawyer's job to solve a problem as quickly and inexpensively as possible. A.I. is a godsend when it comes to this. It allows you access to better information, faster and less expensively. Even when both sides are armed with A.I., it still helps, because when either party has all the information they need, they can resolve the conflict faster.

How do you see A.I. playing a role in jury selection?
It's massively valuable. Today, if a conflict concerns a matter of fact—for example, *did the doctor cut off the wrong leg?*—it's settled out of court. It never goes to trial. Trials concern matters of interpretation. *Did a doctor wait too long before performing a biopsy? Did she make a bad judgment call?* This is why the philosophical makeup of a jury is so important.

Unfortunately, most judges provide little time for jury selection. A few basic questions are asked with yes or no responses. With A.I., however, we can quickly discover more about each potential juror. *Have they served on juries before? What were the verdicts? Are they politically active? What causes do they donate to? Have they been involved in accidents?* A.I. can obtain this information and evaluate whether a potential juror would benefit or threaten a case within seconds.

Along the same lines, analyzing facial reactions and body language can also provide great insight into how a potential juror feels about an issue. If I ask a question, even before the potential juror answers, this person's eyes might move in a certain way, their skin color might change slightly, their body could shift, reflecting an emotional response. Again, an A.I. can interpret these reactions as either good or bad signs for our side. Will judges allow this kind of analysis? Well, remember, most judges are sticklers for fairness. They want to rule out prejudice and bias. So I believe courts will welcome any technology promising to speed up the trial process and facilitate justice.

In addition to trial lawyers, what other areas of the law stand to benefit from A.I.?

Business law, for sure. If I'm going to enter into a large contract with somebody, I want to know everything I can about this person or the company I'm considering doing business with. *Have there been lawsuits against them? How many? What were the reasons?* Relying on A.I. for this information will greatly aid in the decision-making process.

Won't A.I.'s speed and efficiency reduce a firm's billable hours?

Probably. But a lawyer can't just consider one case. If a lawyer can use A.I. to win a case and do it for less than someone without A.I., who do you think the client will choose to work with next time? Consider this scenario. Through A.I., a firm can now take on 12 cases when before they could only take on 3. In this way, they are still making the same money—they are billing for the same number of hours—but they're also greatly expanding their client roster. And creating a lasting practice is ultimately about building long-term relationships.

Do you see a time when A.I. might adjudicate cases, when they might replace flesh-and-blood judges?

No. I don't think that's going to happen. But what A.I. *can* do is provide the judicial system with more and better information to make the process move faster. To put this in context, a hundred years ago, the typewriter was a big technological step up. Forty years ago, computers were a big step up. Now, A.I. is an even bigger step up. Ultimately, some firms will be faster to adopt this technology than others and they will reap the advantages. After that, others will race to catch up. The whole point of good lawyering is to be as effective as you can be and make happy clients. Any relationship between client and attorney is very special. Though A.I. can help as a great tool, it's not going to ever replace that.

A Conversation with L. Song Richardson
Award-Winning Dean of the UCI School of Law
and Expert on Unconscious Bias

In January 2018, **L. Song Richardson** became dean of the University of California-Irvine (UCI) School of Law, thus becoming the only woman of color to head a Top 21 law school. She had previously served as interim dean following the departure of the school's founding dean, Erwin Chemerinsky.

An award-winning teacher and scholar, Richardson's academic research uses cognitive and social psychology to study perception, decision making, and judgment. An expert on bias in the practice of law and in the criminal justice system, her article, "Police Efficiency and the Fourth Amendment," was selected as a "Must Read" by the National Association of Criminal Defense Attorneys. She was the 2011 recipient of the American Association of Law School's Derrick Bell Award, recognizing her extraordinary contributions to legal education through teaching, scholarship, and mentorship.

How did you become interested in the field of artificial intelligence?

I became interested in A.I. through my work on unconscious bias. People often view A.I. and algorithms as objective without thinking carefully about the origin of the data being used in the machine learning process. Biased data is going to lead to biased A.I. When teaching and preparing law students for the legal profession, it is important for them to understand how A.I. works and how A.I. will impact the law.

How are today's law students being trained to deal with the coming world of A.I.?

Law schools must still train students to think like lawyers, which includes developing their critical thinking and analytical skills. That's because A.I. isn't going to replace lawyers. Schools also must prepare students to address the legal, ethical, and policy issues that will arise as a result of A.I. For example, when self-driving cars are involved in an accident, who is responsible? The owner of the car? The car manufacturer? The software designer? These are the types of questions lawyers must be prepared to address.

So, you don't see A.I. replacing lawyers?

A.I. will not replace lawyers, but it will impact what lawyers do. In fact, rather than replacing lawyers, the need for lawyers—good lawyers—will be greater than ever. These technologies are creating a slew of new legal issues regarding privacy, bias, liability, and ethics, just to name a few. Law schools have a vital role to play educating students, lawyers, judges, and policy makers about A.I. so that they will be equipped to grapple effectively and thoughtfully with the host of new legal issues that will arise.

Currently, some courts are using A.I. to determine who receives bail and who doesn't—using behavioral patterns to determine potential flight risk— which is something a judge would normally do. Do you think a time will come when A.I. replaces human judges for other tasks as well?'

I don't think that A.I. will replace human judges. Nor should it. My worry is that judges, lawyers, policy makers, and others will rely too heavily on the outputs from A.I. without paying sufficient attention to how the outputs were generated. The outputs from any A.I. system are only as good as the inputs. Thus, we should not blindly trust that whatever an automated system concludes is just and fair. No matter how sophisticated A.I. becomes, it can't possibly—and shouldn't—replace human decision making.

Some A.I. experts believe A.I. will make better doctors because they will never show up hung over or be otherwise distracted. One could say the same for lawyers and judges. No matter how rational and objective we try to be, people always bring their personal baggage to a job.

That's true. However, A.I. will also bring baggage to the job, so to speak. A.I. systems learn from data and experience, just as humans do. To the extent that the data that is used to train the system is biased, the decisions made by A.I. will also be biased. Additionally, societal biases influence our current reality, and our current social arrangements will influence what A.I. systems learn and the conclusions these systems reach. For instance, there are not as many women in STEM fields as men. Because A.I. learns from currently existing data and experience, it may incorrectly conclude that women are not as qualified as men for jobs in the STEM field.

I can imagine many situations where A.I. can enhance the work that human beings do. For instance, clients may be more honest answering questions asked by an A.I. system because they will worry less about being judged. If true, then an A.I. system can conduct an initial interview of the client while the lawyer spends her time developing a relationship of trust with the client. The lawyer can ask follow-up questions later, once trust is developed. In the interim, she can also act on the information gathered by the system.

Our court system is massively backlogged at all levels. Some people are advocating outsourcing less serious cases to A.I. to relieve the glut and speed things along. What are your thoughts about this?

I consider this to be a misuse of technology. Why does someone become a lawyer? Why does someone become a judge? It's certainly not to become a cog in the wheel of an assembly line system of justice. The fact that we have massive backlogs resulting in a failure to give people the individualized attention their cases deserve tells us there's something fundamentally wrong with our justice system. Expediting the mass processing of people using A.I. isn't the answer.

It's the opposite of justice. We need a system to evaluate each case individually on its merits. When I speak to judges, public defenders, and prosecutors who worry about how overwhelmed the criminal justice system is and conclude that they simply do not have the time to spend considering each case individually, it really disappoints me. We make time for the things we consider important, and giving people the individualized attention they deserve is critically important to the legitimacy of our justice system.

Ultimately do you see A.I. having a positive or negative impact on the legal profession?

A.I. is like any technology. It depends on how it is used. Like the tools that came before it, from typewriters to computers, I think the net impact will be positive. Lawyers and judges are only as good as the information they receive, and A.I. has the potential to increase the quality of this information significantly. But as I said earlier, information will never be a substitute for good judgment.

A Conversation with Silvia Hodges Silverstein
Legal Procurement Expert

The editor and publisher of the *Legal Procurement Handbook*, **Silvia Hodges Silverstein** researches, instructs, and speaks on topics related to purchasing decisions in the legal market and change in the legal industry. She is the executive director of the Buying Legal Council, the international trade organization for legal procurement, and an adjunct professor for law firm management at Columbia Law School.

You have written extensively on the impact of technology on the legal profession. What can lawyers today look forward to in the next 5 to 10 years? Will their jobs become more satisfying as a result of technology, or will they be rendered obsolete?

Technological change is one of the key trends influencing labor markets in many countries, including the United States. I've read studies predicting that up to 800 million people will lose their jobs by 2030, and I believe that the legal profession will be profoundly influenced by automation, A.I., and the continuous substitution of low-cost labor.

But keep in mind that technology and automation aren't synonymous with job displacement. I think we'll see many of these lost jobs replaced by people with different skills. This means they will need to significantly change their skillsets to get these new jobs. Otherwise, a lost job might be lost forever to them. As an example, I would say that a majority of today's lawyers don't know how to code; they don't learn this in law school—but in 10 years, or even sooner, they will need to. I believe the transformation of the legal profession has already started; technology frees us up to do higher-level tasks, including advising clients, negotiating deals, and arguing in court.

Did I understand that correctly? Did you say you think lawyers in the future will also have to know how to code?
Absolutely. I am convinced they will have to do that, just like everyone else. There are many examples now of law firms with incubators, R&D teams, for instance, using legal technology in one way or another. But by and large, firms still behave like they are an artisanal shop. I do believe that knowing coding, or how to use an applied technology, will be needed to deliver services in crucial ways that clients will come to expect in the future.

What are the areas of law where A.I. is likely to be the most impactful? Which are likely to remain beyond the reach of artificial intelligence?
A.I. is typically applied in document review for discovery, in so-called predictive coding, in due diligence review for corporate transactions, for legal document analysis, for legal research, for automated searches, for time-entry data analysis. But beyond the reach of A.I. will be tasks really demanding the human touch: interpersonal skills, social interaction. Being perceptive, offering personal services—anything requiring you to look someone in the eye—will not be substitutable by A.I. Everything else has at least the risk that it probably can be done better by A.I. in the foreseeable future.

I don't expect this to happen in the next 5 to 10 years. But beyond that, it's hard to know what will happen. I do believe certain types of legal cases might be augmented by what could be termed "robotic justice." I can imagine scenarios in which certain types of cases will automatically be decided.

Could you please describe how A.I. is likely to produce a boon in small or even one-person law operations? What will A.I. allow smaller firms to do, things that they can't do now?
A.I. definitely diminishes the importance of having a huge staff, especially in litigation. Until recently, small firms have been really hampered by the tradi-

tionally labor-intensive, human process-driven practice of law. But since A.I. automates tasks once requiring human intelligence to make predictions and areas needing expertise, I believe A.I. totally changes all of that. A.I. will make it easier for small firms to take on cases they otherwise could not have taken on before.

What do law schools need to do to prepare tomorrow's lawyers for the world of A.I.?

Our industry is in transition from a labor-intensive delivery model to a more technology- and process-enabled model. I believe even the elite law schools must totally rethink their approach and prepare students for this new marketplace because fewer and fewer of them will practice in traditional ways.

Law school curricula, the educational tools, and how they deliver knowledge need to change, to be aligned with new needed skillsets and competencies. I find that the gap between what the marketplace demands and the competencies most law grads possess is staggering. Until a few years ago, when I asked students about eDiscovery—and eDiscovery is very standard these days—they didn't even know what eDiscovery was. And that's just unacceptable.

What do the lawyers of today—especially those that may have been practicing for decades, have to do to take advantage of emerging technologies?

If I was in my 60s, I might have a choice as to whether I wish to be part of this development or not. People in their 20s, however, don't have such a luxury. Even those individuals in their 40s, don't have much of a choice—*they need to learn to work* with this technology.

They need to ask themselves, do they want to compete with the new technology or do they want to work with it? Traditionalists who can't imagine how their work could possibly be replaced by technology—they compete. But over time, technology, which initially might just be able to solve some simple problems, will be reaching farther up the food chain. And as technology's reach increases, there's going to be less and less of this work that so-called traditional lawyers do. The better alternative, in my opinion, is to be part of a future in which you help build technology, providing better, faster, and more efficient solutions.

In your own experience, what is the most exciting impact you've seen A.I. have on a particular law firm?

There are a number of firms around the world doing really interesting things, those that have created virtual assistants to help teams make quicker, better decisions; providing insights that would have not been possible without A.I. There are new legal technology examples popping up almost daily. It's a really exciting marketplace offering breakthrough research in areas such as task automation and behavioral analytics. This type of innovation really changes the status quo in all areas of the law.

Do you think A.I. should be used in law beyond individual legal practices? What about in the judicial system itself? Should judges use A.I.?
Some believe A.I. will help reduce, if not eliminate, human failure, even reducing or eliminating bias issues in the judicial system. However, to develop an A.I. algorithm, data sets are needed. Information must be collected and fed to the A.I. to humanize its reasonings. I'm not convinced this will eliminate bias; we might have an A.I. believing itself to be unbiased, but it might still possess this problem issue.

I am reluctant to hand over the reins to technology when we talk about the judicial system. Unless we really know and can control the algorithms, we have to some extent worry about the terror of technology. Right now, the stakes are too high. I personally wouldn't trust A.I. with our judicial systems until we know how it makes choices and how to control it. And even then, if it gets into the wrong hands, that's really scary. I don't want to live in a society where technology companies have power over our freedom and rights.

Best-case scenario: The year is 2050. How has our legal system improved as a result of artificial intelligence? Is America a more just country?
I like the thought of a more just system providing equal access to justice. Even if it's not yet possible, we need to keep working toward it. There is going to be a revolution by the buyers of legal services. It hopefully will mean fewer errors, less busywork, more output.

It is definitely my hope that America will be a country with greater access to law. And to some extent, A.I. can be the great equalizer. Just like with any tool, it can potentially do lots of good. But if it's in the wrong hands, it can also create a lot of damage. We need to continue this journey, but we also need to ask ourselves at every stage of the process: are we doing the right thing in the larger scheme of things?

A.I. AND LANGUAGE

In the Book of Genesis, the Bible speaks of a time when all humanity spoke the same language and could cooperate on a massive scale. The Tower of Babel, designed to reach Heaven, was the ultimate symbol of this cooperation. But the Tower offended God, who caused humankind to fracture and speak hundreds of languages so individuals could not understand each other and confusion ruled the land. This ancient allegory is meant to explain humanity's instinct for tribalism and nationalistic warfare. But in the twenty-first century, artificial intelligence may finally overcome this ancient curse, allowing people to understand each other regardless of their native tongues.

A Conversation with Danny May
Cofounder of Lingmo International
and Pioneer in A.I.-Powered Language Translation

Australian native **Danny May** is the CEO and cofounder of Lingmo International, a global leader in A.I.-powered language translation. You may recall we featured an interview with non-techie Danny May in Chapter 14, describing how he was able to disrupt himself to own the A.I. revolution for his new translation venture. Originally trained as a plumber, he founded Lingmo in 2014, having previously founded Muscit Industries, a social networking site based in China, in 2013, the same year he founded Global Creations, an organization assisting foreign companies to expand their operations and sales internationally. Since launching Lingmo, he has been featured in publications such as *Business Insider* and the *Daily Telegraph*. In 2017, his company's flagship product, Translate One2One, an earpiece capable of interpreting eight different languages in real time, went to market after being featured at the United Nations' Artificial Intelligence for Good Summit in Geneva.

How did you come up with Lingmo, and how is it different from other language translation applications?
It so happened I was in China on a business trip. After someone stole my passport, I needed to find the consulate. Not knowing where this might be located, I walked up to a Chinese police officer. Once I realized he didn't speak English, I downloaded a popular translation app into my phone and tried to use it to ask for help.

The problem was the app mistranslated my request to the Chinese equivalent of "I love you." Needless to say, things got pretty awkward from there. I thought about this problem during my entire flight back to Sydney. As soon as I arrived home, I started doing market research and learned that even the best language translation apps had only 50 percent accuracy. But why? As I subsequently discovered, everyone has been focusing on the translation aspect of the problem, when the real issue is voice recognition. If an app can't clearly understand what you're saying in the first place, it can't provide an accurate translation. That's where I decided to focus.

Your professional background isn't in artificial intelligence. Can you tell us how you got into this field?

No. I'm a plumber by training. Before Lingmo, I spent much of my time commuting to Sydney from the coast. But after my experience in China, I decided to invest my time and $100,000 of my life savings into my vision. It helps that I am also an entrepreneur and knew how to connect with the right people to provide the necessary technical expertise.

What role does IBM's Watson play in the translation process?

Watson's artificial intelligence serves two functions. The first is machine learning: picking up keywords in speech recognition and expediting the learning process. The second part is its ability to pick up nuances and dialects within different languages. Instead of translating word-for-word—which as anyone knows, can result in all kinds of nonsense—Watson actually stops and thinks about what's being said, then translates it in a way to communicate the *meaning* as closely as possible in the listener's language. This way the person on the other end really understands what's being said instead of just getting the gist.

What are some of the ways you trained Watson?

One big way was watching movies with subtitles. But it's not just comparing speech to the translation. It's actually *watching the movie* to see how the other characters react to what's being said. This is how it's able to pick up nuance and emotional context. It also helps with overcoming confusion concerning synonyms. For example, if Watson hears the word "FLOW-er," and sees a picture of a cake, it understands the speaker means "flour," the substance you use to bake bread and pastries. If it sees a colorful plant, it understands the speaker is talking about a "flower," something that blooms and has a smell.

How does Lingmo handle slang or idioms, words or phrases that don't carry their literal meaning? Like saying, "That's water under the bridge"?

This has always been a challenge and demonstrates why artificial intelligence is so valuable. Artificial intelligence can learn through trial and error. And this is just what it's doing. It's a slow process, yes, but it's a process that yields results, something computers merely employing word-to-word translation could never accomplish.

Can Lingmo detect sarcasm?

Again, this is just a matter of training. When you're being sarcastic, your pitch and tone of voice tends to change compared to when you're being literal. Watson is learning how to pick up on these changes and recognize sarcasm.

How do you deal with large conversations involving groups in which the members all speak different languages?

We currently have a system that works via text and voice message. You leave a message in English, and one person in Hong Kong gets it in Mandarin, while another receiver in Buenos Aires gets it in Spanish, and a third receiver in Moscow gets it in Russian. Step two—and we're still working on this—is to make this possible with real-time phone calls and Skype-style video conferencing. No matter what language someone speaks, the receivers will hear it in their native tongue.

What's the accuracy of your system?

When IBM tests it, it usually comes out at 95 to 97 percent accurate, but we say 85 percent just to be safe. We want to account for dialects, slang, and all the other variables we've yet to fully conquer.

What about live person-to-person communication? Are you working toward a technology allowing people who speak different languages to talk face-to-face?

Yes. At first, we tried using Bluetooth earbuds to provide the translation, but the problem was getting the other party to put the buds in their ears. It proved to be very awkward. So instead we went to the smartwatch. You speak into the watch, and its speaker provides your listener with the proper translation.

Besides tourism, what is the market for A.I.-enabled translation?

The market is quite large. Consider the United Nations. There, many professional translators can only work for 20 minutes or so at a time because the work is so intense. A.I. can provide a great relief to these individuals. Newspapers can use it to create editions geared to nonnative speakers. Publishers can use it to quickly and accurately translate books into various languages.

We're working with airlines needing a way to communicate with international passengers. A.I. can be a real boon to companies using chatbots on their marketing sites needing to communicate with foreign customers. In the legal field, accurate translation can also be essential when drawing up contracts, especially to someone charged with a crime in a foreign country.

What do you see as the ultimate expression of this technology?
I can easily envision a time when anyone visiting a foreign country wears these little earbuds. The A.I. instantly recognizes the local language being spoken and provides an accurate real-time translation to the listener. And, of course, everyone else is wearing these, too, so everyone can communicate instantly with each other, no matter where they're from.

Like Star Trek's universal translator? Or Hitchhiker's Guide to the Galaxy's Babelfish?
Only it's not science fiction anymore. It's real.

A.I. FOR GOOD

Although many people fear the effects of artificial intelligence—whether it be losing their job to a robot or witnessing a Terminator-led Armageddon—there are just as many who view it as a force for good. Many leading experts in the field believe that A.I. will usher in a new age of prosperity, leveling economic inequalities and combating scarcity. Numerous innovators have dedicated themselves to making some form of an A.I.-driven utopia a reality. Or the closest thing to this ideal. And they are already starting to produce measurable results.

A Conversation with Ben Goertzel
Blockchain Visionary, Robot Designer,
and Proponent of Artificial General Intelligence (AGI)

Ben Goertzel is founder and CEO of SingularityNET, a blockchain-based A.I. marketplace, as well as the chief scientist for Hanson Robotics, creator of the android Sophia. A former child prodigy, Ben left high school after the tenth grade to attend Bard College at Simon's Rock (in Great Barrington, MA), where he earned a BS in Quantitative Sciences before obtaining his PhD in Mathematics from Temple University at age 22. Chairman of the Artificial General Intelligence Society and an advisor to Singularity University, he is particularly optimistic about A.I.'s profound ability to improve the lives of people worldwide.

Sophia is probably the best-known robot around today. What was the purpose behind developing her?

One of our commercial goals at Hanson Robotics is to create a whole generation of service robots. We're working with folks in South China to create a factory to manufacture them, first for business purposes, then for the general consumer. Right now, Sophia is both an R&D platform and a showcase, a "spokes-robot." But our long-term idea foresees service robots being as ubiquitous as desktop computers, telephones, and cars today.

I'm talking about human-like robots we can interact with easily and who can help us in our everyday lives. These have been a science-fiction staple for decades, but there's no reason we can't achieve such a phenomenon using available technologies. One thing to keep in mind is that the intelligence driving these robots won't be in the robots themselves. It will be distributed among a vast, decentralized computer network accessible anywhere.

You have been a big proponent of artificial general intelligence (AGI), as opposed to the more prevalent artificial narrow intelligence (ANI) we see now. Why is that?

Decades ago, when anyone thought about machine intelligence, it was in terms of AGI. You wanted a machine capable of thinking like a person, who could deal with all kinds of problems up and down the spectrum. But as A.I. developed, people discovered narrow intelligence to be much easier to achieve. You could create an A.I. offering the best way to maneuver through traffic or another capable of recognizing faces or writing music. But narrow A.I. has limits, because it lacks context. For instance, such an A.I. may recognize who I am but still not understand that I'm a person, and what this actually means.

So, at some point, for narrow A.I. to function optimally, it must take in more and more information from a wide variety of sources and be able to integrate all this information to make contextually appropriate judgments. And soon you're talking about AGI. When I first introduced the term *AGI* in 2004 or 2005, people didn't really understand the difference between AGI and ANI. Or they figured that true AGI wouldn't be achieved for thousands of years. Now the development community understands that AGI isn't only achievable, but necessary.

When we have sentient robots, who is going to own them? Can people "own" other sentient beings? And if we can't own them in the legal sense, what's the purpose of building them?

I find this whole question kind of mystifying. I have children whom I have helped create and whom I am raising, but I don't "own" them. AGI needs to be seen in the same way. Robots will be the children of our minds. Also, their consciousness is likely to be very different from ours. Human consciousness is itself barely understood, and we're going to have to do a lot more research into this area to understand what and how our intelligent machines "think."

You're also a big proponent of transhumanism, the theory suggesting that the human race can transcend its current physical and mental limitations through technology. Do you see something like this occurring within our lifetimes?

Well, in a way, it's already started. Look at me. I'm wearing these glasses. Without them, I'm badly impaired. Many older people wear electronic hearing aids. We use cars to augment our legs and get us rapidly from point A to point B.

We're all addicted to our smartphones. Go to Hong Kong and you'll see everyone looking at their phones instead of the street around them. Now, it's not that much of a leap between what we have now and wiring these machines directly into our brains. Yes, it's going to take some work, but these techniques are being developed even as we speak. And once it starts, it's going to catch on fast. I mean, your teenage daughter isn't going to sit idly by while her school friends IM each other via telepathic Wi-Fi, right? She's going to demand an implant too. We all are.

One imagines that, at least initially, these enhancements will be expensive and thus only available to the super-rich. Is that a fair assumption, and, if so, how is that going to impact the divide between the world's rich and poor?

I don't think enhancement will just be available to the super-rich. It will be available mostly to the upper and middle classes. That's about 20 percent of the world's population, which is still an issue, but this is the way things are now. I mean, the smartphone took millions of dollars to develop, but now you use the same smartphone that Bill Gates uses. Viagra took billions to develop, but everyone gets the same blue pill, regardless of their status. Billionaires may fly around in private jets, but they're not any faster than a commercial 747, just a bit more comfortable. Having a private yacht is nice, but there's no real economic advantage to having one, and, in the end, going out in your private yacht may not be any more fun than having a party with your friends at the local public swimming pool.

It will be the same with these enhancements. The only way to make them profitable will be to make them scalable, to make them available to the masses. The real challenge will be getting these new products to underserved areas like Africa. There are a lot of issues in these places that our current socioeconomic interests seem not inclined to solve because we're wrapped up with other issues like fighting wars over oil, or conducting trade wars between relatively rich countries like the United States and China.

What do you see life being like 100 years from now?
Obviously, it's impossible to predict with any accuracy. If you had asked someone from 1920 to describe what life in 2020 would be like, they would probably have missed the mark by a wide margin. What I can tell you is what I'd like to see. I'd like to see people have the option to basically upload their minds into a transhuman mind matrix and become part of a global brain, which would involve giving up your individual identity and a lot of what it means to be human, but then gaining a great union with other minds and an ability to have experiences and thoughts that go well beyond what an individual mind can fathom.

I'd also like to see people have the ability to remain in a human form while ridding themselves of physical and mental sickness. Imagine an environment where the tedious necessities of everyday life are taken care of by narrow A.I.s. In this future, robots are happy to take out the garbage, make you dinner, and 3D-print you whatever you want. There are a lot of books to read and musical instruments to play and mountains to climb and relationships to have.

So much more depth to the human experience would be possible to achieve than we can right now because we're too concerned with accumulating material resources and playing social status games while staving off death. When we solve the material scarcity problem and having "things" no longer becomes the be-all of human existence, I suspect that 95 percent of people will spend 95 percent of their time in virtual reality of some kind (if that's what they choose to do). I may well not be one of them, though. I am eager to enjoy what advanced VR has to offer, but I'm still also highly interested in building things in the real world.

A Conversation with Kriti Sharma
Pioneer in A.I. Ethics

Born in Rajasthan, India, **Kriti Sharma** is a world leader in artificial intelligence focused on applying machine learning and chatbots for social impact. Named by *Forbes* magazine as a top "30 under 30" in 2017, she is the founder of AI for Good (www.aiforgood.co.uk), a U.K.-based social enterprise. A board member at the Centre for Data Ethics and Innovation (appointed by the U.K. Secretary of State), an advisor to the United Nations and a participant in the Obama Foundation Summit, she holds a bachelor's degree in Engineering and a master's in Advanced Computer Science from the

University of St. Andrews. In 2010, she was awarded the Google India Women in Engineering Award for excellence in computer science and her work in promoting diversity in the tech industry.

Can you give us some details about your work in A.I. ethics and your involvement with AI for Good?

I have been involved with building technology for good since I was a child. Growing up in India, I saw technology as a means to scalably help solve social issues. It can be used to address some of the most pressing humanitarian challenges facing the planet today. For example, I am currently using A.I. to help people going through domestic violence and abuse, young people who don't have access to sexual and reproductive health services, and those without access to general healthcare. I find all this really, really exciting.

Could you speak more about how A.I. is helping in the area of domestic abuse?

Sure. One of my friends was a victim of domestic abuse, and this led me to do extensive research on the subject. I learned that one in three women will suffer abuse from their domestic partner at some time during their lifetime. Also, most victims are very reluctant to talk about the experience or ask for help. They're afraid of being judged.

So, I wondered, what if women could talk to a machine instead of a person? Would this change anything? I went down to Johannesburg, South Africa, where the rate of femicide and violence against women is the highest on the planet, to do some trials with women experiencing such abuse. Initially, I was afraid the women would be confused or even offended by the idea of talking to a machine—they'd want sympathy from a flesh-and-blood human being. As it turned out, the opposite was the case. These women really loved talking to an unbiased, nonjudgmental robot. They really opened up and started asking for help. We have very high engagement rates. I see great potential here, especially in countries where being the victim of sexual abuse carries a heavy social stigma.

Can you describe the organization you worked with and how it's helping the underserved through A.I.?

I worked with an amazing social justice institute called Soul City Institute for Social Justice in South Africa. They've been working in this field for decades. They bring all this expertise in communicating with victims. They know what works to drive behavioral change. We adapted their methods to our new technology. For example, they found one of the most effective ways to affect behavioral change is storytelling. People like to hear narratives about people who have gone through things similar to what they're experiencing.

This is something our bot, rAInbow, is able to do. It picks up key cues about a victim's situation and then draws upon a variety of scenarios, complete with established characters, to provide an instructive tale about next best steps. But it's done on a very personal level. For example, rAInbow will say, "I'd like to tell you a story about my friend, Amanda, and what happened to her." And then you'll follow Amanda's journey.

What were some key moments inspiring her to take action? What was the impact on her children?
Abuse is a complicated issue. Often, alcohol is involved and sometimes even incest. It's very difficult on the victim, especially those experiencing self-doubt. There are all of these different components that A.I. can weave into stories to personalize them so it's therapeutic to the person experiencing such trauma.

And people are really comfortable talking to a machine?
It usually takes someone unfamiliar with the experience a few minutes to get acclimated. But after that, it tends to go quite smoothly. There's a lot of pent-up need for something like this. In many cultures, abuse is not only common, but expected. Women, by tradition and necessity, are afraid to speak up. Doing so usually puts them in further danger. So, a safe, nonjudgmental, 24x7 bot is a desperately needed refuge.

Could you tell us about your involvement with A.I. ethics?
In my work, we tend to look at algorithms through a number of lenses. Perhaps the most important are the datasets. Are they truly objective and unbiased? I'll tell you a funny story. I was working on a face recognition panel, and the developers were having trouble getting their A.I. to recognize nonwhite women. I asked what datasets they were using to recognize Indian women. "Bollywood Films," one of the developers said.

Unfortunately, I don't look like a Bollywood actress. Most Indian women don't. Those females are ideals. A similar thing occurs when big corporations use A.I. to recruit senior management candidates. Most companies have a history of hiring older white men, disproportionately biasing the selection process based on past decisions.

If A.I. is really going to do its job, it's important to have as wide and varied a dataset as possible. Most of the time this kind of discrimination isn't intentional. It's just the result of following years of precedent. A racist, sexist database will produce a racist, sexist A.I. But if we're aware the problem exists, we can fix it.

You were selected to be one of the U.N.'s young leaders. What is the U.N. doing to improve the world, and what is your role in it?

The U.N. has created a list of 17 sustainable development goals it wants to achieve by 2030. These are very broad, audacious goals, like ending hunger, poverty, and disease worldwide. We know we are going to have to apply our most advanced technologies to these problems if we are going to solve them. I would love to make sure we use this new technology for global good instead of, you know, getting more ad clicks or making better cat videos.

Can you give us an example of how A.I. can be used to achieve one of these goals?

Certainly. Let's look at healthcare. In India, we are in the process of rolling out universal healthcare. Currently, 500 million people don't have access to doctors or healthcare services. The country has limited resources and not nearly enough doctors or other trained medical personnel to take care of everybody.

Here's where A.I. can help. We have already developed amazing diagnostic algorithms to identify diseases and other issues, even remotely. This way we can quickly and efficiently identify cases requiring immediate attention. A.I. can also provide information and guidance to human workers in the field, increasing their efficiency and efficacy exponentially.

Another area is education. With A.I., we can custom-tailor learning programs to the individual. This will help encourage more women to enter the tech field, especially those who feel intimidated by tech the way it is traditionally taught. I have found that when young people start to understand and master this technology, they immediately see ways to use it to solve social problems. They're not interested in just creating video games or building killer robots, but in using it instead to help people in need.

This is something that needs to get more media attention. We're always hearing sensational stories about how A.I. is going to take our jobs or start World War III, but not enough about how it's been applied for good. And that's where the real action is.

Right now, a lot of people are saying how important it is for young people to learn to code. I think that's a mistake. Pretty soon, computers will be able to code themselves and humans will be left to do the human stuff. That's where vision and creativity come into play. Think about the things humans are good at: emotional intelligence, problem solving, reasoning, empathy, connection. This is what people should be focusing on. We can use machines to do everything else.

A Conversation with Irakli Beridze, Frederic Werner, and Reinhard Scholl, Leaders of the U.N.'s AI for Good Initiative

Irakli Beridze, Frederic Werner, and Reinhard Scholl are key thought leaders for the United Nation's AI for Good initiative. Created jointly by the International Telecommunications Union (ITU) and XPRIZE, AI for Good promotes the use of artificial intelligence to address the most pressing global challenges, such as poverty, healthcare, and the environment.

Irakli Beridze heads the United Nations' Interregional Crime (UNICRI) Centre for Artificial Intelligence and Robotics. In 2014, he initiated the U.N.'s first A.I. and robotics program, bringing together representatives from nations throughout the world to establish training, educational, and monitoring protocols to manage the development of artificial intelligence for the benefit of all mankind. He continues to work for the peaceful and lawful development of A.I., helping stakeholders pursue new opportunities for advancement while identifying and mitigating risks.

Frederic Werner is the ITU's Head of the Strategic Engagement Division. He previously served as Communications & Program Director of ETIS, The Global IT Association for Telecommunications. He has helped the telecom industry create a pan-European community of cybersecurity experts. Currently responsible for communications and membership for ITU's standardization bureau, he was pivotal in the creation of the landmark AI for Good Global Summit. He also is heavily involved with innovation, digital transformation, financial inclusion, 5G, and A.I. through many ICT industry projects and events he has developed.

Dr. Reinhard Scholl is Deputy Director of the ITU-T Secretariat (TSB). He previously worked with Siemens in Munich, Germany, and with the European Telecommunications Standards Institute (ETSI). He holds a PhD in Physics from the University of Illinois and served on the Board of ICANN (Internet Corporation for Assigned Names and Numbers).

Could you provide a little background on the AI for Good summit?
FW: It grew out of the IBM Watson XPRIZE challenge, which is a highly leveraged, incentivized prize to motivate people to compete and originate A.I. solutions for good. The summit brings together people from various U.N. agencies as well as a broad cross section of industry and academia. A.I. experts will tell you this technology is too important to be left to the "experts," which is why we're trying to involve as many people as possible.

We have individuals from Silicon Valley, leading researchers from Harvard, MIT, Stanford, and Oxford, as well as representatives from the Red Cross, Amnesty International, and other organizations possessing a good understanding of problems at the ground level. It's important to recognize this isn't just talk and panel discussions. We're looking for practical solutions to real problems. The years 2020 and 2030 aren't that far away, so we have to start acting now.

RS: The U.N. has published a list of 17 sustainability goals it hopes to achieve by 2030. Accordingly, much of the summit's attention is focused on these areas, which range from poverty and education to healthcare and the environment.

Can you explain the A.I. Repository, what it is, and who participates?
RS: It's pretty simple. It's a database open to anyone who would like to submit a short description for a project they believe can use A.I. to meet one of the sustainable development goals. Much like open-source software, we are crowdsourcing ideas and insight to expand our knowledge base. As a result, we encourage the public to contribute their thoughts and solutions.

Do you see A.I. development ever becoming akin to the Cold War arms race or the space race, with countries vying to become the first to develop artificial general intelligence?
IB: I have been involved in issues of nonproliferation, working to control weapons of mass destruction involving chemical, biological, radiological, and nuclear weapons, so I know what an arms race looks like. Based on this experience, I can say, no, nothing like that is happening now. You can't have a race when no one knows what the finish line looks like. Yes, countries are working to extract the most out of A.I. for their own benefit, but this isn't like the race to be the first to build an atomic bomb or land a man on the moon. Every country has its own needs and is developing its own strategies for developing and adapting this technology.

FW: The U.N. represents 193 countries. They all have the same view, which is why they're supporting AI for Good. We've held summits for two years now, and there's a great sense of cooperation.

RS: AI for Good has worked to be as inclusive as possible. We're encouraging the participation of as many countries as we can get, as well as private companies and academia. We currently have over 30 U.N. organizations as partners, as well as the XPRIZE Foundation and the ACM (Association for Computing Machinery, a learned society for computing). For future gatherings, we hope to get more speakers from countries like China, Japan, and Korea. We don't have many Russian or Latin American participants yet, but we're working to improve this. We also need to make a big effort to reach out to developing countries. We're also trying to get more women involved. At the 2nd summit in 2018, about one-third of our speakers were women—that's pretty good for a tech conference. For the 2019 summit, we're hoping for a 50/50 ratio.

There's already a widening gap between the developed and developing worlds. Is there a danger A.I. will only accelerate this trend—rich countries will just get richer and leave everyone else behind?

IB: Yes, this is a possibility. The nations possessing the resources—intellectual and financial—are likely to develop more sophisticated levels of artificial intelligence first and reap most benefits as well. That's why we must work to make sure these advantages are not concentrated among a select few but shared by the whole world.

FW: Actually, it's probably the least developed countries with the most to gain from A.I. Conversely, they have the most to lose if we don't chart a responsible path for A.I. development and implementation. The U.N., being the U.N., is working to keep A.I. development inclusive and transparent, and to make sure A.I. helps all segments of society equally.

To be effective, A.I. needs to consider as many data points as possible. This often requires access to vast amounts of personal information. How do you see A.I. development balancing the need for mass data with people's desire for individual privacy?

IB: This is an issue the international community is currently wrestling with. No one wants to live under constant surveillance. Fortunately, there is a growing school of thought suggesting that A.I. may not be as dependent on Big Data as first believed. After all, a child doesn't need to see 10 million pictures of a cat to learn how to recognize a cat. Once an A.I. system achieves a sufficient level of knowledge, it may be able to function quite nicely without having to pry into the intimate goings-on of the entire human population. A.I. and privacy may not be mutually exclusive.

FW: Privacy and regulation are issues we recognize need to be addressed now. If we take a wait-and-see approach, in 10 or 15 years we could find ourselves looking back and saying, we really should have taken this or that into account when we had the chance. There's an awareness, a sense of urgency to create discussions now, before things run away from us. Actually, one of the big issues we've recognized is that while a vast amount of data exists, much of it is being closely held. It's siloed. A lot of it is valuable IP, or intellectual property, and the owners are not going to share it willingly. Our challenge is to merge datasets from different agencies and people who trust each other and can share data anonymously to facilitate a kind of sandbox environment to test different algorithms and see which work best.

The U.N. has developed 17 sustainability goals it hopes to achieve by the year 2030. Which of these do you think will be most positively impacted by A.I.?

IB: I believe A.I. will be particularly useful in delivering healthcare, providing quality education, and ending hunger throughout the world. I can easily imagine A.I. analyzing large quantities of healthcare data leading to scientific breakthroughs that might otherwise take decades to achieve. Analyzing trends, it can make predictions about disease outbreaks to better manage pandemics.

Using A.I., people in remote areas will be able to access medical specialists and treatments otherwise inaccessible. A.I. also has a lot to contribute to education in the form of virtual mentors and in developing learning plans tailored to individual students. In terms of ending hunger, A.I. and predictive analytics can greatly increase agricultural productivity and also help us more wisely and efficiently distribute food to where it's needed most.

FW: I see A.I. having a large impact on healthcare very quickly. With A.I., we can use mobile phones to detect conditions like skin cancer or even poisonous snake bites. There's already an app to analyze suspicious skin growths. And this isn't just for use in developing countries.

It's helpful in developed countries, like the U.K., where it can take up to one year to get an appointment with a dermatologist. I see lots of possibilities for A.I. to facilitate early detection and get people the treatments they need before little problems become big ones. We're also likely to see lots of focus on wearable tech, sensors offering real-time readings on heartrate, blood pressure, blood sugar, and so on. These will be used to incentivize people to pursue more healthy behaviors, leading to a lowering of healthcare costs as a whole.

RS: Let us look at an example of how A.I. is used to address the elimination of poverty. Step one is to discover where the poorest people actually live. It seems obvious, but it's actually a difficult task. The old way to do this was simply to go door-to-door, but this is time consuming, expensive, and often dangerous. A more modern way is to use satellite imagery relying on nighttime images, but that doesn't allow you to differentiate grades of poverty.

However, recently Stanford University used machine learning to show that daytime satellite images were much better than nighttime images for mapping poverty. In principle, their model can make predictions at any resolution by analyzing daytime satellite images.

Many futurists fear that A.I. will lead to massive unemployment, particularly in the area of lower-paying, repetitive jobs robots can accomplish more efficiently. How do we deal with the problem of human irrelevance?

IB: It's no secret that many people worry about this. We regularly see reports predicting A.I. will wipe out 20 to 70 percent of jobs. And we're not just talking about truck drivers and factory workers, but also accountants, lawyers, doctors, and other highly skilled professionals. But then I see reports that A.I. will also create more jobs than it replaces. They'll just be different kinds of jobs. One way or another, A.I.-induced unemployment is a risk we cannot dismiss out of hand.

I believe A.I. is likely to disrupt whole employment categories throughout the world and create millions of economic refugees. This is going to particularly impact social stability in the developing world. This is why we must act now to develop policies and strategies to deal with this inevitable upheaval.

Just as dangerous is the risk of A.I.-enhanced crime. A.I. is likely to make cyberattacks thousands of times more devastating than they are today. A.I. may also be used in political attacks in the form of impersonations, fake videos, face swapping, and other spoofing tools designed to undermine the credibility of political figures. And then there's the threat of criminals or terrorists using A.I. to stage physical attacks, using autonomous drones to attack targets or even individuals.

Finally, there is the existential danger we often read about in science fiction novels. There may come a time when we are no longer the most intelligent species on the planet. We've seen examples of how super-intelligence can go wrong, and how it can pose an existential threat to humanity. This is why we have to start formulating policies now.

To address A.I.-induced unemployment, there are basically three solutions now being discussed. One of the most popular is the universal basic income. This would involve A.I. taxation of some sort and a wealth redistribution to the population as a whole. This solution presents many problems because, to begin with, nobody knows how this wealth is actually going to be generated. There are many perplexing questions: how are you going to distribute it? Will people be generally happy without a sense of real contribution to society? That goes against the values of virtually every society on our planet. As the French philosopher Voltaire said: "Work keeps at bay three great evils: boredom, vice, and need."

The second type of solution involves workforce retraining. The problem here is we don't really know what skills will be needed 10 years from now, nor do we have the resources to continuously re-educate huge portions of our adult population. This becomes even more difficult when dealing with mature individuals—people in their 40s and 50s—who naturally find it harder to acquire a whole new set of skills in midlife.

The third solution is to slow the pace of technological change so societies can adapt to it gradually. Of the three solutions, this is probably the least realistic; when it comes to innovation, no one is going to slow down so everyone else can catch up. But whatever choice we make, many people are not going to be pleased.

RS. Ironically, I think the jobs requiring high degrees of empathy will be done better by machines than humans—jobs like doctors, nurses, or therapists. Humans can quickly get overwhelmed. When they get busy, they get distracted. They get impatient. Computers can focus better. They never get distracted and never lose their tempers. A computer could also be more ethical than a human. Given a set of rules, it's going to stick by them. It will eventually give you better advice on choosing a career path, where to go to school, and whom to marry. I think you'll have a lot of trouble finding an occupation where A.I. would not perform the work better than a person.

As we become more and more trusting of A.I., how likely are our current political institutions to survive in their current form? Why rely on imperfect and corruptible flesh-and-blood leaders when artificial intelligence can make better decisions for us?
IB: I cannot speak for the world, but if we actually develop an AGI capable of making better decisions than we can alone, I think we'll adapt to it. There is precedent for this. Take the stock exchange. We don't use exchange brokers

anymore. A.I. makes buying and selling decisions in fractions of a second, and everybody is happy about it. The same is true for autopilots on airplanes. We don't really question these things anymore.

Ideally, it would not be a bad idea to have some kind of world government ensuring the prosperity, happiness, and health of everyone. But in practice, I don't see us turning to a centralized world government. Instead, I envision national governments looking to A.I. for assistance in their decision-making, then acting locally. Hopefully, we will have some kind of international cooperation in place so we can use A.I. to elevate the status of half the world's population currently suffering.

RS: Actually, trust is becoming a major issue for the A.I. community. As much as A.I. can be used for good, it can also be used for bad. We already know computers can be used to steal identities, plunder bank accounts, and hold data for ransom. But it's going to get worse than that. It will soon come to the point where you can't trust anything you see or hear on the Internet. A.I. is already being used to make fake videos—put words into people's mouths. I don't know how that's going to end.

What are the chances a rogue country or organization develops AGI first and uses it to achieve some kind of economic or political domination?
IB: The reality is that creating something as powerful as AGI—or beyond that, super-intelligence—will require significant resources, a lot of scientific breakthroughs, and computational power beyond the abilities of a single nation or organization. It's far more likely that the wealthy, educated, and connected groups will get there before rogue states, organizations, or individuals bent on doing harm.

If or when A.I. produces solutions to problems like healthcare, hunger, and climate change, how will these solutions be implemented?
IB: That's an issue unto itself. On the ground, there has to be the political awareness and will to make these changes. Beyond that, we need available resources and funding, as well as the technology to demonstrate that the solutions do, in fact, work, and that they're scalable. Fortunately, if these solutions can be shown to work on a small scale, it may trigger a domino effect, initiating a groundswell of demand for these solutions elsewhere.

FW: The big issue is establishing a format for large-scale international cooperation. Data needs to be not only shared, but also shared in a common format. We need to create a standard that is robust, transparent, and stable. You can have data from hundreds of sources, but if it's not in the same format, how can it interact and interface? Technological innovation is evolving exponentially, but the bottleneck is always going to be, how do we share the data? This is a big, big challenge that is not even close to being solved.

RS: Another issue people are talking about is model testing and approval. Say you're a pharmaceutical company with a new drug. Your drug must be approved by your nation's healthcare administration, such as the FDA, before you can go to market with it, right?

This can take years of testing. We need the same process for models. ITU and WHO, the World Health Organization, launched a project at the 2nd A.I. summit to develop a benchmarking framework to allow for a standardized and transparent evaluation of A.I. methods. Imagine you're a start-up with a new model. There should be a place for independent testing. If you encounter problems, your organization can keep working to refine your model for subsequent testing. This back-and-forth will lead to greater effectiveness. Afterward, based on among other things the score in the standardized benchmarking, a model could be marketed as "certified" by medicine regulators such as the FDA (USA), EMA (EU), CFCA (China), or CDSCO (India).

How do you envision the world of 2050 for the average individual as a result of A.I.?

IB: Since we don't know exactly where A.I. development is headed, predictions are difficult to make. But I believe the world of 2050 will be a better one than we live in now. Yes, problems will remain, but I see most people enjoying happier, healthier, and longer lives, thanks to the impact of artificial intelligence.

RS: I think we'll turn to A.I. to make more and more decisions for us. A lot of people are talking about self-driving cars, but reliability in this space is difficult to achieve. Traditional telecommunication networks operate at something like 99.999 percent availability, translating into a downtime of the network of around 5 minutes per year. I suspect people are going to demand even more from autonomous vehicles—after all, mistakes here can prove injurious or fatal.

As a result, it's going to take a lot longer than people think. Overall, the A.I. evolution is going to be a continuous process. It's not going to happen overnight. Young people will probably be able to adapt the fastest. The kids today are growing up with A.I. tools in their smartphones, and for them A.I. will be normal. They're not afraid of it.

A.I. AND EMPATHY

A.I. Robots. Machine learning. It's natural to imagine these technologies as cold, calculating, and without emotion. As time-traveling warrior Kyle Reese tells waitress Sarah Connor in *The Terminator*, "It can't be bargained with. It can't be reasoned with. It doesn't feel pity, or remorse, or fear. And it absolutely will not stop . . . ever . . . until you are dead." Likewise, a common pejorative levied at people who appear coldblooded or aloof is to call them a "robot" or a "drone."

So in spite of the fact machines are well-known to lack feelings, perceptions surrounding this deficit are likely to change in the A.I. age. It may seem far-fetched, but today's developers are creating algorithms to not only detect human emotional states but respond appropriately in kind. A vast market is emerging for computers capable of expressing empathy, sympathy, caring, and even humor . . . without the flashes of anger, impatience, and frustration expressed by flesh-and-blood human beings. Perhaps, in the not-too-distant future, the greatest compliment one might bestow upon a doctor, nurse, or social worker is that they behave like a machine.

A Conversation with Scott Sandland and Todd Banhidy
Pioneers in Empathic A.I.-Powered Sales and Commerce

Scott Sandland is the cofounder and CEO of Cyrano.ai, a company combining artificial intelligence and emotional intelligence in commercial environments. Their algorithm allows machines to engage customers in natural conversations, identifying and responding to customers' emotions, commitment levels, and communication in real time. A Southern California-based entrepreneur, Sandland is a world-renowned hypnotherapist as well as an accomplished innovator and entrepreneur. He has been actively involved in the development and customization of multiple software platforms focused on continued education and professional networking.

Todd Banhidy is the founder and chief product architect of Buy It Installed Inc. The company uses a proprietary technological architecture and an advanced form of A.I., called artificial empathy, to increase online shopping conversion rates and decrease cart abandonment, product returns, and warranty claims. Another entrepreneur located in Southern California, Todd has more than 30 years of international field service experience and attended California State University-Los Angeles.

In the world of contemporary A.I., how do you define **empathy?**

SS: For a long time now, computers possessed decent voice recognition capable of understanding human speech. But language is much more complex than the literal words we use. Meaning is communicated through tone, context, and cultural filters. For example, if I invite you to my Super Bowl party and you say, "I'll try to be there," what you're really saying is, "Thanks, but I probably won't come."

You're being polite, and I understand that based on reading the social cues. What we're doing now is teaching machines to pick up on nuance and subtext containing the real message being communicated. There are all kinds of clues a computer can look for. Length of response. Type and variety of words chosen. Whether or not a response is direct or a deflection. Agreement or disagreement. The presence or lack of commitment words.

In order to train our system to detect these things, we used transcripts from actual sales encounters to look for linguistic clues allowing us to predict how the encounter would end. Once we identified these, we could categorize them and then use them to create a functional algorithm. To be sure, the algorithm isn't 100 percent predictive. It uses weighted averages to determine what you are *probably* saying and what response is *probably* the best. These odds increase as the machine interacts with people and learns over time.

TB: Artificial empathy is very much like artificial intelligence in that everyone in the industry has their own definition. We use empathy to mean the nonactionable part of being able to tell how a person feels. What you do with that information is the second part. With artificial empathy, a computer can mimic a human's ability to empathize or share feelings with another. This means a computer can ascertain what a person is feeling with abilities similar to those people use to do the same thing.

Consider your own empathetic powers. You meet a person and almost instantly feel either at peace or threatened. How do you do that? You're able to pick up cues, like facial expressions, body stance, tone of voice, and so on. And you base a lot of this on your personal experiences since you were a child. You remember dealing with people who were loving or angry or deceitful or sarcastic and what that looked and sounded like. We're doing the exact same thing with computers. There may be thousands or even millions of data points people use when creating empathy; we're trying to identify these, analyze these, and then make a computer do the same thing.

How effective have computers been in this field so far?

SS: Actually, our Cyrano algorithm has found cues and patterns even we weren't aware of. It's like AlphaGo, the self-teaching computer that learned to play Go before becoming even better at the game than its human creators. Cyrano has become better at predicting outcomes based on conversational exchanges than we are.

We see this as a sign of genuine creativity. Things are going on inside the machine's "head" we can't see or explain. To understand what I mean, it might be helpful to consider this analogy. Imagine a creation as being an assemblage of Lego pieces. Creative people—artists, comedians, writers, and so on— seem to have more Lego pieces than the average person, so they can put things together in ways normal people don't immediately consider. Robin Williams is a good example. He could take seemingly incompatible ideas and make a brilliant comedic connection. This is also what the best algorithms can do now. The more data we give them, the more Lego pieces they have to play with, and the more amazing connections and combinations they're able to generate. And, like a good stand-up comic, they work *fast*.

TB: We have found empathetic A.I. to be extremely effective in customer service situations. On the phone, a chatbot can pick up on a personality type just through word choice and tone of voice. *Is the caller someone who likes to chat, or do they just want to get to the point and get things over with? Also, where are they calling from? What kind of language works best for people from New York as opposed to Tennessee?* A.I. can pick up on these factors and be far more flexible than human customer service reps.

What's the advantage of developing empathetic A.I. to work in sales environments?

SS: An A.I. is able to think from a broader perspective than a human salesperson is. Most salespeople are short-sighted. They're looking for an immediate outcome rather than thinking about the lifetime value of the customer. A skillful A.I, on the other hand, can create a sales experience harmonious with the customer's needs and intentions rather than with the salesperson.

TB: We're using artificial empathy in what's called the "installed sales" industry. This involves the sales of both products and installation services for products, like doors, windows, and roofs. It's more like a horizontal market than a distinct industry because it cuts across a bunch of different industries, such as home improvement or business improvement.

With our A.I., people can communicate to a sales bot directly over the Web without the need for a human salesperson. So far, the results have been extremely encouraging. I expect this same tech will become widespread in any industry usually requiring strong human-to-human communication, like mortgage lending, where customers tend to be anxious and insecure throughout the process. Most sales encounters involve something like 5,000 steps before the sale is closed. If there is misunderstanding or miscommunication in any one of those steps, the sale can fall apart. That's why empathetic A.I. has the potential to be so effective. It's not going to become distracted or miss cues the way people can.

Do you believe empathetic A.I. can lead to robot therapists?

SS: Yes, I think that's going to happen. Not next year or the year after that, but eventually. Let's imagine a therapist has the best training and remembers everything and always cares. Now, this a best-case scenario that never happens, but let's say it does. Even then, a human ego can contaminate patient outcomes. Over time, a human's opinions can ossify. They can become close-minded. There will be times when even the best therapist is tired or hungry or eager to leave on vacation. Sometimes, the human therapist is just going through a bad day.

Up until now, humans have still been better than machines because the tech wasn't there yet. But when it is, everything will change. People won't have to go to an office to get help. They'll be able to do it from home, on their phone or computer, or an Alexa-like device. People already seek support from Facebook groups and talk radio shows. It's not a big leap to imagine them turning to A.I. for help instead of human therapists.

TB: I suspect interactions between humans and machines with empathetic A.I. will be better than an empathetic exchange with a human. Why? Because humans have to divide their attention between the other person and their own self-promotion. We all have our own hierarchy of needs.

But empathy is about giving. You have to turn your mind off, you have to let the mirror neurons fire in your mind. Do you really understand what the other person is feeling? I think people, at best, can focus 30 percent of their energy on another person. But computers can focus 100 percent. A computer will also have a knowledge base far outstripping even the most educated, experienced human therapist. And a machine will never be judgmental. It's very hard to open yourself fully to another person for fear of being judged.

All of this sounds positive in theory, but might empathetical powers be used for evil instead of good?

TB: Any technology can be weaponized. You can use a pot of boiling water as a weapon if you choose to. Right now, people use A.I. as a persuasive tool, to induce people to act in a certain way. I suppose you could call this artificial manipulation. But I think the real power lies in using it properly, allowing people to understand each other better, to build trust and cooperation, to persuade individuals to do things beneficial for themselves and for others.

Could an A.I. become conscious or have a soul?

SS: Immediately, this begs the question, where does consciousness reside? Is it just electricity in meat, or is it something grander? I think machines will be able to *simulate* consciousness. For example, they will be able to avoid fire, even though they would never actually experience physical pain. They will be able to *act* joyful, sad, or even angry, but they will never be able to existentially experience joy or sadness or anger. There's an old Russian expression: "Pretend to be a good person often enough and you will fool even God." It means that if you consistently behave a certain way, this is how everyone will perceive you. And ultimately that's the only thing that matters. Even for algorithms.

A Conversation with Leila Toplic
Former Refugee and Head of NetHope's
Program for Refugee Youth

Leila Toplic is a former refugee and refugee school teacher herself. She leads two "tech for good" initiatives at NetHope, a nonprofit technology consortium of 50+ global nonprofits. Emerging Technologies Working Group is a sector-wide approach to integrating A.I. and blockchain in humanitarian, development, and conservancy work. No Lost Generation Tech Task Force brings together the experts in humanitarian response (UN:NGO agencies) with the private-sector expertise and resources to address the needs of refugee children and youth, including education, employment, and protection.

Prior to NetHope, Leila was part of the leadership teams for two social enterprises each focused on using technology to connect people with education and work, in the U.S. and internationally. She spent 13 years in the tech sector, at Microsoft and Adobe.

Could you please tell us about NetHope and its mission?

NetHope is a nonprofit technology consortium of 57 global NGOs, collaborating with dozens of different tech companies. We bring together the largest nonprofits with technology innovators, focusing on addressing specific problems across the humanitarian, development, and conservancy spaces. Founded 17 years ago, the NetHope consortium includes some of the largest and most prominent humanitarian, development, and conservancy NGOs, such as the International Rescue Committee, Oxfam, Save the Children, Mercy Corps, Médecins Sans Frontières, The Nature Conservancy, and the World Wildlife Fund.

We support our members in four ways: One is what we call supporting practical innovation. We specifically help NGOs evaluate, design, and implement tech-enabled responses to improve their work. So, whether it's in disaster response or refugee education, we consider the role technology can play in helping us do good, better.

Second, we simplify and streamline utilization of technology. We make it easier to locate, purchase, and integrate technologies in inexpensive and simple ways. We also share those best practices across our members. Third, we work directly with tech teams at NGOs to build organizational capacity, specifically by helping our members understand the value of technology and how they can best integrate it into their programming. Fourth, we encourage both sector-wide change and sector-wide sharing through learning tool kits, program design, and evaluation frameworks to collectively learn from each other and, again, do good work better.

What's your background? How does it translate to your current work with NetHope, particularly addressing the problem of education?

I'm a former refugee from Bosnia. The war in Bosnia started when I was 14. We stayed until I turned 18, because we were hoping that the war would end and that we wouldn't need to leave our home. Nobody wakes up one day and says they want to flee everything they love and know and want to become refugees. People who become refugees see no other choice.

It became clear in the summer of 1995, given all the terrible things that were happening in Bosnia, that we needed to find a way out to save our lives. We fled on buses through the humanitarian corridor that was set up in the battle zone, and ended up in Hungary, where UNHCR took us to a refugee camp in Southern Hungary. It was former military barracks set up for refugees coming from the former Yugoslavia.

My first significant connection to technology occurred in a refugee camp in Southern Hungary in the mid-90s. There, I had my first experience working with computers, which ultimately led me to study computer science and media arts and sciences at Wellesley and the MIT Media Lab. This led me to work in the tech sector at Adobe and Microsoft. I was really interested in understanding what problems technology can solve and how to implement the solutions.

After 13 years at Adobe Systems and Microsoft, I decided to combine my personal experience as a refugee with my passion for technology and background in the private sector to drive collaboration between the humanitarian and private sectors, with a focus on tech-enabled programs for conflict-affected children and youth.

The common thread in my life has been technology. Technology is an important part of the work I do at NetHope with the No Lost Generation Tech Task Force and Emerging Technologies Working Group. Both initiatives bring together experts in humanitarian response with the technology experts (from tech companies and academic institutions) to explore how technology could be used to help us solve problems ranging from natural disaster response and recovery, to disease outbreaks, poverty, and education for millions of refugees.

Why does A.I. matter for NetHope members? What are some of the examples of how A.I. can help solve humanitarian, development, and conservancy challenges?

According to NetHope's Center for Digital Nonprofit study, nonprofits play a $40 billion role in the delivery of international aid. At the same time, we in the nonprofit sector increasingly see the widening gap between available resources and growing needs. So effective integration of technology into humanitarian, development, and conservancy programs, whether it's connectivity and hardware or A.I. and blockchain, coupled with a strong M&E can enhance the impact of that budgeted dollar to help us close the gap. To give you a sense of what this means, every 5 percent increase in effectiveness of the NGO sector translates into $2 billion of enhanced annual global impact.

While A.I. holds the promise of helping us do good better, its application in international development is still very nascent, raising a lot of questions from our members related to people, process, and technology. The direction of A.I. cannot, and should not, be driven by tech companies and the commercial sector alone. Active participation from nonprofits, from policy makers, from academia, as well as the end users, like refugees, will ensure the problems (or use cases) we focus on are inclusive of some of the highest priority needs, goals, and principles. How we define, design, implement, scale, and maintain technology solutions has an ethical impact on people's lives. Nonprofits have an obligation to have an adequate understanding of what those technologies can do and the implications on their work and populations they're supporting.

What role can A.I. play in connecting displaced children and youth to education?

We're in the early days of applying A.I. in the social impact sector. Many of the current examples of applied A.I. in our sector are in POC stage. In the AI for Good sessions at NetHope's 2018 annual summit, we discussed several examples, including:

- Predicting food insecurity in Malawi
- Detecting online hate-speech content for removal
- Digital credit scoring and agricultural input loans
- Early warning systems for earthquakes in Mexico
- Identifying Zika virus reservoirs in the Americas

One of the POCs I've been working on to productize and ultimately scale is focused on enabling broad access to online educational content by underserved populations, like millions of refugee youth in the Middle East. Making educational content visible and accessible to young people in the region will enable them to access dignified work and contribute to their communities in a positive way as teachers, doctors, or entrepreneurs solving problems their communities face.

While there are many free educational resources available, they are not easily discoverable and accessible by some of the most vulnerable people on the planet. First, discovering what is available and relevant is cumbersome and takes a lot of time, which is a barrier for young people whose time is taken up by work to support themselves and their families, and their access to connectivity is limited as well. Second, to truly access and benefit from the content, content needs to be available in their language. In the Middle East and North Africa, Arabic is a predominant language. Yet a lot of learning resources are not available in Arabic.

This is where A.I., with natural language processing capabilities and real-time translation, can be incredibly helpful. NetHope is working with one of our members—Norwegian Refugee Council—along with Microsoft and University College Dublin, with support from Lero Research Institute to develop a chatbot called Hakeem to enable youth to discover and access relevant learning content like language, entrepreneurship, coding, marketing, and design courses—anywhere and anytime.

We're using A.I. and other capabilities available in Skype to address the issue of discoverability and access to educational content while leveraging what youth are already used to and enjoy doing—chatting in Skype, Facebook, WhatsApp, or Viber. Conversational UI can guide young people from a broad learning category like Business to a specific focus area like entrepreneurship to an exact course—just like a virtual learning companion. Additionally, it provides an experience that is more interactive and tailored than a website— through relevant content and notifications—which we've seen from our testing so far. This compels youth to come back again and again, increasing the likelihood of creating lifelong learners.

You might think of it as a virtual learning companion helping a young person discover what's available and relevant to them in the context in which they live. Instead of spending hours searching for this kind of content on the internet themselves, the chatbot could quickly connect them to the right learning resources so they can actually spend their time on learning.

What can be done to ensure the technology being built—such as A.I.—is truly reaching and benefiting all?

Simply building the technology is not the same as making it relevant and accessible, and also affordable, for everyone. Likewise, keeping the knowledge of how these tech solutions are being created in the hands of a few experts in places like Silicon Valley or Seattle is not going to empower all people to be creators of solutions for their communities. Knowledge of technologies like A.I. needs to be transferred from a few experts at tech companies and research institutions to many, including humanitarian staff and affected communities, so they can become active participants and creators of solutions and better informed about how A.I.-powered products and services might impact them in their work and daily lives. That can happen through training or through the process of co-creation of A.I.-enabled solutions which would in turn inform how technologies might evolve in order to meet a diverse set of needs, across a diverse set of contexts.

Additionally, while technology is a powerful tool and it can be an equalizer, it's never the starting point for doing good. We do not start with how we might use A.I. or a chatbot. It's critical to first understand the needs of the target audience in the context in which they live. The other important thing and one of the best ways to avoid technology missing the mark or becoming irrelevant as soon as a humanitarian agency is gone—is to be inclusive from the start by co-designing with end uses for the communities in which the affected people live.

For example, with Hakeem bot, we started with research conducted by the youth and UN:NGO agencies working in the MENA region. They've been instrumental in the development of a chatbot persona that's both engaging and relevant to them. They gave it the name Hakeem and thought it would be important to provide it the persona of an older brother or sister, not a parent or teacher. They also continually provide feedback on the bot's content and features. Codesigning with the youth helps us ensure the product is highly relevant and compelling, so they will recommend it to their friends, regardless of whether humanitarian agencies or their parents tell them to use it or not.

How do you see educational A.I. advancing over the next 10 years? What do you think educational A.I. will look like in the year 2030?

Personalization is one of the areas where I hope we'll see some change soon. Instead of a one-to-many model where a teacher broadcasts information, we'll transition to a greater level of personalized and individualized learning in which machines can assist in curating (across multiple sources) and supporting custom-tailored learning pathways that make lifelong learning sustainable and accessible to a lot more people. I see Hakeem bot as a node in that personalized experience, making anywhere, anytime access to quality learning possible especially in the places where teachers and mentors are scarce or not available.

Another aspect of future personalized learning is affective computing, where a machine could recognize and interpret human affects (emotions) and apply that to support the individual's learning experience. Let's say someone is struggling while working on a math problem; a machine might adapt the learning experience for more positive learning outcomes.

I also see us improving on the proof of learning and assessment of learning. Proof of learning is currently limited to formal education or some of the online learning opportunities, like Udacity. Yet, proof of learning is an important signal for unlocking future opportunities like jobs or further education. While learning happens everywhere—in school, online, in libraries, in parks – we're currently not capturing learning outside of the formal setting. With A.I. and other tools we should be able to capture learning where it happens, assess it, and document it.

What can technology experts (companies, academic institutions) do to support NetHope members?

In addition to supporting knowledge transfer, which I covered above, resources are necessary for NGOs to explore and incorporate A.I. into their programming. Funding could be in the form of grants, employee volunteering, product donations (e.g., Azure credits).

Involve humanitarian experts in defining how A.I. gets developed, applied, and used. While nonprofits need to learn about A.I., technologists need to be aware of the societal problems that need to be solved, contexts in which they exist, and needs of the populations that are typically not prioritized for emerging technologies.

A.I. capabilities should be made available as externally facing services, which companies like Microsoft are starting to do with their cognitive services, allowing individuals to build their own applications and businesses on top of the platform.

What are the necessary conditions for making tech-powered solutions like Hakeem accessible and usable by all in the contexts in which they live?

There are a number of conditions that should be considered when designing, implementing, and sustaining tech-enabled solutions. I'll mention a few. Certain resources and infrastructure are necessary for making other services possible—NetHope has worked for many years to bring *connectivity* to some of the most remote and destroyed places around the world. Connectivity empowers local communities as well as those who are serving them with access to life-saving information. Connectivity enables a teen in Jordan to actually use the Hakeem chatbot. Another condition that is critical for inclusive design of tech-enabled solutions is having *data* that is representative of the populations we're supporting, and data context. There are 3.9 billion people that are not connected to the Internet, which means that our understanding of their lives, needs, behaviors is limited.

Another condition is *identity*. Over 1 billion people around the world lack a way to prove who they are, which makes it difficult for them to access things like education, healthcare, and other services.

So, the first focus must be solving some of the baseline problems that have been around for decades. One of the key ways to tackle those problems is through a *collective impact model* for action. In order to deliver both immediate but lasting impact, it's important to coordinate intervention through collaboration. For the humanitarian agencies, this means shifting from implementing as an individual NGO to working together or incubating and sharing with all agencies. For example, we're incubating Hakeem bot with the Norwegian Refugee Council for 30+ U.N. and NGO agencies. For the tech sector, it means collaborating with other tech companies and humanitarian agencies to ensure that the intervention is complementary vs. duplicative, additive vs. one-off, relevant vs. wasteful.

Technology may not be the solution to everything, but it is an important tool in our toolbox for making the world a better place for all. It is our collective responsibility—technologists and humanitarian experts, alike—to ensure that what we build, how we build it, and who gets to participate in the creation and usage of technology is inclusive and empowering.

A Conversation with James Campbell, Steve Hellen, and Erwin Knippenberg, Working in Partnership with Catholic Relief Services Working in Africa

James Campbell is a monitoring, evaluation, accountability, and learning technical advisor in the Southern Africa Region for CRS. Possessing more than 20 years of experience, he provides leadership to strengthen organizational, staff, and partner capacity to design and implement effective monitoring and evaluation systems. He has worked in the aerospace industry as a systems engineer, as an applied researcher with a focus on contemporary public health and biomedical issues in developing countries, and as a lecturer in the Department of Community Medicine at the University of Zambia. Campbell holds a bachelor's degree in civil engineering and a master's in biostatistics.

Steve Hellen holds a master's in environmental science and policy, a bachelor's in engineering science, and a graduate certificate in Geographic Information Systems (GIS). With over 20 years of IT experience, he joined Catholic Relief Services (CRS) in 2012, where he heads the agency's ICT4D (Information and Communications Technologies for Development) and GIS practice. In 2016 he led an update of CRS's ICT4D strategy to focus on data analytics, scale, and enabling programs and partners. Prior to joining CRS, Hellen served as an IT Director at Johns Hopkins University. He taught computer science courses at Loyola University and an undergraduate GIS course at Johns Hopkins.

Dr. Erwin Knippenberg is Lead Economist at Cooper/Smith, a D.C.-based start-up using data to drive innovations in public health and food security.

Knippenberg holds a PhD in Applied Economics from Cornell University, where he wrote his dissertation on resilience and food security in the context of climate change. As a consultant at the World Bank, he used machine learning algorithms to inform poverty targeting. His analytical work on the MIRA project forms a cornerstone of his ongoing research. Prior to teaching at Cornell, Knippenberg was an Overseas Development Institute Fellow at the Liberian Ministry of Finance. He helped establish the development coordination unit, working closely with donors on aligning projects with national priorities. Knippenberg holds an MSC in Economics for Development from Oxford (2012) and a joint BS/MA from Georgetown University's School of Foreign Service (2011).

Could you please describe how A.I. is helping Catholic Relief Services provide needed humanitarian aid to people in Malawi and Madagascar?
JC: The biggest problems faced by most of the households in both of the countries we work with are high levels of poverty, combined with a chronic vulnerability caused by food and nutrition insecurity. This is exacerbated by the effects of climate change and impacts the livelihoods of the people we serve.

We're employing A.I. technology to help us develop a more detailed understanding of the shocks and other stressors inhibiting households from moving up the pathway to prosperity. A.I. allows us to identify conditions that explain certain outcomes in the face of shock. More specifically, it explains variations in recovery from shocks observed over time across a set of well-being outcomes, like food security and poverty.

We started one study in Malawi in 2016, following a flood that displaced 250,000 households. We wanted to determine the impact that some of our project activities would have in relation to households recovering from such a covariate shock (major floods, drought, hurricane, cyclones). We're using machine learning to predict certain outcomes, explicitly how households can recover from covariate shocks and other kinds of stressors.

SH: Our work in Malawi specifically uses machine-learning algorithms to predict at an individual household level how likely they are to deal with some of these external stressors. Having such a visibility into a specific family is a dramatic improvement over some of the tools that have been generally available providing a sense, in a larger geographic area, of where vulnerabilities might occur. Achieving more precise predictions can be a helpful tool to improve how interventions are delivered.

How did you go about creating your predictive models?

JC: To ensure the data we're collecting is complete and accurate, we've developed a community engagement component for this study. The data is collected monthly from a total of 2,200 households in Malawi and about 600 households in Madagascar during a two-week period each month.

Once the data is synced and uploaded to the server, our team reviews it for accuracy and completeness. If there's any inconsistency or clarification is required, the team liaises with the enumerators and community members to address errors and validate the findings. We work together closely with these communities to try to get them to take ownership of the system. We also coordinate with the village development committees, who are engaged by the community to identify and develop mitigation plans.

We share the results with them, and they in turn share the results with other community members, leaders, and so on, as well as with district-level personnel. We want the local citizens to take ownership because if they see the usefulness of this information—and not as something being imposed on them by outsiders—we think the positive consequences will perpetuate.

EK: I was formerly a PhD candidate at Cornell University; I graduated this May. This project is the cornerstone of my thesis. I contributed to the data collection, but I also designed a lot of the analytics. The idea was to develop a predictive model based on relatively sparse data, knowing that needed information was hard and potentially expensive to collect, especially monthly.

We wanted to see how we might best predict future shocks and future food security as experienced by the households themselves based on a limited set of indicators. There's a growing literature in development around proxy means testing, which is essentially based on the question that if you can only choose 10 or 15 or 20 indicators to predict poverty, how do you determine what the best 15 or 20 indicators are?

Traditionally it's been more linear regression; but increasingly entities like the World Bank and various researchers have started using more sophisticated algorithms, including lasso, random forest, and neural networks. We wanted to use the data we're collecting here on the ground in Malawi to identify the best predictors of food security and of poverty, based on those indicators. I narrowed it down to two algorithms best suited to our needs, lasso and random forest, and essentially trained my data on the first set of observations, the first 10 months or so of the year. We then inferred the predictive power on the subsequent months of the year to see how well we could forecast forward, compared to the actual outcomes. What this allowed us to do is narrow it down to a set of 10 to 12 key indicators, some of which were sort of obvious things, like where people lived and how much livestock they had, but some were less obvious, including how far people had to walk to get to drinking water.

How did the results from your predictive models jibe with realities on the ground?

JC: They matched up extremely well. Some of the other things the model doesn't provide for are social networks, social cohesion, and specifically household incomes and how these may affect resilience at household levels and vulnerability to shock. Although we did include some of these issues in our questionnaires, it's not really reflected in the predictive models. And some of these things are difficult to get at, especially in a resource-poor setting, things like incomes—because most of these people don't have incomes—you have to look at productive assets, and it varies. They have a barter system, so it's pretty difficult to learn some of these things.

Do you see leaders in impoverished countries being able to eventually use A.I.-enabled modeling to help themselves rather than depend on the largess of international agencies and groups like CRS?

SH: Yes, absolutely. You know, if we look at where A.I. is getting the most frequent use, I would argue that it's in tools where the fact that there's A.I. or machine learning behind the scenes is completely obscure to the end user. I'm thinking of consumer tools like Google Translate and Alexa. I think the application of A.I. to the aid and development sector will move more quickly when the tools are democratized, meaning when they are more accessible to users without deep expertise.

One of the developments I'm really optimistic about in this space is some of the work that Microsoft is doing. They have, for a number of years, been packaging a number of A.I. tools in what are called Azure Cognitive Services. They're now taking a step further and embedding those tools into a data-visualization product called Power BI. This will put things like image recognition, text analytics, and key driver analysis into the hands of many, many more people.

Having said all of that, in the current state, artificial intelligence still requires a lot of customization to meet the needs of specific contexts. Taking what we did in Malawi is not as easy as cutting and pasting to apply it to Madagascar. We have to figure out what those predictors are in the Madagascar context. Until these tools become more packaged, there's still a lot of customization that's needed to apply them to a specific context.

It's all about the enabling environment. From a nation's policy perspective, having effective institutions, having an education system that's preparing citizens who can take advantage of these tools. There are really impressive things coming out of some universities in the global south—for example, at Makerere University in Uganda, they have a center focused on artificial intelligence and data science that's already doing impressive work to meet the very contextual needs of that particular country.

JC: As I mentioned before, the majority of areas that we work in are resource poor. There's limited infrastructure, like no paved road or electricity. The other issue is that in some cases there is no network coverage, although this also has improved over the past seven to 10 years. Additionally, literacy is a problem in some of these areas. All this is to say that we're constrained in the types of technologies we can introduce in the communities we serve since our goal is to empower the people using the resources they have at their disposal. This is the only way we can sustainably help communities develop without causing any internal conflicts.

Many A.I. experts predict that this technology will eventually—perhaps sooner rather than later—lead to a general improvement in living standards worldwide, with the developing world looking to particularly benefit. Do you see an eagerness in Africa to embrace A.I.? If so, do you think the spoils will indeed be shared equally?

SH: I'm an optimist, so the answer to both would be yes. You know, what really struck me most when I started work in the aid and development sector is that there's this absolutely incredible drive and ambition, particularly among the burgeoning youth population.

There's a new generation that has access to information, frankly, like no other before and that's eager to use any and all available tools, like A.I., to improve living standards. As with any innovation there will be positive as well as negative results. And we can make analogies to the Internet. I would argue that the positive outcomes in terms of access to knowledge and communication tools have outweighed downsides that are very real, such as information bubbles and the digital divide. We need to constantly strive to address those shortcomings, but not try to prevent that innovation from having a greater overall purpose.

And I think in the A.I. space, it's a tool to create automation. If we look at history as a precedent, humanity realizes more benefits from automation than downsides, but there have been downsides, and the results have not been equally shared. I would attribute most of that to greed at some level, but the aggregate improvement to the human condition has been positive. We will always have those forces of greed or selfishness that are at odds with the common good, but it's up to us to choose to be on the right side of that, to support equity, to support inclusion, and to uphold human dignity.

A.I. AND EDUCATION

In an economy increasingly demanding specialization from its participants, education is key to both personal success and overall societal well-being. As well-paying manufacturing jobs become just a distant memory, possessing a bachelor's degree is, at minimum, now all but required to pursue the American Dream. At the same time, traditional educational methods fail to work for large segments of the population. An estimated 50 percent of today's elementary and high school-aged students cannot read at their grade level. Worse, 20 percent of today's teenagers will never finish high school. And, of the two million people who start college every year, more than half, 54.8 percent, drop out before earning their diploma.

For decades, professional educators have sought a way to make education more effective. Realizing that not all people have the same level of intelligence, or learn the same way or at the same rate, personalization is considered a promising approach to improving educational outcomes in the twenty-first century. But personalization is labor-intensive and expensive. Behold, Artificial Intelligence. It may hold answers that educators have long been seeking.

A Conversation with Jay Connor
Leader in A.I.-Powered Education

Jay Connor is the founder/CEO of Learning Ovations, a company dedicated to solving today's education challenges through technology. Since 2005, his company's learning assessment software, a2i, has been developed, evaluated, and scaled with support from the U.S. Department of Education, principally IES, the Institute of Education Sciences, as well as the National Institutes of Health/National Institute of Child Health and Human Development (NIH/NICHD).

Needed research was conducted in multiple locations, including the University of California–Irvine, the University of Michigan, Arizona State University, and the Florida Center for Reading Research. a2i is presently used in hundreds of schools across the country with the goal of improving students' literacy outcomes. Learning Ovations is implementing the United2Read project following the announcement of a five-year EIR expansion grant totaling $14.65 million. The EIR award provides funding to expand and evaluate innovative, evidence-based programs designed and proven to improve student achievement at a individual level.

It's no secret that helping children to read early is a major challenge for our educational system. Can you describe why this is such a catastrophe?
Yes, it's a huge problem in the United States. Fewer than 50 percent of our children are reading at their grade level, and if you're talking about high-need or high-poverty populations, this number is below 20 percent. If you're not reading successfully by the end of the third grade, you're consigned to being behind the rest of your life. According to research, failing to achieve early learning proficiency can cost you a quarter of a million dollars in lifetime earnings. Plus, you're six times more likely to get involved with the criminal justice system. You will also have poorer health outcomes over the course of your life. In this area, we as a society have been failing for over 30 years.

And your A.I. is designed to improve these outcomes?
Our a2i program has been around for almost 15 years, long before A.I. reached the stage where it is today. We partnered with the Department of Education and the National Institutes of Health to support and scale research from observing children performing in classrooms. Our objective was to discover what kinds of instruction enable students to read at the appropriate grade level.

This allowed us to support teachers and make recommendations about the curriculum. Where A.I. comes into play is that our approach is tremendously human-centric. We needed to have lots of human hours and vast amounts of data to make our determinations. The real value of A.I. technology in our project was our ability to support numerous teachers to individually respond to students via indexing.

What is "indexing"?
Indexing means taking what is already in a school's curriculum—items the school system has already invested heavily in—and using these proprietary activities in just the right amounts to get a specific child up to grade level. Skills vary significantly between individuals, so you need to be able to respond to individual needs.

Our A.I. takes the resources a classroom has available, such as textbooks and multimedia assets, and converts them so they can be individualized instead of using them to teach everyone the same thing the same way. We have done this manually, but it was just too time-intensive to allow us sufficient cost leverage to make this breakthrough method of achieving outcomes affordable for all school districts across the country. A.I. reduces a year's worth of work to minutes. To be clear, though, we're not asking schools to throw out everything they've paid for or developed and start from scratch. Instead, we are showing them how to use what they already have more effectively.

Are you up and running?

We first had to ensure that Watson could actually learn all our research protocols, and we established it could. The next step was to train it to use a variety of media. Currently, we've only used PDFs. But there's also video and other media we want Watson to apply to various situations. That's where we're at now. We're very close.

Using algorithms you developed, what kind of outcomes have you achieved?

We worked with many high-needs populations where only 20 percent of the students could read at grade level. In these same populations, we now have 94 percent of kids reading at their grade level. The average reading outcome is a fifth-grade reading rate. So all children struggling are able to improve at their own rate.

Has there been push-back from teachers who don't like being told how to do their jobs?

There's often resistance at some level. A teacher who has been teaching the same way for 25 years isn't going to want to change overnight. But most teachers understand our A.I. to be a helpful tool to get them to where they want to be faster and with far less frustration. Most of them are eager to get on board with this.

Could you use this same system with adults to improve adult literacy?

To some extent, yes. We could skew younger or we could go older, but we've focused on this sweet spot of K-3 because this is where we get the best results. Having said that, using this same thought process, we could make the level of achieving adult literacy much better than what's presently in place.

Could this same A.I. be used in other education environments, such as in private industry or the military?

With adjustments, yes. The first step is always to properly characterize the current situation. Then you have to be able to describe the ideal situation. The A.I. then acts as a bridge between the status quo and what you want things to be.

How do you know your technology works?

The way we know it works is much like if you were going to test out an artificial heart implant. To do so, the FDA would insist you go through a number of randomized trials. Our work with the U.S. Department of Education and N.I.H. has undergone the same level of rigor and research. More importantly, the data speaks for itself. As I mentioned, in those same at-risk populations, the new literacy achievement rate is 94 percent. It's important to note that I am not a politician. I am not trying to secure governmental buy-in. My organization is focused on collaborating with teachers on the ground.

Recently, I was in upstate New York, and we had about 40 teachers together. Now in the past, what officials tried to do was talk teachers out of using their own materials. That just creates resistance. Instead, what we can do now with A.I. is say, "Let's just have IBM Watson look at it. Watson will tell us whether this activity achieves the research rigors, what the standards covered are, what it'll accomplish." Then, provided the activity conforms with what the research tells us, you can make the choice whether you want to include it in your curricular activities and/or make it available to other teachers across the country.

How was this received? I am happy to report the energy level in the room couldn't have been higher. The teachers were ecstatic. Why? At that moment, no one was thinking about politics or educational philosophies. Everyone was focused on the one thing that matters: a solution—learning what it takes to get all our kids reading.

A Conversation with Joe Adams
Head of California's Discovery Cube

Joe Adams is chief executive officer of the nonprofit Discovery Science Foundation and president of the renamed Discovery Cube Orange County science center in Santa Ana, California, south of Los Angeles. He is a former theme park designer for the Walt Disney Co., who helped raise $25 million for the Cube's expansion starting in 2003.

Please give us a quick overview of the Discovery Science Foundation,
its history, and its mission.

The Discovery Science Foundation has been around for over 30 years. We started as a hands-on learning center attached to an elementary school. About 20 years ago, we established a permanent center at our current site, just off the I-5 Santa Ana Freeway in Orange County (O.C.).

When I joined as CEO 15 years ago, my principal challenge was to create exhibits and experiences supporting the education students were getting at schools here in O.C. We wanted to help kids understand the scientific principles and concepts they were learning in the classroom. We now have three sites: the Discovery Cube here in Santa Ana, another Discovery Cube in Los Angeles, and Ocean Quest down in Newport Beach. All fall under the umbrella of the Discovery Science Foundation.

Over the years, we've grown beyond just supporting classroom science to focus on science in the world around us. We have a big emphasis now on environmental sciences as well as science for healthier living. We also have a subset for early learners, kids still in their very formative years. I firmly believe getting a head start is the only way to achieve success later in school. This is true for people of all ethnic backgrounds.

We have four levels of programs. A Level 1 program just involves hands-on learning in the center itself. By the time we reach Level 4, students have taken what they've learned into their homes and schools. For example, we have a Level 4 conservation program responsible for saving 50 million gallons of water since its inception.

We're now part of a nationwide network of more than 200 community science centers working with states and school districts to establish the next generation of science standards and promote the use of sound scientific principles in the community and at home. Our mission is to promote scientific literary and to make scientific thinking a part of everyday life.

How are you using A.I. as part of your scientific curriculum?

Right now, we're still trying to figure out the best ways to apply artificial intelligence. I believe we can use A.I. to make our exhibits more dynamic and flexible, and to take visitors to places they've never been before. It's important to note that we're not a collection-based museum. We're not here to look at the past, but to focus on the future. And A.I. is certainly a big part of that.

How do the Cube's educational programs differ from what's being taught in traditional K-12 classrooms?

For one, our staff works with the state of California when creating new science standards, so we're among the first to roll these programs out when they're introduced in the schools. Beyond that, elementary teachers tend to be generalists. They teach math, history, and social studies in addition to science. We're purely science-focused, so our programs tend to go into far greater depth compared to what students learn in the classroom. We want to make science really cool and exciting, so when the kids go back to school, they're more eager than ever to learn.

Who is your target market?

Our target market is the sixth- to eighth-grader. By middle school, you're sophisticated enough to grasp complex concepts, but still young enough to be malleable and still have an active imagination. In the eighth grade, a strong, positive experience with science education, including tech and A.I., today's emerging tools, can have a great impact on the course of the rest of your life.

Which is not to say that we're not concerned with impressing our younger visitors. We are. We not only want to get them excited about science, we want to teach them good habits that will stay with them into adulthood. For example, we want them to learn to eat nutritious foods, to think about where their food comes from, and to consider how their behavior impact the rest of the planet.

How do you see young people today interacting with technology?

Today, kids are interacting with computers and with iPads and such at a very early age. By age five or six, they're already masters. They're not afraid of pushing the wrong button or things like that. When they get to middle school and high school, they're going to be amazing. They're going to embrace artificial intelligence and quickly make it an integral part of their lives. That's one reason why we're putting a big focus on young children. They can harness this technology faster with virtually no resistance.

What kind of thinking goes into building your exhibits?

The exhibits that are most successful and win the most national awards are those that are "hands-on." They don't just discuss a topic but require you to *use* the knowledge you've just gained to solve a problem, achieve a goal, or receive a reward. When you use a technology, you advance your understanding of the scientific principles behind it. So we create these games based on scientific principles.

The real challenge with any science center is to create engaging exhibits that impart knowledge that changes behaviors, impacting the way students act at school and in the home, using science to improve the world around them.

Also, it's key to understand that being successful with teaching doesn't always mean being new and unique. Sometimes it just involves combining existing ideas in new ways. Back when I worked for Disney, we developed what became the Soarin' Over California experience. It involved an Imax screen and a swing, technologies that already existed. But put them together and you've got something new and cool. I can see the same thing being done with virtual reality (VR) and simple environmental simulators like fans or space heaters. Take people to a solar farm in the Mojave Desert or make them feel what it's like to work on a wind turbine 300 feet in the air. By combining A.I. with other established technologies, we can create a whole catalog of thrilling educational experiences.

How do you think A.I. will impact the lives of your students?

A.I. is very much a near-future thing. It's going to be integrated into every part of our lives, from the way we drive, to how we shop, to the entertainment we consume. Science centers can be used to introduce today's youth to what's coming down the pike just a few years hence. *Meet the robots who'll be cleaning your homes. Feel what it's like to ride in an autonomous car.* Kids need to be shown what A.I. can and can't do, how it works, and how to make it work for them.

How do you think A.I. will impact society as a whole?

When I was a kid, if we wanted information, we went to the encyclopedia. When the Internet came along, it changed all of that. Suddenly there was *all* this information available. The problem was, it wasn't being presented in a way that was necessary, thoughtful, and useful. I think A.I. is going to change that.

A.I. has the capacity to present information in ways that will be understandable to the younger generation. It can make learning fun and weed out the stuff that isn't important. Because it has the power to anticipate, it can begin with a simple question and then lead you down a learning path that is deeper and richer, but still relevant to your initial inquiry.

How can we get the general public more aware of A.I.—and less afraid of it?

It starts with young people. If they see A.I. as some super-computer that's going to take over the world, of course they are going to be afraid of it. But if kids see it as something friendly and helpful that can make their lives better and easier, well, they're going to love it.

A.I. AND SPORTS

When you think of sports and computers, your mind is likely to conjure up the rock-'em/sock-'em robotic pugilists in 2011's *Real Steel*, or the bionically enhanced Six Million Dollar Man and Seven Million Dollar Woman of classic 1970s TV. But artificial intelligence has a legitimate and vital role to play in today's athletic environment. From devising optimized training regimens, to keeping real-time data on athletes' metabolic signs, to designing sports-specific menus, A.I. has the potential to produce a new generation of super-athletes. And that's all without implanting titanium limbs or telescopic eyes.

A Conversation with Yasuto Suga
Leader in Sports Training and Athletic Performance Enhancement

Yasuto Suga is cofounder and president of Kadho Sports, headquartered in Irvine, California. Suga and his team create A.I.-driven software to train athletes to see better, think faster, and optimize decisions during high-pressure gameplay. Kadho Sports worked with USA Volleyball to develop a custom volleyball training platform for the National Team players, improving on-court visual recognition and decision-making skills. Kadho Sports also works with professional and collegiate baseball teams with a platform customized to improve baseball-specific skills.

Can you describe how your company uses neuroscience to train athletes' minds for optimal performance?
The easiest way to explain what we do is "brain training for athletes," targeting the mental areas responsible for high-speed, instinctual decision-making. Over the last 100 years, sports training has followed a similar pattern. The focus centered on making athletes faster, stronger, and more explosive through nutrition, weight training, and highly tuned methodologies based on physiology and biomechanics. But practitioners weren't evolving their methods. They were largely relying on practices conducted the same way 50 years ago—by drawing on chalkboards and talking during practice.

At Kadho Sports, we're closing the performance gap by combining over 50 years of neuroscience research into how athletes make high-speed decisions, creating a technology to help them refine these skills to be even faster and more effective.

Our platform utilizes video clips to re-create mental reps for athletes. This has created a unique demand for large quantities of video. This process is currently done through people watching film and breaking it down, but we believe that in one or two years this process will be completely automated by a machine-learning-based solution.

There's a great line in the movie *Rounders* where Matt Damon's character Mike McDermott narrates, "Listen, here's the thing. If you can't spot the sucker in your first half-hour at the table, then you ARE the sucker." And we believe this is true in terms of A.I. If you're not a company that can leverage A.I. and this coming wave of technology, then you run the risk of being swallowed up by it.

Your platform is based on decades of neuroscience research on game-time decisions. How did you compile this into actionable software athletes can use to improve their performance?

Now that individualized, A.I.-based training is being used by elite athletes, we're able to gather data on how these athletes make decisions. The evolution of analytics prompted by the book and movie *Moneyball* and the waves it made in the sports world have really pushed the envelope of what's possible by crunching numbers.

Though many savvy people have taken to breaking down data from actual gameplay, there's still a major gap in our understanding of a specific athlete's strengths and weaknesses. For example, in baseball, we know Player A may be prone to striking out against a curveball. What analytics can't tell us is if Player A needs to improve his decision-making or his swing. One is a mental issue; the other is physical. Right now, coaches have no choice but to try to teach both.

Through our platform, athletes and coaches now have the ability to analyze a player's decision-making strengths and weaknesses with real quantitative data. This means we can now discover if someone is making poor choices, or if she's making the correct choice and not making good contact because of a mechanical flaw in her swing.

This opens the door to utilizing data to find a specific course of action best suited to help a player improve. As we continue to gather data and fine-tune our training, we believe A.I. can be leveraged to predict the best training course for each individual based on their strengths and weaknesses, both mental and physical. This can really accelerate player development and improvement in specific areas much faster.

Can A.I. teach someone how to hit a fastball even if they are terrible at sports (or if they're a child and have never played before)?

Unfortunately, the answer is no. It's not like the movie *Limitless*, where Bradley Cooper develops into an expert fighter just because he becomes suddenly smarter and can draw on all of the action movies he has ever seen. There still is no amount of mental training that can teach the brain and muscles how to actually swing a bat or throw a ball. There is no artificial replacement for muscle memory, and the brain learns best through real experience.

How do you see A.I. transforming the professional sports world in novel and unusual ways?

It's difficult to say where A.I. will become prevalent in sports, since sports is the only arena in which we like to watch people perform with as little artificial assistance as possible. We enjoy watching a basketball player dunking a ball because they have to do it with their own leg strength. If we added artificial legs to each player so they could jump 20 feet, it wouldn't have the same level of excitement.

Instead, the first shift may be subtle and strategic. A football coach may employ A.I. to determine what type of play to use or which player to draft. Is there a day coming when we won't use coaches at all and instead rely on A.I.? I don't think so, because coaches are much more than tacticians; they must also be master motivators, creative, as well as leaders to their teams. I don't predict a future in which A.I. can replace these human factors.

When it comes to AR and VR enhancing the sports world, I think the fan experience will be greatly improved over the next decade in many ways. It'll be fascinating to see what AR can do to optimize real-world performance. Athletes will be able to practice with goggles on, reacting to new levels of stimulus to develop their skills in exciting ways. These ideas are still in the concept stage, so we can't get too specific, but we're excited for this day to come.

In what ways will the next generation of athletes be different due to advances in neuroscience and A.I. technology?

There will be a massive difference in twenty-first-century athletic performance resulting from our growing understanding of the brain. This understanding, combined with modern technology, will allow athletes to improve their performance by leaps and bounds over previous generations. As our understanding of the brain and cognitive performance improves, we believe that mental training will have the same impact that physical training has had on the modern athlete.

Since the dawn of sports, we've equated training to improving physical strength and endurance. The mental aspect of the sport has been largely ignored, and this is exactly the area that technology like ours is targeting. In parallel to developing artificial intelligence, our understanding of real intelligence and the brain is just beginning, and this will lead to major differences in the way the next generation of athlete trains and prepares.

How do you see professional scouts changing in the future, with new technologies such as A.I.?

Scouting has some of the same inherent problems as sports training, in that we haven't had the proper tools to gauge the mind and its full impact on athletic performance. We may know an athlete's 40-yard dash time and how much he bench-presses. What we don't know is how he'll deal with pressure, how well he'll make instinctual decisions, or how quickly he'll adopt a playbook.

This leads to the question of whether data and A.I. will ever replace human scouts. I'm not an expert in either field, but I think the organization that manages to find the right balance between qualitative and quantitative data will always have an advantage. There will never be a perfect combination of A.I. and data points always leading to the best draft choice, but I think it can get pretty close. My hope is that the last part still comes down to human scouting intuition and feel.

Where do you see your company 15 years from now? 50 years from now? How do you see A.I. meshing with this future?

We feel we can use a mobile app to get the young generation not only more interested in sports, but also to encourage outside play more. There's an obesity problem in the United States, and much of it is attributed to video games and children playing sports less often. It may sound funny, since we are using screen technology, but we believe that through our app, we can actually harness video gaming to get players back onto the field and playing sports again by generating interest and boosting their confidence.

Even though "sports" is in our company name, we're thinking beyond athletics. Much like reading a pitch or anticipating a blitz, police officers, firefighters, and emergency responder personnel are required to make high-speed gut decisions on a daily basis. The general public is wholly dependent on them making these decisions accurately and quickly in highly stressful situations. Through the same mobile technology we developed to help athletes improve their critical decision-making process, we can also assist first responders to make faster and better split-second decisions to save lives—both their own and the people who depend on them.

A.I. AND FINANCE

Historians tell us that the oldest surviving written records are Sumerian accounting ledgers. It now seems certain that literacy itself was invented to help people keep track of trades and financial transactions. Five thousand years later, electronic computers—originally designed to help break military codes and plot ballistic trajectories—gained their commercial foothold in the financial industry, which needed the machines' speed and power to store and process records pertaining to savings, investments, loans, sales, and purchases. Today, finance is again a prime target for the latest technological frontier: artificial intelligence.

A Conversation with Leon Kotovich
Entrepreneur and Commodity Price Forecasting Specialist

Leon Kotovich is CEO of TerraManta. His company uses A.I.-driven software to forecast commodity prices by analyzing news reports and data from publicly available sources. By combining the analysis of energy- and currency-relevant news, fundamental factors such as supply, demand, inventory, distribution, and geopolitical drivers, and price actions, TerraManta provides key insights to commodity traders, industry analysts, and procurement specialists.

An experienced software executive and entrepreneur, Kotovich was formerly Chief Operating Officer at a late-stage software start-up, Vice President of Engineering at OpenText, and CTO at agileSEQUENT. His career includes management consulting at ATKearney's strategic information technology practice and PepsiCo, where he first became aware that commodities truly run the world.

How did you train your commodity analysis system? How did you acquire the baseline data to develop your technology?
Let's start with oil. The price of oil is based on four things: global supply, global demand, global inventory, and the status of the currencies used to trade oil, principally the U.S. dollar. The challenge for the human analyst and our software is identical: how to aggregate hundreds or even thousands of potentially

conflicting themes and isolate important trends (called *themes* in TerraManta). What we did was build software doing three things: First, it analyzes all relevant energy news, all relevant market news, and all news regarding events directly or indirectly influencing the oil market fundamentals and the value of international currencies. This comes to about 4,000 news items a day. For example, a news item about an OPEC meeting can mention an agreement to cut production to stabilize falling crude oil prices. Yet, at the same time, other important events could be influencing oil inventory in China.

Second, it reads what the industry calls fundamental reports on supply/demand inventory, distribution, exports, imports, and reports from OPEC and agencies, such as the U.S. Department of Energy. Then, it records the daily close of WTI (West Texas Intermediate) oil prices, which is one of the leading petroleum benchmarks.

Third, using this information, the software looks for patterns affecting price changes three months out. And it learns more with each new monthly cycle. The data collection process started on January 1, 2013, so we now have about six years' worth of data to work with. This is why we think we're on the right track.

What's your biggest challenge?

Overfitting. This refers to the phenomenon when you start with a false premise and allow it to work its way into your learning model. Like confusing causation with correlation. Events can seem related but only be coincidental. We developed a proprietary process to eliminate the chances of overfitting, so we get a truly accurate model of how the market functions.

Besides commodity investors, who else can benefit from your software?

Any large manufacturing or transportation company. The price of oil is built into everything, be it for use in making plastics and pharmaceuticals, or in the cost of transportation. To hedge their bets, many large companies, particularly airlines, buy oil futures contracts to lock in prices months in advance.

This can be great if prices go up, but horrible if prices go down and you're stuck paying more than market rates. Just getting out of these contracts can be very costly—in some cases, tens of millions of dollars are involved. So it can be a huge benefit to a company to know with reasonable accuracy where the price of oil will be three months from now.

Of course, this isn't a perfect science. A lot of oil is produced in the Middle East, which is geopolitically unstable. A lot of oil also ships through the South China Sea, which China can easily blockade if it wishes. Any sudden military action in any of these areas can have a huge impact on crude oil prices. And such events tend to be wholly unpredictable.

At the same time, the big oil-producing nations, like Saudi Arabia and Venezuela, have an interest in maintaining a certain level of instability to keep oil prices high. It's interesting to observe how economic conditions force oil-producing and oil-consuming nations to do certain things. That's what we call "motivational analysis," and we're working to incorporate this into our forecasting model.

What is the accuracy of your current software?
It's 70 percent on forecasting prices 10 days ahead. And it has been improving steadily because it's been learning since January of 2013.

Besides oil, what other commodities do you want to forecast?
We're looking at industrial metals, such as lithium, cobalt, nickel, and copper. These minerals are essential to today's electric car manufacturers, such as Tesla. As other companies, like BMW and Mercedes, get into the EV business, having insight into industrial metals prices will be essential to their long-term profitability. Another area involves commodities, like sugar and orange juice concentrate, which are essential to soft drink manufacturers, like Coca-Cola and PepsiCo. These commodities can fluctuate in price and therefore expose companies to millions of dollars annually in additional costs. To these companies, and to any analyst who follows them, being able to forecast commodities prices with any accuracy is a big leg up.

The Uncertainly Principle tells us that the mere act of observing a phenomenon affects its outcome. By forecasting a price, you could be influencing it, right? Does your A.I. compensate for this?
Right now, our influence is so small I don't see this being an issue. If every company in the world used TerraManta and we were 90 percent accurate, then, yes, it could be a problem, but coming even close to this happening would take years and years. Even if a large company, like BASF, was to make a major trade based on our forecasting, it would likely be viewed as an isolated trade, not a trend. Our goal is to help companies manage risk, not necessarily bring total transparency to the market.

What do you mean by "transparency"?
In this context, I mean the ability to draw information not only from current events, but to consider the past to make solid correlations. I'll give you an example. For years, the Nigerian government paid local rebels billions of dollars not

to attack the country's oil transportation infrastructure. Then, a new president was elected, and he announced that he would no longer pay this extortion.

It took about six months for the militants to realize this new guy meant business, so they started blowing up oil pipelines. The result: In 2016, Nigeria's oil production fell to a 27-year low. Now, if people had sufficient understanding of Nigerian politics and presidential cycles, they might have been able to predict this. But few people do and therefore they couldn't. TerraManta could. That's the difference.

We understand you're also creating software to analyze corporate quarterly earnings calls.

Yes. These calls are supposed to supply analysts with the information they need to make prudent investment decisions. But in reality, they're used to hide information as much as they are to provide it. A great case in point is Enron, back in 2000 and 2001. Analysts were asking tough questions, but the Enron CEO kept skillfully deflecting them.

Good software can pick up on these evasions. It has an excellent memory for identifying the topics a company constantly emphasizes and those it avoids. If a new CEO is brought on board, it can also research and remember how this individual behaved in the past, what were the results, and compare this information to what's happening now. Armed with this information, a good analyst can obtain more actionable information from a quarterly earnings report than just the call itself.

At the end of the day, do you really see a market for honesty in the geopolitical sphere, where honesty always seems to take a backseat to narratives?

Narratives are powerful. Politicians depend on them. Even when the facts are all laid out, it's hard for most people to connect the dots and understand what's really going on. I'll give you a great example. When Russia invaded Ukraine and took the Crimea back in 2014, the Kremlin said the purpose of the invasion was to "protect" Russian-speaking nationals there. Of course, no one believed them. Instead, we bought the counternarrative that Russia wanted to secure its warm-water naval base there. Which was partially true. Ukraine was charging Russia millions for rent and preparing to demand more.

What wasn't part of the story is the fact that Exxon/Mobil had recently won rights to drill for oil off the coast, beating out a Russian oil company. Russia depends on oil for approximately 40 percent of its revenues. The invasion was principally motivated by economics and detailed exhaustively in an article published by the *New York Times*. The real tragedy was that no other news outlet picked up on this analysis. That's why software like TerraManta is so valuable. It connects the dots, revealing the truth. And truth is ultimately the most powerful weapon there is.

A.I. AND MENTORING

In literary scholar Joseph Campbell's classic book *The Hero with a Thousand Faces*, he makes the claim that all great stories follow a similar narrative pattern called the "Hero's Journey," in which a character goes on a quest or adventure. After suffering a number of challenges and setbacks, he or she triumphs and comes home transformed as an individual. The Hero's Journey can be seen in the plots of *Star Wars* or *Harry Potter* or even *The Deer Hunter*. Campbell also suggests that there are archetypal characters that pop up in tale after tale, one of which is the mentor. King Arthur had Merlin as mentor. Harry Potter had Professor Dumbledore. Luke Skywalker had both Yoda and Obi-Wan Kenobi. And where would the Teenage Mutant Ninja Turtles be without Splinter?

Today, A.I. is helping connect students with mentors who can similarly help them along their personal hero's journeys. In the not-too-distant future, people of all ages are likely to turn to A.I. itself for wisdom, insight, and moral guidance as well as basic education. A.I. will become the universal guru, showing us the path to success, personal fulfillment, and perhaps even spiritual enlightenment.

A Conversation with Paul Lu
Founder of MentorMint

Paul Lu is a Southern California-based engineer turned entrepreneur who cofounded the company MentorMint in 2015. Part MasterClass, part interactive Ted Talk, the company describes its mission to create products that form a "supportive community comprised of students, alumni, and professionals from a wide range of industries and backgrounds, who are primed to help each other succeed." Using A.I. technology, MentorMint connects subject matter experts in a wide variety of fields with students requiring insight and guidance in their area of expertise. Their current Introdeck product is an online platform supporting online calling, live chats, file sharing, and video conferencing.

How did you come up with the idea for this service? What need did you see was not being fulfilled?

My former partner Eddie and I had graduated from college and were always struggling to make inroads into our chosen career fields. We realized that networking was essential, but how do you start? How do you connect with the established experts you need to help you along? One thing led to another, and we came up with this service helping people to match up much like they would in a dating site—only in career fields.

We're starting slow and not just letting anybody sign up. We began in San Diego with the Honor Foundation, which is a veterans' group. Now we're working with the City of Los Angeles' STEM program, helping female entrepreneurs meet up with college students and assist them on their career paths. And we're setting up another program with local colleges and universities.

How do these interactions take place?

Everything is done online. There's even live chatting. Messaging occurs between the mentors and mentees, and they can conduct live sessions using video.

Do the mentors get paid for this?

Not at the moment. Right now, we're selling it to institutions and these pay their cohorts. There is a paywall. If a university pays us, only their students and mentors can use the platform.

This goes beyond just students and professors.

Yes. Very often college alumni are involved. The advantage here is the mentors don't have to be physically present at an event or conference to participate. Students can access their experience and wisdom remotely, even if the alumnus now lives thousands of miles away.

Are your relationships always one-to-one?

No. As a mentee, you can reach out to multiple individuals to access the information and insight you seek. You aren't technically assigned a single mentor for life. You can connect with other mentors when you wish and then disconnect when you want to as well.

You use IBM's Watson as your A.I. interface. What does this offer you?

Watson can do much more than just identify what information or assistance you need. Based on your request, it can deduce your personality type. Your category of assertiveness: Introversion. Extroversion. The level of mentorship you actually need. It can also pair you with one or more mentors who work best with your personality type. It can then monitor your session and judge the results, determining if the session was useful or not—even suggesting when another mentor may be more appropriate for you. We couldn't have done this type of analysis five years ago. The technology just wasn't there.

What do you have planned for the future?

We're planning to offer people the ability to stage TED Talk-like miniconferences online. A given expert can talk to 30 or 40 people live. Everyone in the audience will have a computer microphone so they can interact with the presenter. Using Watson, we can monitor each viewer's voice and facial expression to determine if the presentation was successful, when and how the speaker was engaging the audience, and to offer constructive feedback for future events.

How do you see A.I. impacting the small business landscape in the next 5 to 10 years? What opportunities does it offer entrepreneurs that didn't exist a decade ago?

That's easy. Data science and market research-on-demand is going to be a big thing. In the past, you needed a huge research team to identify and analyze your market. With A.I., it can be done with a much smaller team, and the results are much more accurate.

What advice would you give to upcoming entrepreneurs?

Pick the right team. Businesses come in all shapes and sizes. What kills an endeavor is the team not working together and not getting along. People kill businesses. Second, go out there and discover all of the A.I. tools now available. A.I. offers a whole range of shortcuts to success, and they're already built. You don't have to start from scratch.

A.I. AND COMPUTING

And now we're back to the foundation of artificial intelligence, the computer itself, without which A.I. is not possible. A.I. is expected to make its own contributions to the progress of computer hardware technology. In the not-so-distant future, expect A.I.-enabled computers to design and even program their descendants, perhaps finding ways to provide future generations of machines with speeds and capabilities that exceed human comprehension. As some A.I. experts have declared, true AGI may be the last invention humankind ever creates. Or, at least, needs to. Yet what is the path forward to AGI?

A Conversation with Lars Wood and Lisa Wood

Lars Wood is a pioneer in high performance computing and machine learning (8 patents), EHF analog mixed-signal integrated circuits and algorithms, and solver of intractable challenges for the U.S. DoD and industry through novel invention, development, and application of hardware/software systems since the 1980s.

Lars built a diverse career in A.I., machine learning, novel algorithms, quantum physics, therapeutic small molecule drug discovery, *ab initio* quantum chemistry, brain cancer fundamental mechanism basic research, microelectronic, optoelectronic, superconducting and analog and hybrid VLSI design, and extremely low-temperature and semiconductor solid state physics including quantum computing research. He was founder and director of the GTE Advanced Machine Intelligence Laboratory and was responsible for the first large scale ANN program for the U.S. DoD in the late 1980s.

In 1993, Lars designed and built the first optoelectronic FCCM machine, which was presented at the first IEEE conference on field reconfigurable computing. The NSA- and Intel-invited IEEE paper he published on that machine is considered the original vision-reference for the FCCM computing industry.

Lisa Wood, Lars's business partner and life partner, is a longtime supporter and early funder of Lars' research, dating back to the mid-1990s. Lisa's background is originally in big business media.

Together, they are working on the development of new super-Turing analog recurrent neural network semiconductor machines that will exceed the capabilities of current digital and proposed quantum computers. Super-Turing machines will compute in ways digital and quantum machines cannot. They will compute like human brain neurons.

What are the most significant achievements in A.I. since the 1990s?
Lars: A.I. covers many things, such as image and speech processing, voice and pattern recognition, game playing, robotics and other kinds of automation. Probably the greatest advances so far have been made in facial and speech recognition. However, the fundamental machine learning ANN algorithms have not substantially changed in decades. What has changed is that both computer memory and processing performance have greatly increased and become less expensive due to advances in semiconductor technology, which is key. This has resulted in applying machine learning algorithms to larger problems. It is important to understand that current technologies like deep learning networks

and so forth were understood decades ago. I built an award-winning machine learning application development environment in the 1980s, written in a logic programming system that provided for deep learning network implementation. The challenge decades ago was that computer processing performance was a fraction of what it is today, so it was not feasible to exploit deep networks and other machine learning technologies, as is possible today.

How have our expectations of A.I. changed over the last 30 years?
Lars: A.I. narrow applications abound; however, attempts to build adaptive A.I. systems to date have failed. There are several reasons for this. First, although digital machines offer excellent high precision, they are energy-inefficient and structurally bulky from a semiconductor perspective. Second, the processor is separate from the computer memory. This is completely orthogonal to the structure and function of real analog brain neural networks. The nature of digital circuits, with separate processing and memory, does not afford the ability to implement analog brain neurons, which seamlessly combine processor and memory together. Third, and most important, digital machines are constrained to rational number computation, whereas analog brain neurons have full real number degrees of problem-solving freedom. Computation is a continuum and current digital machines can only approximate real number computations. In this context, digital machines will never be able to implement truly adaptive A.I. and will be relegated to narrow A.I. applications indefinitely. These digital computing A.I. constraints have become known as the "Turing limit," after the founder of modern-day digital computing, Dr. Alan Turing.

What, in your opinion, is the path to adaptive machine intelligence?
Lars: The path forward to adaptive intelligence is to develop new analog super-Turing semiconductor neural machines. Let us explain. Current digital and indeed quantum computing machines (which are still not scalable) are both constrained by the aforementioned Turing limit because their functionality is based on bits, i.e., they are both forms of digital machines. The path forward to adaptive machine intelligence must exceed the Turing limit. This is what is known as super-Turing analog neural computation. In the mid=1990s Dr. Hava Siegelmann and Dr. Eduardo Sontag described a continuum of computation now called the *Siegelmann-Sontag hypothesis*. In their highly mathematical treatise, they proved that adaptive intelligence implemented by biological brain neurons must exceed the Turing limit imposed on digital computation through real number calculations. They called this super-Turing computation

and unlike other so-called hyper computing machine architectures (which are not feasible to build) that exceed the Turing computational limit, super-Turing analog neural network machines are buildable.

However, until recently non-silicon analog composite semiconductor technology was not sufficiently refined to implement super-Turing machines. Super-Turing machines break through the Turing limit to enable new machines with adaptive intelligence, which learn from experience without having to be completely retrained, which is what is called catastrophic forgetting. Real brain neurons and their recurrent neural networks are not subject to catastrophic forgetting. They learn continuously. The development of super-Turing machines eliminates the challenges to achieving the adaptive A.I. we discussed earlier.

Do you see us achieving artificial general intelligence any time in the foreseeable future?
Lisa: We believe it's possible with super-Turing machines. This is a fundamental paradigm shift from the use of digital or quantum machines based on binary computation, using zeros and ones. We're focused on building this new technology to implement the self-organizing real number processing functionality of biological brain neurons and their networks. Super-Turing machines will exceed digital and quantum computation through wireless analog neural network real number computation, including adaptive neural processing.

A Conversation with Jeanna Matthews
Professor of Computer Science

Jeanna N. Matthews is an Associate Professor of Computer Science at Clarkson University (in Potsdam, New York). She has written several popular books including *Running Xen: A Hands-On Guide to the Art of Virtualization* and *Computer Networking: Internet Protocols in Action*. Her research interests include virtualization, cloud computing, computer security, computer networks, and operating systems. At Clarkson, she leads several hands-on computing laboratories, including the Clarkson Open Source Institute and Clarkson Internet Teaching Laboratory. Jeanna received her PhD in Computer Science from the University of California at Berkeley in 1999 and her BS in Mathematics and Computer Science from Ohio State University in 1994.

What do you see as being the next big transformation in A.I.? What are the obstacles we have to overcome to get there?

I see the future as being about a partnership between humans and A.I., between human decision-making and computer decision-making. There will be an increasing demand for transparency in computer decision-making, whether it involves medical diagnoses, personnel hiring, criminal justice decisions, autonomous vehicles, or aircraft.

The focus needs to be on transparency and correctness even for rare cases, not just on efficiency for common cases. What kind of data is involved? Those answers are not as easy to get as you might think. Algorithms are intellectual property and their owners are not eager to reveal their proprietary secrets.

The Association for Computing Machinery (ACM) has proposed a set of principles designed to promote algorithmic transparency and accountability. It has established principles allowing stakeholders to understand and improve A.I. systems.

Where do you see A.I. being applied most effectively?

There are many cases where A.I. can prove very useful. Take medicine, for example. On occasion, doctors encounter patients with conditions falling outside the norm. Some treatments work well for most people, but not for everyone.

A.I. has the potential to customize treatments for outlier individuals. Resource management is another area. A.I. has the potential to be far more adept at governing the generation and distribution of power than humans are, helping to minimize or even eliminate waste. As we have seen with ride-sharing apps, A.I. can aid with transportation, matching passengers with drivers. Overall, A.I. will allow people the information they need to choose alternative paths and make better, more measured use of resources.

What is the greatest misconception about A.I.?

Its infallibility. That it's logical and unbiased. Computers learn from the past. In spite of all of the futuristic perceptions around A.I., it's a backward-looking technology. Here's an example: Want to hire a great CEO? It's best to seek the kind of people who were great CEOs in the past. Though there's some sense in predicating your information on precedent, it also leads to bias creep.

Predictive policing is another danger. If you go into a neighborhood looking for crime, chances are you'll find it in many of the same places again and again. Profiling becomes a self-fulfilling prophesy. For A.I. to be truly effective, it must go beyond established limits, to try what hasn't been tried before.

What are some of the greatest dangers that A.I. poses?

I worry that A.I.'s implementation will lead to a lack of personal accountability. When you eat at a restaurant or eat food obtained from a supermarket, you don't give much thought as to where the food came from, right? What about the slaughtered animals or the migrant workers who sweated all day in the fields to pick the fruit?

You're removed from all that. I think A.I. will encourage people to act the same way when it comes to decision-making. "Well, the A.I. said this or that, and I just followed it." A.I. threatens to relieve individuals of karmic responsibility for the decisions they make. And I think this is a place for mischief, for injustice and unfairness, especially because the interests of those making the decisions are usually different from the interests of those being decided about. This is true even in regulated areas, like hiring, housing, credit, healthcare, and criminal justice. We really need to focus on accountability and transparency to create the kind of just and equitable society we want.

Do you see A.I. leading to a more equitable society?

It has this potential. The issue of data ownership makes it problematic, however. The power A.I. has could end up concentrated in just a few hands and could become oppressive. Models of data ownership need to be changed so they return value to individuals who contribute to it. A.I. "black boxes" are a great place to hide mischief that further controls, surveils, and oppresses. Without the societal will to control our governments, to hold corporations accountable for the things they're building, we risk losing our liberties to special interests.

I'm all for incentives for people to work hard and innovate. But when innovations rely on the surveillance of individuals—when they're contributing to the information driving these innovations, then they need to be justly compensated for them. Not only would I like this scenario better than the current one, I think it's only just.

A Conversation with Andy Chen
Industry Watchdog and Regulator

Andy Chen currently serves as President Elect, Institute of Electrical and Electronic Engineers Technology and Engineering and Management Society (IEEE TEMS), an organization he has served for more than 25 years. He is also director of the Federation of Enterprise Architecture Professional

Organizations (FEAPO) Board, a member of the Digital Africa Global Advisory Board, and a member of the Technical Advisory Council for Financial Roundtable Services' FinTech Ideas Festival.

He is internationally recognized for his expertise in information technology and nuclear facility network security systems. Recently, he was the keynote speaker for the AI for Good Global Summit organized by XPRIZE and the International Telecommunication Union in Geneva. He has also been selected as a distinguished moderator at the 2018 World CIO Forum and the 2017 FinTech Ideas Festival and as a keynote presenter at the 2016 Digital Africa Conference, the 2015 World Computer Congress, and the 2014 World CIO Forum.

Could you describe the so-called "Three Waves" in the development of artificial intelligence and computing?
First wave: Good Ol' Fashioned A.I. (GOFAI), or what DARPA calls "Handcrafted Knowledge." This was the old symbolic models, which suffered from brittleness and an underestimate of how complicated human cognition actually is. Their big success was in expert systems, and there were even Lisp machines that ran . . . only Lisp. Then came "A.I. Winter."

Second wave: we have the power, what DARPA calls "Statistical Learning." Neural networks have enough computational energy to properly digest tons and tons of data. Great successes in narrow disciplines like game playing, automated driving, image recognition, text-to-speech-to-text. Unfortunately, these are "black boxes" and all you have to work with are matrices of numbers.

Third wave: context context context, DARPA harping "Contextual Adaptation." Understanding where you're coming from, to be able to contextualize information in order to properly reason with wide-ranging corpora of data. A general intelligence that understands like the previous two waves did not. "Context" is MIND.AI's middle name. (Almost literally, look at our model!)

Is there going to be a fourth wave? And what would it look like?
We don't know for sure, but I think it will involve using computers to create synthetic realities or deploying them to augment and amplify human senses.

Some people see A.I. as mankind's savior, others as its existential threat. Where does the IEEE stand on this question?
I think it will be a bit of both. Technology has always been a double-edged sword. Any technology can be used for good or it can be weaponized. We've done this with many past inventions, and we will with A.I.

What do you say to people who fear A.I. will cause them to lose their jobs?
A.I. is just a tool. Tools always make things simpler and easier. With some new tools, jobs that once took 10 people now just take 5. With A.I., maybe one person can now do the job, but there's always a need for people. On one hand, some people are displaced. They have to find new jobs. But on the other hand, goods and services become better and cheaper. And everybody wants that, right?

What kind of ethics need to be built into artificial intelligence to keep it benign?
Obviously, we need to have standards and regulations. We have rules governing the safety of food, cars, and aircraft. Even household appliances like toasters. We want our technology to be safe. A.I. will need to be regulated in the same way.

We know why humans need computers. But what happens when computers no longer need humans?
This is a tough question. In a way, we are creating a whole new race. We have to ask ourselves, how are we going to care for it? Then again, A.I. may still need us for sustenance, such as its need for electricity, so we will never be obsolete.

What, in your opinion, are the areas in which A.I. can improve life?
One is infrastructure. Without infrastructure, you can't communicate. You can't move anything. So any innovations improving infrastructure will be of great benefit. Then there's medicine. A.I. will find new cures and medicines, improving humanity's overall physical well-being.

Third is education. A.I. will not only help just in classrooms, but in places where there are no schools. It's a way of really leveling the playing field. Jobs, as we have discussed, is the fourth area. A.I. can also relieve us of a lot of menial occupations, like dishwashing, cleaning, and picking crops. I think it will also lead us to policies improving the economy overall. Slowly, steadily A.I. will make its way into our everyday lives. It's just going to be there making everything so much easier that we're going to eventually take it for granted.

Chapter 16

Tomorrowland Is Here Today

We have come to our final chapter. Before parting, we wish to offer you a vision of life in the future using A.I. in unprecedented ways. But instead of merely telling you how the businesses of tomorrow are already employing this technology, or gearing up to implement it in their operations, we are going macro in the final portion. By way of two case studies we are going to present to you how entire *populations* are latching onto A.I. to generate smart cities teeming with robotics, predictive analytics, and the Internet of Things. Run by mind-boggling amounts of data and herculean computer processing power, these metropolises—one extant and one in development—appear at first glance to be torn from the pages of science fiction novels, but they're not. They demonstrate in real-life technicolor the farthest reaches of human imagination and practical ingenuity.

OUR BOOK IN REVIEW

Before previewing Hangzhou, China, what some are calling "A.I. Town," as well as NEOM (the New Enterprise Operating Model), dubbed "the world's most ambitious project: an entire new land, purpose-built for a new way of living," let's recap what we covered in the previous pages. At the outset of this book, we learned the history of artificial intelligence, beginning with computing milestones, such as the formulation of Moore's Law, the Turing test, DARPA's intervention, the Garry Kasparov vs. Deep Blue showdown, and the

Ken Jennings vs. Watson challenge, to witness how far A.I. has come within just a few decades.

After describing landmark innovations and technological breakthroughs, we discussed what makes our present computing wave different from previous epochs. Do you remember the difference? The first two waves featured large, bulky computers more akin to processors and calculators as opposed to today's predictive thinking machines capable of learning and therefore intelligence. To better understand how A.I. works in practice, we investigated leading consciousness theories put forth by scholars, psychologists, and theoretical experts before zeroing in on the two types of artificial intelligence currently in development: artificial general intelligence and artificial narrow intelligence, so far, the only type of A.I. in use.

With a better understanding of what constitutes intelligence, we unmasked A.I.'s defining features: how modern computers have crossed the threshold from cold, programmed responses toward some simulacrum of human thought and feeling through the implementation of ground rules and the processing of Big Data. Since teaching and learning go hand in hand, we provided the fundamentals for both when it comes to A.I., including a robust discussion of natural language processing, a subfield encompassing the ways in which computers decode the symbology behind the words, sentences, and phrases humans use to communicate. Surpassing the limitations of first and second wave computing, we observed how today's computers can not only understand speech but are capable of "machine learning," a method by which computers gain data and understanding beyond their initial programming. (Think: AlphaGo learning to best past adepts of the ancient Chinese game Go by playing millions of games against itself to attain total mastery.)

Recognizing that such unprecedented aptitude is bound to breed apprehension—or at least misgivings—about the emerging technology, we spent considerable time diagnosing humanity's metathesiophobia (or fear of change) concerning A.I. Also cognizant of the fact of robots displacing human jobs remains a paramount societal concern, we examined the perceived threat from multiple angles, including historical, social, and political perspectives, to determine if the concerns around A.I. are valid and how best to adapt to the technology. With a more grounded understanding in place, we next looked at ways in which A.I. promises not just to free up humans for more creative work, but the novel avenues it offers to make our lives more productive and fulfilled.

Before turning our attention in the last couple of chapters toward real-world examples of companies using A.I. in areas such as sales, supply-chain planning/logistics, business dashboards, farming, cybersecurity, resort and casino management, and marketing, we examined the importance of two recently improved digital tools. What we saw is that both increased data storage and increased processing power have truly unlocked A.I.'s technology. Meanwhile, plummeting costs for both, coupled with proper training, are the primary drivers for unprecedented innovation in the twenty-first century. At the same time, we extolled A.I.'s ability to limit the pitfalls of groupthink. (Aware that any serious discussion of A.I. must include a discussion of bias dangers, we included multiple interview questions on this topic in Section II.) Last, we also painted a picture of A.I.'s use on an individual level—as an outsourced artificial mind capable of acting as a business's closest confidante. Now before we conclude, let's look at what A.I. can offer populations on a grand scale.

CHINA'S HANGZHOU

Located at the southern part of the Grand Canal of China running toward Beijing in the south-central region of the Yangtze River Delta, Hangzhou is the capital city of Zhejiang Province. Nearly 10 million individuals occupy this beautiful land listed as one of the Seven Ancient Capitals of China. In 2016, Hangzhou mayor Zhang Hongming, together with Wang Jian, chairman of retail leviathan Alibaba's Technology Steering Committee, and the founder/CEO of Foxconn Technology Group, Terry Gou, launched what they coined the "City Brain Project."

An artificial intelligence hub, City Brain set out to use Big Data to help Hangzhou make decisions—to *think* much like a person would. "City Brain is an unprecedented experiment of bringing artificial intelligence into city management," said Jian in a statement at the conference. "The core of City Brain will use the ET artificial intelligence technology of Ali cloud, which can conduct overall real-time analysis of the city, automatically deploy[ing] public resources, and amend[ing] defects in urban operations."

The comparison of Hangzhou to a thinking person cuts to the core of any so-called smart city's effectiveness. As we have seen throughout this book, humans differentiate themselves from their animal compatriots by virtue of our ability to synthesize tremendous amounts of actionable information from our environment. Where smart cities excel—how they can transcend the abilities of the most intelligent human being—is their ability to draw on seemingly unfathomable streams of data to make their decisions.

According to an article in *IFL Science*, this is just what this metropolis does so well. It metaphorically lives and breathes on an A.I. bent on absorbing "every last drop of data it could get its virtual hands on." Though the way Hangzhou operates may seem offensive to Western sensibilities—in particular, in light of our high regard for privacy— it has been hailed in scientific circles as a success in urban planning. Modern frustrations, including traffic congestion and crime, have been reduced with the aid of wholesale tracking and therefore informed responsiveness, on a vast scale. Of course, achieving such real-time reactivity requires nothing short of constant surveillance, achievable in a country comfortable with monitoring its citizens through millions of CCTV video cameras and a controversial social credit system.

However we choose to view such innovation from an ethical point of view, it can still be highly instructive to understand what Hangzhou's City Brain Project affords its citizens. According to Chia Jie Lin, writing for *GovInsider* in July 2018, it uses numerous "camera systems and sensors across the city to collect data on road conditions in real time. The data is fed to an A.I. hub, which then manages traffic signals at 128 intersections, and helps city officials make better decisions at a faster rate." Unlike a human, the City Brain never sleeps and can analyze the real-time movements of millions of automobiles racing across streets and tunnels, contemplating traffic flow to inform signals at numerous intersections, something no person—or even groups of persons —could possibly do without aid from this groundbreaking technology.

So are such privacy trade-offs warranted? Does 24-7 A.I. monitoring and decision-making lead to better lives for its citizens? Since what constitutes a good life is subjective, we won't try to answer this question. Instead, we will list some of the features Hangzhou's proponents point out. Safety is enhanced via alerts displayed on everyone's phone whenever danger exists. When it comes to health, City Brain has reportedly halved drive times for ambulances by turning red lights in their paths to green when approaching. Commute times are down, too, since the system can dynamically respond to traffic conditions as needed. Policing has also improved, according to officials. "The City Brain can detect accidents within a second, and we can arrive at the site in five minutes," said Zheng Yijiong, China's traffic policeman who controls traffic flows with aid from an A.I. partner.

Since a good life well-lived involves more than fending off traffic inconveniences and even feeling safer from crime, we will look at one more component of modernity in Hangzhou, what its famed hospitality has to offer. If we recall from Chapter 13, traditional hotel and resort management is just one vertical that A.I. is disrupting. With this in mind, let's consider how Hangzhou's FlyZoo Hotel treats its guests. At this luxury resort visitors can check in with the help of facial recognition technology and dine on food delivered by robots. In fact, robots make up much of the "staff." Instead of human servers, robots work in the restaurant and at the bar. Even the rooms possess their own robot butler called "Tmall Elf" capable of providing for their nearly every need.

Undoubtedly, there are many wonderful elements Hangzhou offers its citizens, as well as causes for concern even if nonstop surveillance promises a more responsive and safer city. In addition to this metropolis, other Chinese cities are pushing the envelope of technological possibilities, including Shanghai and Xi'an.

Shanghai

To solve the problem of parking in a city containing 24 million is no easy task. In fact, finding a place to leave one's vehicle has become such a vexing challenge that the tech company Huawei generated a smart parking network allowing users to find, book, and pay for nearby parking spots from an all-in-one smartphone app. To facilitate the technology Shanghai placed smart chipsets under spaces in more than 300 lots across the city, transmitting up-to-date information concerning parking availability.

Xi'an

In an effort to respond to one of the largest migrations occurring in the world today, China's city of Xi'an has turned to Big Data. Analytics allow authorities to observe and track population movements from rural areas to this city of approximately 8.7 million. City officials see tremendous value in learning the demographics of its new citizens, including their ages, ethnicities, backgrounds, and occupations, as such information can be used to inform civic decision-making as well as to better cater public services to a dynamic, growing population.

SAUDI ARABIA'S NEOM

Saudi Arabia is the world's largest petroleum exporter. Fully 87 percent of its budget revenues currently come from this one commodity. Yet in recent years the ruling party members, in particular Crown Prince Mohammad Bin Salman, have set their sights on an ambitious plan to massively reduce the country's dependence on oil for income while diversifying the country's economy and developing key public service sectors, including education, tourism, and health. Dubbed Saudi Vision 2030, the project's details were made public by Bin Salman in 2016 with a media relations rollout centered on spurring capital investment as well as widespread attention for the endeavor.

One of the most interesting—and certainly most audacious—aspects of Saudi Vision 2030 is the $500 billion mega project NEOM (which stands for New Enterprise Operating Model) backed by the kingdom's lucrative public investment fund, as well as outside investment groups. According to *Arab News*, "NEOM will operate as an independent economic zone powered solely by regenerative energy spanning three countries, complete with its own self-governing laws and regulations and all strategically designed for economic stimulation."

Currently under construction in Tabuk, in the northwest corner of Saudi Arabia intersecting Egypt and Jordan, NEOM is a futuristic conclave the likes of which the world has never seen. Though Bin Salman came under immense fire in 2018 for his alleged role in the death of journalist Jamal Khashoggi, until this incident he was well on his way toward transforming global perceptions surrounding his kingdom, including, among many other things, a series of high-profile tech/business conferences, such as "Davos in the Desert," attended by numerous investors, executives, and officials from around the world.

In spite of the fallout from the controversy surrounding Khashoggi's death, Bin Salman's government is determined to press forward with plans for NEOM. Demonstrating Saudi Arabia's commitment to wean the country from oil, NEOM will be 100 percent powered by wind and solar power, giving it a zero-carbon footprint. Beyond this bold infrastructural gambit, NEOM plans to make its mark as a new scientific and technological center. "NEOM aims to foster innovation through an open-source policy platform, where the world's top scientists will have an open invitation to conduct research in the fields of medical science, artificial intelligence, and virtual reality," again according to *Arab News*. "By adopting a regulatory framework that fosters technological growth according to the highest international standards, guidelines, and practices, scientists will have the luxury of having NEOM itself as a scientific testing ground for next-generation genomics, gene therapy, nanobiology, bio-engineering, and stem cell research."

Spanning 10,000 square miles along the Red Sea coastline, it appears that Bin Salman wishes to divorce his city from the kingdom in other meaningful ways. It will be independent from Saudi Arabia's governmental body, including its regulatory, tax, and labor laws. Advancing a utopia-like agenda to improve the world, it is focusing on key industries for growth and development: energy and water, mobility, biotech, food, advanced manufacturing, media, entertainment, technological sciences, and digital sciences. Meant to attract the world's greatest minds through the audacity of its aims and the technology on display, it has been described by *Bloomberg News* as "a city from scratch that will be bigger than Dubai and have more robots than humans."

Much like China's Hangzhou, NEOM is also designed to connect with a plethora of smart devices through artificial intelligence while raising the bar for other forms of technology. As Bin Salman has said, "Everything will have a link with artificial intelligence, with the Internet of Things—everything." NEOM wishes to advance the field of mobility with autonomous transport solutions, including self-driving vehicles and drones. It also views 3-D printing as the future of manufacturing and will be deploying robotics to develop new materials in composites and metals. In order to push the envelope on food production, NEOM will foster what it has termed "an international innovation center" for emerging technologies, including seawater and desert farming, aeroponics, and hydroponics.

Intrigued yet by the promise of NEOM? According to the *Saudi Gazette*, here are some more technological goals it intends to pursue as the consummate city of the future:

- **Next generation healthy living and transport.** NEOM will feature an unprecedented transportation infrastructure built on future travel technologies.
- **Automated services/e-government.** NEOM government services will be fully automated and easily accessible to residents.
- **Digitization.** NEOM will provide "digital air," free highest-speed Internet, and online continuous education.
- **Sustainability.** NEOM will be solely powered by renewable energy and buildings will have a net zero carbon footprint.
- **Innovation in construction.** NEOM will serve as a laboratory for innovative construction techniques and materials.

ONE FINAL WORLD ON RACING
TOWARD OUR A.I. FUTURE

Adapting to new technologies takes time. Today we take electricity-on-demand for granted, but it took nearly 50 years, from the early 1900s to around 1950, to bring electricity to all parts of the United States. In a similar fashion, although large companies began using computers for data processing in the mid-to-late 1950s, computers only became useful—and affordable—for most small businesses in the mid 1980s to early '90s.

As we have seen, technological innovation and adaptation is happening at a rapidly accelerating pace. Consider this: Facebook launched in February 2004. It took four and a half years to acquire 100 million active users, and just another five and a half years afterward to reach 1 billion people. Apple introduced the first smartphone in June 2007. Less than 10 years later, more than 2 billion smartphones were in use worldwide. That same year, both Netflix and Hulu began streaming TV shows and movies on demand. A decade later more than 70 percent of all Internet traffic was devoted to video streaming. Tesla delivered its first all-electric car in 2008. Today's most prescient forecasts suggest electric car sales will grow from 3 million in 2018 to 125 million by 2030.

Today, A.I. is roughly where computers were in the 1950s. Most of the benefits are going to large companies like Google, Facebook, eBay, and Amazon. But don't expect it to take 40 years for commercial A.I. to go mainstream. Already, numerous A.I. applications abound for small-to-medium-sized businesses to use right now. And as the technology matures and economies of scale drive prices down, we can expect more companies to jump on the A.I. bandwagon. In fact, many businesses already view A.I. adoption as critical to their economic survival.

We have said it before, but it bears repeating. If you are a business owner, the biggest threat to your bottom line is complacency. If you see no possible benefits of artificial intelligence, or, worse, you *fear* technological change, then you are leaving yourself vulnerable to those who are bolder, more imaginative, and more open to transformation. Remember Frank Herbert's words from *Dune*, "Fear is the mind-killer." To thrive in the coming decade, you must embrace the promise of artificial intelligence and actively seek ways to harness this emerging technology to your benefit.

Before concluding, here are the six steps you need to take to adapt A.I. to your business, starting now:

1. **Educate yourself.** Beyond this book, read up on where A.I. is today and how it's being used for business. A simple Google search will

yield dozens of articles on the latest commercial applications. By continuing to survey the landscape, you will better understand how A.I. is developing on an ongoing basis.

2. **Think big but start small.** As we've discussed, there is as yet no such thing as human-level artificial intelligence. Artificial general intelligence (AGI) is still in its early development stage and may never be achieved in our lifetimes. What we do have is artificial *narrow* intelligence (ANI), algorithms designed to apply A.I. and machine learning (ML) to specific problems. To adapt A.I. to your business, you also need to think as narrowly as possible. *Exactly what do you want A.I. to do? What specific problem do you want to solve? What question do you want to answer?* The sharper you define your parameters, the more useful A.I. is likely to be.

3. **Look for off-the-shelf solutions.** If you want to use your computer for word processing, desktop publishing, spreadsheets, photo manipulation, music editing, or web surfing, you don't need to go out and hire a team of programming specialists to create a customized application. Dozens of such applications are available off-the-shelf—and have been for years, often for little or no cost. Likewise, some basic A.I. applications suitable for business uses are already available from far-sighted developers. Some platforms, including Facebook, already use sophisticated A.I. as part of their advertising services, allowing you to intelligently target customers based on an almost limitless range of factors. Expect the number of prepackaged A.I.-boosted business applications to grow exponentially in the years ahead, with prices dropping accordingly.

4. **Perform a cost/benefit analysis.** Right now, most A.I. applications don't come cheap, and their ROI is difficult to ascertain. Before investing in A.I. for your business, you should perform a cost/benefit analysis, balancing the cost of your application against any potential gains you expect to see. To do this, you will likely need the help of an outside consultant, someone who understands A.I., the needs of your business, and the efficiencies artificial intelligence has the potential to deliver.

5. **Assemble a team.** If off-the-shelf solutions aren't available to meet your needs, you really must build your own application. To do this, you will need specialists trained in artificial intelligence and machine learning. (An "A Team" may also be necessary to adapt an existing

product to the specific needs of your operation.) Today, such expertise comes at a premium. There is only a small universe of individuals who are trained in A.I., and the demand for their services greatly outstrips the current supply. (However, expect this void to be filled quickly as more and more computer engineers and coders shift their focus to this burgeoning field.)

6. **Be prepared to disrupt yourself gradually.** Like the parent of a newborn baby, you must nurse your A.I. along during its first weeks of operation. Like an infant, a newly minted A.I. is something of a blank slate. It needs to be educated, trained, and given the opportunity to fail. But the whole point of A.I. is to be able to learn from one's mistakes, and to become increasingly powerful and efficient with each new experience. In time—and we are talking just a few months, in most cases—your A.I. will grow from infancy into adolescence and finally into mature adulthood.

OFF AND RUNNING

So, are you at last ready to disrupt yourself to own the A.I. revolution? We sure hope so. It's been our intention all along to get you to this point. Change is coming—and you can be the driver rather than the passenger. We hope things go swimmingly well for you in your journey. But, just to make sure you're well prepared to make the A.I. leap, we have included one last section in our book, an Afterword offering our final thoughts on the A.I. Revolution and what it portends for the future and the present. We thank you for reading and congratulate you on taking the first step to transforming your business—and, ultimately, your life.

Afterword

"The only thing we know about the future is that it will be different," said Peter Drucker, the business icon, consultant, and foundational mind behind the practical foundations of the modern corporation. The appealing thing about life is getting to experience how our future will manifest. We happen to live in interesting times. Unprecedented times. Never in the history of mankind has there been so many people, never has there been so many challenges, never before has there been so much incredible promise.

Scrolling through the day's news can upset people. Scorning our present era, they offer to tell anyone who will listen how much they wish we could return to simpler times. To them, the rise of artificial intelligence supplies yet more proof that life is deteriorating—that the world is falling apart. That A.I. offers one more reason to be cynical or, worse, afraid.

It is my hope that despite so much negative coverage surrounding A.I., we can find reason to view its development in a different light. A hopeful light. Also, contemplating Drucker's words can't help but lead us to another truth: life's only constant *is* change. No matter how much we try to slow Earth's spinning, no matter how much we cling to familiar modes of thinking, we must face the fact that everything is transforming all the time.

In order to stay relevant, in order to keep in step, in order to maybe even lead, we must change within. The beautiful yet mutable nature of daily life calls upon us to respond in kind. It requires us to *think differently*. That's the underlying message we have tried to convey throughout this book. More than half a millennium removed from the invention of Gutenberg's printing press, with the advent of the Internet in our rear view by only a few decades, we are fortunate to live in this time. The Web's digital ability to spread ideas far and wide, coupled with a book's analog capacity to teach, offer us the opportunity to empower ourselves with tremendous knowledge faster than ever before.

It's mind-blowing just how far we have come in recent years and how much the pace of technology promises to accelerate our understanding even more. Profound knowledge is within our grasp: knowledge of our environment, our solar system, the way animals function, the way plants grow, and ultimately, what may be the most profound mystery of all—why we are who we are and our life's purpose. To this end, though this book is primarily a business book, it's also meant to question our ideas about our abilities, limitations, and what is yet to come.

Thinking differently about such questions is a matter of mindset. The mindset of an individual or company successfully using A.I. to its fullest capacity can mean transcending commercial ends and affecting humanitarian change. Throughout these pages we have read of innovative companies, such as Zinx, who are employing new medical approaches powered by machine learning and biometric data to foster a cultural shift from sickness to wellness. Similarly, activist Kriti Sharma opened our eyes to how A.I. is being used to treat victims of trauma and abuse. We also absorbed fascinating philosophical ideas from modern tech prophets, including Peter Diamandis, Steven Kotler, David Hanson, and Ben Goertzel upending traditional notions as to what makes us human in the age of thinking machines.

As a result of these kinds of insight, researching and writing this book has been an incredible journey. From the outset, my goal was to help people. Yes, this book will not dispel everyone's questions, concerns, and fears surrounding A.I., but it can at least lead to needed conversations. As part of my work as a subject matter expert (S.M.E.) for the United Nations and consultant to tech start-ups, I routinely come into contact with individuals confused or curious about A.I. (Most often, a bit of both.) However, it's been my experience that there aren't enough resources to answer people's questions or mollify their fears. Instead, too much ignorance and differing viewpoints surrounding the subject of A.I tend to exacerbate what is already a challenging situation.

In order to meet the challenges facing us—whether they be personal, professional, or global—it's incumbent we learn as much as we can. The twin pillars of education and empowerment cannot be overstated. Possessing knowledge allows us to understand and direct our destiny. If this book helped you at all to glimpse what's coming (and what's already here), then may I say with the humblest appreciation, I feel gratified.

On another personal note, I must confess, I, too, learned a lot from cowriting this book. Creating each of the sections and chapters helped crystallize my thoughts, allowing me to better shape and share stories with others in meaningful ways. Interestingly, though Michael and I wrote a lot about artificial intelligence, a significant amount of our content concerned "real intelligence." *How do people think? How does consciousness work and influence what we do?*

Pondering such ideas led me to consider new takeaways; for instance, while we recognize that machines process data/information differently than we do, in some regards we may be constraining how machines can "think" through our own limited beliefs. To bring this idea home, think about driving a car. People drive very much through visual input. However, beyond using mere vision, self-driving cars can use radar, audio, and even heat sensors to navigate. (A good example of this is Tesla's A.I.-based autopilot mode, which uses radar in addition to cameras.) Is it possible that possessing access to greater sensory input makes for a safer driver (human or otherwise), and if so, what else might (artificial) consciousness be able to do with greater access to diverse sensory inputs?

Beyond big-picture ideas like this raised in this book, its ultimate purpose from a strategic level is to offer guidance to businesses seeking to harness A.I. technology: first to disrupt yourself, then to seize this opportunity and disrupt your competition. In order to accomplish this feat, there are four key takeaways to remember:

1. A.I. is not just the realm of technologists. Business and domain knowledge are also critical to understanding the pain points of your customers, allowing you to develop value-added solutions. (Think: LegalMation's legal software.)
2. You really do have to *think differently* to leverage A.I. capabilities. No one is going to get you there but yourself. (Think: Danny May's story about launching Lingmo.)
3. Think big but start small . . . too often people focus on the "sexy" solution, which can be incredibly complicated, costly, and time consuming. Just one mistake can derail all of your ambitions. Instead, focus on acquiring the low-hanging fruit. Afterward, continue building momentum through a series of successes. (Think: TerraManta's slow but steady growth.)

4. Fear is the mind-killer. In order to avoid its sway, we must be open to the fact that machines can do *some* things better than humans. (Think Cyrano's empathy-wielding bots.)

Regardless of all of the amazing ways A.I. can improve our lives, it's still not a magic bullet solution. It therefore behooves us to exert caution when considering adoption. The fact is there may not be enough value added to justify the cost and resources to implement it into your business. (For now.) It's also key to understand that A.I. just can't do anything out of the box. As we have detailed throughout the book, really getting started requires extensive amounts of data. Sure, A.I. can be a game-changer. It can enable incredible outcomes, but it also needs a strong, cohesive training strategy.

In closing, I wish to say how thrilled I am by the ways in which the world is poised to change in the coming years. It excites me to know I cannot even begin to fathom what is coming—even after interviewing so many great thought leaders. In particular, the topic of artificial empathy really interests me. Not just because it adds a new dimension to human-computer interaction, but because it proactively forces us to think about what it means to be empathetic . . . to have emotional intelligence . . . to be human. When it comes to the future of work, there's been much focus on developing STEM skills. However, from what I've seen, read, and experienced, I believe there's a strong need for more skills in philosophy, critical thinking, and, of course, creativity.

Before we part, my final advice to readers on how to disrupt yourself and own the A.I. Revolution is this: change your thinking. Whether we like it or not, change happens. It is inevitable. And it seems to be happening faster and faster. But empowerment is within our reach. We can be passengers and go along for a life's ride (with little say as to where we're going), or we can choose to be drivers and shape the future we want. You don't need a $1 billion idea. You don't need a huge game-changer. I challenge people to think big but start small. Find those "small" opportunities to use A.I. and add value. Then, keep finding them. In the end, small changes add up to big things!

—NEIL SAHOTA
in the skies above
the Pacific Ocean,
May 2019

Index

About the Authors

Neil Sahota (萨冠军) is an IBM Master Inventor, United Nations (UN) Artificial Intelligence (A.I.) subject matter expert, and Faculty at the University of California at Irvine. With 20+ years of business experience, he has worked with Global Fortune 500 companies to create disruptive products/solutions powered by emerging technology. His work experience spans multiple industries including legal services, healthcare, life sciences, retail, travel and transportation, energy and utilities, automotive, telecommunications, media/communication, and government. In his free time, Neil helps non-profits and NGOs to fulfill the UN Sustainable Development Goals (SDGs).

Michael Ashley is the coauthor of several books, including *It's Saturday Morning: Celebrating the Golden Era of Cartoons* 1960s–1990s (becker&mayer!), *Catch the White Tiger, The Six-Figure Writer, Fiction in A Weekend, This Works Marketing,* and *Evolution by God*. A columnist for *Forbes*, he writes about A.I. and tech. He holds a Master of Fine Arts Degree in Screenwriting from Chapman University and worked as a professional reader for Creative Artists Agency's Literary Department, a reporter for the *Columbia Missourian*, and a screenwriting consultant for Disney.